Shakespeare in the Theatre: Nicholas Hytner

SHAKESPEARE IN THE THEATRE

Series Editors
Bridget Escolme, Peter Holland and Farah Karim-Cooper

Published titles
The American Shakespeare Center, Paul Menzer
Nicholas Hytner, Abigail Rokison-Woodall

Forthcoming titles
Patrice Chéreau, Dominique Goy-Blanquet
Trevor Nunn, Russell Jackson
Cheek by Jowl, Peter Kirwan
The King's Men, Lucy Munro
Mark Rylance at Shakespeare's Globe, Stephen Purcell
Shakespeare and the National Theatre, 1963–1975:
Olivier and Hall, Robert Shaughnessy
Propeller, Carol Chillington Rutter and Emma Poltrack
Peter Hall, Stuart Hampton-Reeves

Shakespeare in the Theatre: Nicholas Hytner

Abigail Rokison-Woodall

Bloomsbury Arden Shakespeare
An imprint of Bloomsbury Publishing Plc

B L O O M S B U R Y

LONDON · OXFORD · NEW YORK · NEW DELHI · SYDNEY

Bloomsbury Arden Shakespeare

An imprint of Bloomsbury Publishing Plc

Imprint previously known as Arden Shakespeare

50 Bedford Square	1385 Broadway
London	New York
WC1B 3DP	NY 10018
UK	USA

www.bloomsbury.com

BLOOMSBURY, THE ARDEN SHAKESPEARE and the Diana logo are trademarks of Bloomsbury Publishing Plc

First published 2017

British Library Cataloguing-in-Publication Data
A catalogue record for this book is available from the British Library.

ISBN:	HB:	978-1-4725-8161-7
	PB:	978-1-4725-8160-0
	ePDF:	978-1-4725-8163-1
	ePub:	978-1-4725-8162-4

Library of Congress Cataloging-in-Publication Data
A catalogue record for this book is available from the Library of Congress.

Series: Shakespeare in the Theatre

Series cover design: Dani Leigh

Cover image: *Othello*, by Shakespeare; Adrian Lester; Olivia Vinall; at the National Theatre, London, UK; 2013
Credit: Johan Persson/Arena PAL www.arenapal.com

Typeset by Fakenham Prepress Solutions, Fakenham, Norfolk NR21 8NN
Printed and bound in Great Britain

CONTENTS

List of Illustrations vi
Acknowledgements vii
A Note on the Text viii
Series Preface ix

Introduction 1

1 The Early Days 5

2 Hytner and The RSC – 1987–1991 37

3 1991–2001 83

4 The National Theatre Years: Hytner as

   Director 107

5 Conclusion 169

Appendix 183
Notes 185
Bibliography 223
Index 237

LIST OF
ILLUSTRATIONS

1   *As You Like It*, directed by Nicholas Hytner, the Royal
    Exchange Theatre, Manchester 1986. Photograph by
    Kevin Cummins 33

2   *Measure for Measure* directed by Nicholas Hytner, the
    Royal Shakespeare Company, 1987. Joe Cocks Studio
    Collection. © Shakespeare Birthplace Trust 41

3   John Wood in *King Lear* directed by Nicholas Hytner,
    the Royal Shakespeare Company, 1990. Joe Cocks Studio
    Collection. © Shakespeare Birthplace Trust 68

4   James Laurenson and Rory Kinnear in *Hamlet* directed
    by Nicholas Hytner at the National Theatre, 2010.
    © Johan Persson/ArenaPAL 141

5   Deborah Findlay and Simon Russell Beale in *Timon of
    Athens*, directed by Nicholas Hytner at the National
    Theatre, 2012. © Johan Persson/ArenaPAL 150

ACKNOWLEDGEMENTS

I would firstly like to thank Nicholas Hytner who has generously given of his time to talk to me about his work.

Thank you also to Simon Russell Beale and Alice King-Farlow for talking to me about their experiences at the National Theatre.

Thank you to everyone at *Bloomsbury Arden Shakespeare* – in particular Margaret Bartley for her constant support and Emily Hockley and to Peter Holland, Farah Karim-Cooper and Bridget Escolme, the General Editors, for inviting me to write this book and for offering advice and words of wisdom along the way.

I am very grateful to everyone at the archives that I have visited: Exeter University, Manchester Royal Exchange, the Shakespeare Birthplace Trust, The National Theatre archive.

Thank you to the staff of the Shakespeare Institute Library and to Rosalind Fielding, for chasing those references.

Thank you to my husband, Andrew Woodall, for his love and encouragement.

A NOTE ON THE TEXT

All quotations from Shakespeare's plays are taken from *The Arden Shakespeare: Shakespeare Complete Works*, revised edition, eds Ann Thompson, David Scott Kastan and Richard Proudfoot (London: Arden, 2011).

All Theatre reviews of productions in Stratford-upon-Avon and London are taken from *Theatre Record*, unless otherwise stated.

Abbreviations

ADC   Amateur Dramatic Club

BAFTA   British Academy Film and Television Award

BBC   British Broadcasting Corporation

CUOS   Cambridge University Opera Society

ENO   The English National Opera

FT   *Financial Times*

NT   National Theatre

RSC   Royal Shakespeare Company

RST   Royal Shakespeare Theatre

SERIES PREFACE

Each volume in the *Shakespeare in the Theatre* series focuses on a director or theatre company who has made a significant contribution to Shakespeare production, identifying the artistic and political/social contexts of their work.

The series introduces readers to the work of significant theatre directors and companies whose Shakespeare productions have been transformative in our understanding of his plays in performance. Each volume examines a single figure or company, considering their key productions, rehearsal approaches and their work with other artists (actors, designers, composers). A particular feature of each book is its exploration of the contexts within which these theatre artists have made their Shakespeare productions work. Thus, the series considers not only the ways in which directors and companies produce Shakespeare, but also reflects upon their other theatre activity and the broader artistic, cultural and socio-political milieu within which their Shakespeare performances and productions have been created. The key to the series' originality then, is its consideration of Shakespeare production in a range of artistic and broader contexts; in this sense, it de-centres Shakespeare from within Shakespeare studies, pointing to the range of people, artistic practices and cultural phenomena that combine to make meaning in the theatre.

Series editors: Bridget Escolme, Peter Holland,
Farah Karim-Cooper

Introduction

When Nicholas Hytner was appointed Artistic Director of the National Theatre (NT) in September 2001, Sir Christopher Hogg, chairman of the theatre's board, stated of their new appointment:

> He understands and loves the big stages. He will involve all who can help in making theatre in our time vital and relevant.[1]

Vitality and relevance have been key to Hytner's achievements at the NT both in his evident commitment to new work and in his revival of the classics. In the first year of his Artistic Directorship, the theatre mounted nine new plays, including the contentious *Jerry Springer the Opera* (April 2003), which held up to scrutiny the morality of the contemporary television talk show, and Kwame Kwei-Armah's *Elmina's Kitchen* (May 2003), a family story of gun crime, drugs and racism, set in Hackney. Of the nearly thirty productions that Hytner has directed himself at the NT in his twelve years as Artistic Director, over half have been new plays, many of which have engaged directly with key contemporary issues and specific sections of contemporary society, including David Hare's *Stuff Happens* (September 2004), which dramatized events leading up to the Iraq war in 2003; Samuel Adamson's *Southwark Fair* (February 2006), set in the multicultural world of London's South Bank; Ayub Khan-Din's *Rafta, Rafta* (April 2007), about an immigrant Indian family living in Bolton, Lancashire; Richard Bean's *England People Very Nice* (February 2009), which charts the lives of four generations of immigrants – Huguenot, Irish, Jewish and Bangladeshi in Bethnal Green,

East London; and Richard Bean's searing satire, based around the hacking trials, *Great Britain* (June 2014).

In keeping the finger of the theatre on the nation's pulse, Hytner has not been afraid of causing controversy. Choosing *Jerry Springer the Opera* for the start of his first season at the NT, may have seemed 'sheer insanity'[2] given the levels of profanity and, to many religious people, inflammatory appearances of Jesus, Mary, Adam and Eve, as guests on Springer's show in the third act. However, the production attracted a vast new audience to the NT ('55% of the opera's 71,000-strong Lyttleton audience were first-time NT visitors')[3] and won four Olivier awards, including Best New Musical. In fact, the famous furore surrounding the piece was only initiated when the BBC screened a performance in January 2005, generating a campaign by Christian groups and 47,000 complaints.[4] Although Hytner admits that he found the television broadcast 'unfunny and not particularly comfortable',[5] he nevertheless defended it against detractors, making the common-sense assertion that, 'If you don't want to see it, then you should not be watching it.'[6]

Hytner's ability to ride the storm created by *Jerry Springer* appears to have given him and his team at the NT the confidence to mount other willfully contentious productions. Reading Bean's *England People,* for example, Hytner was fully aware that the play was likely to prove controversial.[7] Rather than avoid it, he elected to direct the play himself, vigorously defending it in the press against attacks of perceived racial stereotyping.[8] In bringing his next production of a Bean play – *Great Britain* – to the NT in 2014, Hytner risked accusations of contempt of court, libel and even the possibility of the play's not being able to open at all.[9] The very existence of a play that alluded to the events at the *News of the World*, whilst the trial of Rebekah Brooks, Clive Goodman and Andy Coulson and others continued, was dangerous, the play remaining *sub judice,* with the theatre unable to advertise any performances or even give the play a title until after the delivery of the verdict.

Hytner's work with Bean on *England People, One Man Two Guvnors* and *Great Britain* over a period of five years is illustrative of the sort of ongoing collaborative relationships that he enjoys with writers, the most notable of these being with Alan Bennett, with whom Hytner has had a particularly close and productive working relationship over a span of twenty-five years. However, more so even than Bennett, the playwright with whom Hytner has been most closely associated in his NT career has been William Shakespeare. Shakespeare's plays have, in accordance with the original NT Memorandum and Articles of Association,[10] remained a key part of the theatre's repertoire, with, on average, one Shakespeare production being staged each year in the Olivier auditorium during Hytner's regime. Of these, Hytner has directed seven, his Shakespeare productions displaying similar traits to his work on new plays – a desire for political and social immediacy, the creation of concretely defined stage worlds and a desire first and foremost to make the plays accessible and relevant to twenty-first century audiences.

This volume is particularly concerned with Hytner's work on Shakespeare, from his first forays into Shakespearean acting at school, to his impact on the perception and programming of Shakespeare at the NT under his artistic directorship. It explores his professional Shakespearean productions from *As You Like It* at the Manchester Royal Exchange in 1986 to *Othello* at the NT in 2013, examining his relationships with actors and designers, his rehearsal techniques and his key ideas about Shakespeare on the contemporary British stage. However, it examines this work on Shakespeare in the context of Hytner's theatrical career as a whole, in particular his early work in the medium of opera and his preoccupation in more recent years with new writing.

1

The Early Days

Like his predecessors as Artistic Directors at the NT – Peter Hall, Richard Eyre and Trevor Nunn – Hytner is a Cambridge University graduate, having read English at Trinity Hall between 1974 and 1977. However, his passion for theatre and, in particular the work of Shakespeare, was aroused before his time at Cambridge, through his study and performance of the plays and at trips to the theatre throughout his teenage years.

Asked if he recalls when he first became aware of Shakespeare, Hytner immediately responds – 'Yes, I do, very vividly. I remember *Comedy of Errors* – either at the Opera House or the Palace in Manchester.'[1] This was Clifford Williams's RSC production, starring John Normington and Ian Richardson as the Antipholi, which began at the RST in 1962. Drawing on commedia dell'arte and stressing 'the self-conscious theatricality of the play',[2] Williams's production was praised for its 'unflagging invention and verve'[3] and for its successful balancing of seriousness and farce. Hytner would have seen the production, aged nine in 1965, when it visited the Manchester Opera House – his first experience of seeing Richardson, whose work was to have a major impact on his enjoyment of Shakespeare. Indeed, when the RSC and Richardson returned to Manchester three years later, with Terry Hands's 1968 production of *The Merry Wives of Windsor*, in which Richardson played Ford, Hytner states that the experience 'turned me on to Shakespeare for life'.[4]

Although Hytner recalls seeing the production at the Palace Theatre,[5] it actually toured to the Manchester Opera House from 28 October to 2 November 1968. It was, he recollects, 'the funniest thing I had ever seen', and he reacted by 'howling with laughter' and 'falling off the seat', such that 'a Latin teacher who'd been sitting in the same row complained that my performance in the audience … was bigger than anything on stage'.[6] It was with this production that Hytner realized 'that the plays themselves were only half the story. It depended who was in them, and how they were done',[7] a lesson which has clearly informed his own productions of Shakespeare, which he states have always been about the actors – 'the thinking about the play starts with: "Is there somebody I would like to think this through with?"'.[8] It was Richardson's performance as Ford, visiting Brewster Mason's Falstaff disguised as Master Brook that Hytner remembers in detail:

> The situation is neat, the dialogue no more than serviceable. Ford says very little. Ian Richardson seized on Ford's silence. He turned red with suppressed rage, then crimson, then purple. Literally. He changed colour like the Fairy Godmothers in Disney's Sleeping Beauty. Then he stopped breathing, and changed size: from wizened husk to Michelin Man, and back again.[9]

In 2006, Hytner directed Richardson as Sir Epicure Mammon in *The Alchemist*, shortly before Richardson's death. In a moment of coalescence, as Richardson laughed with delight at Simon Russell Beale and Alex Jennings as 'Subtle' and 'Face', Hytner recalled his own laughter, forty years before – laughter generated by actors following in the grand tradition of 'start[ing] with a play and ma[king] theatre out of it'.[10]

Growing up in Manchester, Hytner was able to see a number of Shakespeare productions, not only at the Opera House and the Palace but also at the University Theatre, where Braham Murray's Century Theatre was initially the resident company, followed by the 69 Theatre Company (established in 1968), run by Murray, Michael Elliott and Caspar Wrede. He recalls, in particular, seeing Century Theatre's production of *Romeo and Juliet* in 1968, with Tom Courtenay and James Maxwell as Prospero in 69 Theatre Company's production of *The Tempest* in 1969.

In the late 1960s, Hytner also began going once a year, with his family, to Stratford-upon-Avon, to productions at the Royal Shakespeare Company (RSC). He saw but has, he says, little memory of Peter Hall's 1965 *Hamlet*, with David Warner in the title role, which he would have seen aged nine. However, he does remember 'going to see *Measure for Measure* for the first time' in John Barton's 1970 production, once again starring Richardson (as Angelo), having his 'mind blown by a Trevor Nunn production of *The Winter's Tale* with Judi Dench doubling Hermione and Perdita' (Nunn's 1969 production in the RST) and Alan Howard as Henry V (in Terry Hands's 1975 RST production).[11] This introduction to Shakespeare was, Hytner asserts, 'totally conventional'. However, it inspired in him a love of Shakespeare, such that he 'couldn't wait to do English A-level'.[12]

Manchester Grammar School (1967–1974)

Surprisingly, Hytner had not studied Shakespeare at school until A-level, something that he believes 'must have been an English department policy'.[13] It is striking – and a potent lesson to those who advocate the curriculum-based study of Shakespeare from an early age – that Hytner's enthusiasm for Shakespeare was aroused not from reading and analysing the plays in class but from seeing them on stage, and from performing in them himself.

Manchester Grammar School offered boys the opportunity to perform regularly in plays and it was here that Hytner was in his element – 'The place that seemed most alive was backstage, the rehearsal room, the school play... That's when I felt happiest.'[14] Hytner's earliest memory of a school Shakespeare production is, however, tinged with bitterness. Having watched a number of Shakespeare productions in the professional theatre, he was keen to start performing Shakespeare himself, and thus, when *Romeo and Juliet* was announced as the school play, he was 'completely thrilled':

> I thought – I am an absolute shoe-in for the Nurse and maybe even, although I wasn't a particularly well-favoured child, maybe even Juliet. And then it was announced that this would be the first ever very exciting production with the Manchester High School down the road [the local girls' school].[15]

Hytner was cast as Samson and utterly resented the girl cast as the Nurse who had, in his view, stolen 'my part'.[16] However, the following year, the girls' school experiment clearly not having been deemed a success, Hytner was cast as Mistress Quickly in a compilation of the two parts of *Henry IV*, a role he relished, partly for its comic potential. Although he then graduated to playing male roles, Hytner doesn't recall performing in any more Shakespeare at school. What is striking, however, are the plays in which he does remember performing and the close correlation between the Manchester Grammar School repertoire and those plays that Hytner has chosen to direct himself at the NT. As well as acting in *Henry IV Parts 1 and 2* which he directed at the NT in 2005, Hytner performed at school as Mr Toad in A. A. Milne's *Toad of Toad Hall*, a stage version of *The Wind in the Willows*, later influencing his decision to ask Alan Bennett to write a new dramatization of Kenneth Grahame's book for his second production at the NT in 1990, and as Truffaldino in Carlo Goldoni's *The Servant of Two Masters*, a play which he also staged in updated form in his award-winning 2011 production of Richard Bean's *One Man Two Guvnors*. Hytner's A-level study also appears to have had an influence on his later directing work, the plays that he studied at A-level – *King Lear* and *Measure for Measure* – being two of those that he elected to direct for the RSC: *Measure for Measure* in 1987 and *King Lear* in 1990.

Cambridge University (1974–1977)

Hytner never doubted that he was going to read English at University and matriculated at Trinity Hall in 1974. His study of Shakespeare – both for the Part 1 Shakespeare paper and Part 2 Tragedy paper – was, he asserts, 'mainstream' in its focus, a style of teaching that he associates with his supervisor at Trinity Hall, the Shakespeare scholar Peter Holland.[17] By 'mainstream', Hytner appears to mean a clear, straightforward approach, unencumbered by some of the more radical theoretical approaches of the 1970s, which in his view Holland accomplished 'brilliantly': 'I kind of sniffed around one or two of the rebel Structuralist lecturers and thought "Oh no, this hurts my brain, I'm not doing this."'[18] Alongside Muriel Bradbrook, whose lectures Hytner found exciting, Holland was and remains a profound influence on Hytner's work on Shakespeare, writing programme notes for many of his productions and offering textual advice.

Hytner was also encouraged and 'much helped by Graham Storey',[19] fellow of the college and Lecturer in English, who encouraged him to pursue his theatre activities alongside his academic work. Indeed, Hytner's view is that:

> Graham Storey and Peter Holland, and I suspect whoever else kept an eye on me at Trinity Hall … took a collective decision that I was serious about working in theatre, and let me get on with it.

He recalls going to his tutors to ask whether he could, 'prioritise whichever show I was directing for six weeks [he thinks that this was probably *The Rise and Fall of the City of Mahagonny*] and promis[ing] to make it up during the vacation and they said "OK fine"',[20] something which seems remarkable even back in the late 1970s. In an interview in the *Weekend Telegraph* in 1989, Hytner asserted that his 'deepest debt to Cambridge is simply a way of thinking', adding, 'I still approach everything initially from quite a sharply academic angle.'[21]

Hytner continued to perform at Cambridge – predominantly with the Cambridge Footlights for whom he was Vice-President in 1976–7, appearing regularly in the Footlights 'Smoking Concerts', late night reviews, including *All's Well That Ends* (ADC 2–6 March 1976), directed by Chris Keightley, and *An Evening Without* (8–12 February 1977), directed by Jimmy Mulville, and Footlights Summer Tour/ Edinburgh shows – *A Kick in the Stalls* (1976), directed by Douglas Adams, and *Tag* (1977), directed by Griff Rhys Jones (televised on BBC East). He also acted in two ADC pantomimes: *Robinson Crusoe* (ADC, 25 November – 7 December 1975) in which he played Squire Farthing and *Snow White and the Seven Dwarfs* (ADC, 23 November – 4 December 1976) in which he played Ruby, the Dame – continuing the trend begun in school of playing women's roles. He also did some classical acting, continuing in that comic vein established at school and in the Footlights, by playing Trinculo in the future novelist Michael Arditti's production of *The Tempest* for the European Theatre Group, 1974 tour. Although the production itself received a lukewarm review from *Varsity*, the Cambridge student newspaper, Hytner was picked out, along with the actor playing Stephano, for 'some fine comedy' and, in the view of reviewer Nigel Chapman, 'in alliance with Prospero and Ariel' came 'nearest to attaining the standard of the arrogant programme note – "we attract the best actors and directors in Cambridge"'.[22]

Hytner claims, however, that he soon realized that he was 'a poor actor',[23] his involvement in the Footlights in particular teaching him that 'the only kind of acting I was

good at was broad comic acting'.[24] Certainly this seems
to have been his forte, a review of *All's Well that Ends* in
the *Cambridge Evening News* naming Hytner as one of
three 'artists' by whom the director was 'exceptionally well-
served', Hytner demonstrating 'a remarkable ability to suggest
any upper-crust, terribly-British "type" to hilarious effect'.[25]
Indeed, Benedict Nightingale confirms the fact that Hytner
did not excel at serious acting, asserting that the Cambridge
theatre scene was, importantly, where 'undergraduates learnt
what they couldn't do', Hytner 'reduc[ing] his audiences to
unwanted hilarity with his playing of a tyrannical general in
Betti's *Queen and the Rebels*'.[26]

Although he recognized that he wasn't going to act, Hytner
knew that he wanted to work in the theatre. Even though he
had spoken of directing as a compensatory choice – 'If you
can't act, and you direct, it's the next best thing ... It gives you
the impression of first-degree creativity'[27] – it was at university
that he came to the realization that he had the skills necessary
to be a director: 'the ability to direct and the clarity of vision
to see a production as a whole'.[28] The ADC was 'a wonderful
apprenticeship' – one which allowed him 'to make all the
elementary mistakes in ... a protected environment'.[29] Hytner
may have abandoned his acting aspirations at university, but
he has clearly retained an instinct for and understanding of the
techniques of comedy, as displayed in the smart visual comedy
and impeccable comic timing of many of his productions.

Hytner directed only one Shakespeare play at Cambridge –
Love's Labour's Lost in Trinity Hall Fellows' Garden in June
1976. One of the continuing traditions of the Cambridge post-
examinations 'May Week' is the performance of Shakespeare
outside in college gardens and Hytner managed to secure
the Trinity Hall garden for a co-production between the
Preston Society (Trinity Hall's drama society) and the ADC.
For Hytner, this production epitomized his 'main stream'
approach to Shakespeare. It was inspired by the sort of work
that he had seen at the RSC and was set in 'the long hot
summer of 1914', a concept which he thought was 'a stroke

of genius', but which he now concedes was 'an idea so obvious that I've seen it done three times since, and I almost certainly ripped it off from some previous production that I'd read about'.[30] It is difficult to know whether Hytner is being modest in his rather derogatory comments about this production; May Week shows were not reviewed in *Varsity*, the productions falling after the final edition of Easter term. Certainly, as Hytner is only too happy to relate, one audience member who disliked the production intensely was the eminent literary critic I. A. Richards. One of Hytner's abiding memories of the production is that 'Richards was very distressed'.[31] Hytner had decided, for some reason that he no longer recalls, to cut the last lines of the play: 'The words of Mercury are harsh after the songs of Apollo. You that way, we this way' (5.2.921–2). On the opening night, he found himself stuck behind Richards as he made his way out of the gardens furiously muttering the final words of the play over and over, and 'telling anyone who'd listen' that 'I was a fool and a vandal'.[32] Hytner freely admits that with the arrogance of youth and the 'blissful self-confidence' of an undergraduate director he 'didn't care' (he does now!).[33] Although he now admits that 'the problem was less with the play than with my understanding of it',[34] this may be seen as an early example in Hytner's career, of his willingness to tamper with the Shakespearean text in order to make it work for him and for his audience – something that he has continued to do, though less rashly and with a good deal more understanding than in his university days.

In addition to *Love's Labour's Lost,* Hytner also directed George Bernard Shaw's *Mrs Warren's Profession* (ADC, 29 April–3 May 1975), a late night *Victorian Music Hall* (ADC, 14–18 October 1975) and Thomas Middleton's *A Chaste Maid in Cheapside* (ADC, 2–6 November 1976), the last of which he remembers as being 'quite good'. Actually, *Chaste Maid* received the least positive reviews of the three productions in the student paper *Varsity*, *Mrs Warren's Profession* being praised as 'a memorable version of Shaw's most infamous play'[35] and the reviewers of *Victorian Music Hall* writing, 'Rarely has the ADC produced anything so hugely enjoyable, with the opportunity for a hippopotamine wallow in professionally presented nostalgia.'[36] The reviewer of *Chaste Maid* described the production as 'extremely competent', but appeared to take issue with Hytner's concept for the production – 'Don't be fooled: true, his engineering tries to angle the *Chaste Maid* into an "uncompromising debunking of romantic ideas and a determination to find a rotten core in everything", but even if he were successful (which he isn't) he has little justification for such an interpretation of the text.'[37]

What is clear is that even by late 1975, little more than a year after his arrival in Cambridge, Hytner was already regarded as a highly accomplished director. A preview article in *Varsity* anticipated the success of his *Victorian Music Hall* stating that 'the combination of Nick Hytner's musical talent and his ability as a director' bode well for the production. On a more ironic, but equally telling note, Hytner's biography in the programme for the Footlights, *A Kick in the Stalls* (presumably written by his fellow students), cites his 'Favourite Sport' as 'Trying to find people less talented than himself',[38] whilst that for *Tag* asserts that 'Nick is probably the most talented third year undergraduate theatre director in the whole Hytner Household',[39] a comment that satirically suggests that Hytner's directing talents extended far beyond the walls of the Hytner home.

Cambridge also proved a fertile ground for Hytner's developing love of opera and musicals. Having directed Kurt Weill and Bertold Brecht's *The Threepenny Opera* (ADC, 18–22 November 1975), a production that sold out every night and established Hytner as 'the doyen of "popular theatre" in Cambridge',[40] he went on to do a full-scale production of their opera *The Rise and Fall of Mahagonny* – a 'ludicrously ambitious'[41] student production mounted in promenade on the vast floor of the Cambridge Corn Exchange and later taken to Edinburgh. Whilst the student review of the production in *Varsity* was not particularly positive, highlighting, 'despite the excellent organization, the mammoth publicity, the midnight-oil rehearsals ... and the impromptu but efficient staging',[42] problems with acoustics and awkward exits and entrances, the production received a positive review in the professional publication *Opera Magazine*, in which Elizabeth Forbes described the Corn Exchange as 'an especially well-chosen venue' which, in spite of creating certain 'problems of balance, audibility and ensemble' created an 'immediacy from close contact between cast and audience'. For Forbes, Hytner achieved 'smooth, swiftly flowing action' and succeeded in keeping 'the dramatic tension fully taut' through his judicious cutting.[43]

Hytner speaks of the production as, in part, 'a gesture of protest against the Cambridge University Opera Society's engagement of a professional director for its shows'.[44] He and Nicholas Till 'formed their own company ... Cambridge Music Theatre'[45] for the venture and managed to secure guarantees against loss from Eastern Arts and the Footlights in what the Footlights secretary, Charles Shaughnessy, described as a 'horrid' but 'hideously clever' plan, which demonstrates Hytner's early talent for innovative theatrical fundraising.[46] However, less than a year later, having graduated, Hytner returned to Cambridge to take up the very role against which he was rebelling, directing Monteverdi's *Coronation of Poppaea* for CUOS in the Music School's newly-built concert hall.

The opera years

When Hytner graduated from Cambridge there were few of the schemes and resources that exist now for young directors: 'There was no National Theatre Studio, no National Theatre Studio directors' course, no Young Vic directors. Nothing.'[47] He applied to one of the few available schemes – the Thames Television directors' course – but was rejected. Although a number of former Cambridge graduates had become professional theatre directors, Hytner felt that being a Cambridge graduate was possibly an obstacle to becoming a professional director – 'People wanted recent graduates to get their hands dirty ... to temper their cleverness and self-confidence with real experience.'[48] One person who was prepared to give a young Cambridge graduate a chance to gain such experience was David Pountney at Scottish Opera, himself a Cambridge graduate. Hytner had written letters to both repertory companies and opera companies in the hope of an assistantship, and found opera more of an 'open door',[49] with Pountney offering him his first paid job assisting on a revival of *Madam Butterfly* (April 1978), which Pountney had first directed for Scottish Opera in 1973.

The opera scene that Hytner encountered was relatively unsophisticated – 'before Pountney had come down to London and turned London opera into something that was theatrically forward looking'.[50] Hytner entered the world of London opera in 1979 as a staff producer [a term used for an assistant director] at the ENO, a role that he gave up in 1982, having re-directed a disastrous revival of John Copley's *Aida*.[51] By then, however, he had already achieved his first big break, which came in 1979, when Norman Platt invited him to direct Britten's *The Turn of the Screw* for Kent Opera (November 1979). According to Platt, Hytner 'radiated intelligence and awareness and I thought this was a risk worth taking with the Screw. Afterwards there was no doubt.'[52] Hytner was to direct two further productions for Kent Opera – *The Marriage of Figaro* in 1981 and Tippett's *King Priam* in 1983 which, he claims, remains 'the happiest opera production I ever did, and probably in many ways the best'.[53] For six years, Hytner worked mainly in the field of opera, directing, in addition to his work for Kent Opera, Benjamin Britten's *Peter Grimes* (1981) and Tchaikovsky's *The Queen of Spades* (1982) for New Sussex Opera, Franco Alfano's *Leggenda di Sakuntala* for Wexford Festival Opera (1983), Giovanni Pacini's *Maria Tudor* for Camden Festival (1983) and Wagner's *Rienzi* (1983) and Handel's *Xerxes* (1985) for ENO. This last production, which was mounted to mark the 300th anniversary of Handel's birth, helped to establish Hytner's name as a director and a translator of librettos, winning both the Olivier and Evening Standard awards for Best Opera. Looking back on it, Hytner has some reservations – 'There's an awful lot of me standing up on that stage, saying, "Hi folks, aren't I clever? And now, another gag from the House of Hytner!".'[54] Max Loppert, reviewing the production in *Opera Magazine*, concurred with Hytner, sometimes finding 'the cleverness being overdone as the work progressed to its more serious moods'. However, he felt that 'it would be a sad, stuffy prude who failed to take some pleasure in the cleverness and bright humour of the production'.[55]

After *Xerxes*, Hytner mounted another Handel opera, *Giulio Cesare* at the Paris Opera (1987), following this with Aulis Sallinen's *The King Goes Forth to France* (1987) and Michael Tippett's *The Knot Garden* (1988) at the Royal Opera House and Mozart's *The Magic Flute* at the ENO (1988) – a production that stayed in the repertoire until 2012. Loppert, writing in 1991 described Hytner as 'the richest, most theatrically equipped, and most intellectually wide-ranging British directorial talent of his generation', asserting that his work 'had come to represent what was freshest and most exciting about opera in Britain in the 1980s'.[56] Throughout the 1980s Hytner had worked to try to find 'a stage world' for each of his opera productions, 'rarely a simple updating':[57] for *Rienzi* a non-specific twentieth-century totalitarian state, for *Xerxes* an eighteenth-century-style garden filled with anachronistic props and for *Giulio Cesare* a triple-time dimension described by Loppert as 'part Tintin, part Carry on Up the Nile'.[58] However, this is something that he found more and more difficult, concluding eventually that 'there's no use trying to create a real stage world in opera, where singers can give the illusion of spontaneity. It's not useful to them; to the opera ... nobody behaves in any recognizable world by belting out top C's at the top of their lungs.'[59]

Indeed, by the second decade of the twenty-first century,

Hytner had more or less stopped doing opera all together. Loppert suggests that one reason that he moved away from this medium, is that he is drawn towards new work with a contemporary resonance, something that, even by 1991, he was worried that opera was lacking – characterized by a dominance of 'style' over 'content' and communicating 'with the few, not the many'.[60] Another is that Hytner is increasingly drawn to the creation of recognizable on-stage worlds, in which all involved understand 'the rules – social, physical and psychological' that govern the location and which he now realizes is a futile goal in opera where 'the last thing ... you need to do is say "this is happening in a world something like ours"'.[61]

Hytner's early experiences in opera have clearly had a profound impact on his subsequent work as a theatre director, one that he recognizes particularly in his work on Shakespeare: 'Opera has helped: on large-scale Shakespeare, or the big plays I did at the Manchester Royal Exchange ... or big-stage productions like *Ghetto* or *Miss Saigon*.'[62] However, it also, in Hytner's view, made some of his early Shakespeare productions – in particular those at the RSC in the 1990s – 'over-inflated'.[63] He recalls, for example, '*Measure for Measure* having a big overbearing set' and 'clothes which told you who the characters were; not clothes that the characters might live in, but clothes that said "pimp"',[64] something that would have worked for opera but not for Shakespeare, a writer whom, Hytner now firmly believes, conceives of his characters in combination with 'the physical reality of the world around them'.[65]

In 1988, Hytner wrote a piece for *Opera Magazine* about acting in operas, in which he discusses the challenges of producing a 'realistic' performance in an opera, of finding a style 'consistent' with the world of the opera that allows the singer, no matter what the piece, to make their 'apparently odd way of behaving seem natural'. The article provides insight both into Hytner's desire to create something tangible on the operatic stage and his thoughts about acting for the theatre. In discussing how a theatre actor might approach a role, Hytner provides a series of questions: 'What was my intention when I came on stage? How is it changed by the action of the scene? What is my journey through the scene?', suggesting that 'if the right questions are asked in rehearsal, a performance should be emotionally specific'.[66] This is key to Hytner's approach to directing all theatre, including Shakespeare – the creation of emotional and psychological specificity within 'particular circumstances'. He acknowledges that, as with opera, the type of 'reality' will be different depending on the nature of the play, providing as an example Othello's journey into 'the grip of hysterical jealousy', which he must achieve 'in verse' and which will be a different 'reality' from that of a film, or a naturalistic piece of theatre;[67] however, he was, even at this early stage of his career, before he had tackled much professional Shakespeare, intent on finding a way to imbue what are essentially non-naturalistic verse dramas with a some form of reality, albeit not that of the television soap opera.

Early theatre productions

In spite of beginning his career in opera, Hytner has always felt that theatre was his true métier – 'if I'm asked what I am, I've always said theatre director'.[68] By the early 1980s, in addition to directing opera, Hytner was also directing plays: five productions at the Northcott Theatre in Exeter, none of which, according to Hytner, he chose to direct[69] – Anthony Shaffer's *Murderer* (1981), *Aladdin*, adapted by Hytner's Cambridge Footlights contemporaries Rory McGrath, Jimmy Mulville (Book) and Peter Fincham (Music and Lyrics) (1981–1982),[70] George Farquhar's *The Recruiting Officer* (1982), Alan Ayckbourn's *Absurd Person Singular* (1982) and Neil Simon's *Barefoot in the Park* (1983); four productions at the Leeds Playhouse – John Morrison's adaptation of *Tom Jones* (1983), Peter Barnes's *The Ruling Class* (1983), *Alice*, a rock musical of *Alice in Wonderland* by Richard Scott and Anthony Phillips (1984) and Arnold Wesker's *Chips with Everything* (1985); Tom Stoppard's *Jumpers* at the Manchester Royal Exchange (1984) and an adaptation by Beverley Cross of Baroness Orczy's *The Scarlet Pimpernel* at the Chichester Festival Theatre (1985). This last production transferred to Her Majesty's Theatre in London in December 1985, marking Hytner's West End debut.

These early productions helped to establish some key working relationships that Hytner has maintained throughout his career, with actors including Julian Wadham,[71] Iain Mitchell,[72] Desmond Barrit[73] and Alex Jennings;[74] designers Mark Thompson,[75] David Fielding[76] and Di Seymour;[77] lighting designer Mark Henderson[78] and composer Jeremy Sams, a friend of Hytner's from Cambridge.[79] Hytner's tendency to work repeatedly with the same actors and production team is illustrative of his collaborative ethos and his belief in the centrality of the actor in the production process. Again and again in interviews and articles, Hytner cites working closely with actors as the most important and satisfying part of his job.[80] However, he also considers it important to have 'an open conversation with a casting director' and 'to work with new people ... who challenge you in different ways and work in different ways'.[81]

Although the fact that Lyn Gardner, reviewing the London production of *The Scarlet Pimpernel*, referred to the director as 'Nicholas Hayter' (*City Limits*)[82] suggests that he had not yet become a universally recognizable name in the professional theatre, a number of the reviewers alluded to Hytner's already established reputation as a director, John Barber referring to him as 'the brilliant Nicholas Hytner' (*Telegraph*) and Michael Billington asserting that 'Nicholas Hytner brings to this Edwardian tat the same brand of pictorial guile he has shown in his opera house productions' (*Guardian*). This was not the last time that Billington was to refer to Hytner's 'pictorial' style. Indeed, his strong sense of the visual dimension of a production is one of a series of Hytner 'tropes' noted in these early productions, which have became characteristic of his work in the theatre, commented upon in reviews and articles – an emphasis on visual spectacle (sometimes described as operatic),[83] a rapid pace,[84] clarity[85] and intelligence.[86]

Hytner's ambition in terms of staging is evident from this early stage of his career. Correspondence contained in the show file for *The Recruiting Officer* indicates that Hytner was determined to have live farm animals on stage, in a market scene also involving 'vegetable stalls, butcher's [sic.] stalls, carts, pens, straw etc.'[87] According to the press notice issued by production manager Alastair McKenzie, Hytner had in mind '2–4 chickens, 2 piglets, 1 dog and 1 goose or turkey'. In the end he succeeded in getting two goats, two collie dogs and three chickens to produce a scene described by Nicholas Cottis, as showing 'a Hogarthian eye for a lively crowd scene and the telling touch of squalor'.[88]

Jumpers was a theatrical coup. Hytner had in his leading roles two British actors who had both, as the production opened, been nominated for Academy awards: Julie Walters (for *Educating Rita*) and Tom Courtenay (for *The Dresser*). As a result, the production sold out within two days of tickets being put on sale. However, the reviews were mixed, both in relation to the acting and the staging. The primary problems with *Jumpers*, in the eyes of the critics, was that it was 'ill-suited to a theatre-in-the-round'[89] and that Hytner's production made 'maladroit use of the stage space',[90] trundling in two noisy trucks at regular intervals to represent George's study and Dotty's bedroom. This was Hytner's first production at the Manchester Royal Exchange – a challenging space for a director, with 750 seats arranged over three levels around a circular auditorium. Although he later admitted that he felt that he 'did it very badly',[91] the fact that he got on well with the cast, production team and theatre management meant that he was asked, in August 1985, to join the theatre as an associate director. This allowed him ample opportunity to become accustomed to the stage space, learning to use it to great effect – as noted in reviews of Marlowe's *Edward II* (1986), which effectively drew on 'the three-dimensional, gladiatorial nature of theatre-in-the-round';[92] Wycherley's *The Country Wife* (1987), which, in using a revolve on the circular stage, conjured up 'some sort of sexual circus';[93] and Schiller's *Don Carlos* (1987), which made the space 'intimate and epic at the same time', by using a narrow traverse stretching across the circular auditorium.[94] Indeed, when tackling his next production in the space after *Jumpers* – *As You Like It* (1986) – Hytner extolled the virtues of the round, explaining that 'the round only presents problems when you're doing a play where a detailed interior setting is required'. For *As You Like It*, 'a play ... which is totally fluid and requires virtually no furniture', the space proved 'very liberating'.[95]

The Manchester Royal Exchange

Hytner's appointment as an associate director of the Royal Exchange committed him to six months per year working for the theatre.[96] Between 1986 and 1987 he directed five productions, including *As You Like It; Mumbo Jumbo* – a new play by Robin Glendinning, playing initially at the Exchange from 8–31 May 1986, before transferring to the Lyric Hammersmith in London in Summer 1987; *Edward II*; *The Country Wife* and Schiller's *Don Carlos*, in a translation by the actor James Maxwell (whom Hytner had recalled seeing as Prospero in 1969) who also appeared in the production as The Grand Inquisitor.

The productions were all favourably reviewed, the critics reiterating some of the features of Hytner's direction already noted in his earlier productions: visually spectacular staging – often pictorial or emblematic, sometimes flamboyant and camp;[97] an operatic quality;[98] a tendency towards the outrageous or contentious;[99] tightness and pace.[100] The reviews also noted Hytner's fondness for stage 'business', occasionally overused at the expense of the subtleties of a play. Michael Schmidt, reviewing *As You Like It* for *Kaleidoscope*, criticized the fact that 'the production time and time again seems to me to camouflage the language of the play, and to fuss and to replace the very vivid and very accurate language of the play with business' – often repetitive in the case of the actors playing Rosalind, Touchstone and Celia.[101] However, Grevel Lindop, reviewing *Edward II* for *TLS* found that the 'elaborate stage business' enriched rather than detracted from the text, drawing comparisons with 'Peter Brook's legendary *Midsummer Night's Dream*'.[102]

This period of Hytner's directing also helped to establish his aims as a director, aims which seem to have changed little in the intervening years. His choice of repertoire shows a particular fondness for large-scale theatre – 'I'm not a useful director for tiny naturalistic plays. I get frustrated by the lack of ambition'[103] – and for innovation. Although *Mumbo Jumbo* was 'his first crack at directing a brand-new play',[104] it is noticeable that, of his other productions, the script of *Murderer* had been 80 per cent rewritten, such that Harvey Crane, writing in *The Stage,* asserted that the production would 'be taken as a world premiere'.[105] *Jumpers* had not been performed in Britain since its first production in 1972, his *Edward II* was 'the first professional production … for a decade'[106] and his *Don Carlos* was the play's British premiere.[107] Even when directing established classics, the critics noted Hytner's ability to find a way to energize them, making them feel 'new'. *Edward II* was described by Michael Coveney as 'modern and outrageous',[108] *The Country Wife* as 'energetic and up-to-date'[109] by John Peter and 'fresh, exciting and up-to-date' by Robin Thornber,[110] whilst Lindop, writing in the *TLS* described it as seeming 'almost a "new play" in itself', so innovative was Hytner's direction and Mark Thompson's design.[111] These reviews epitomize one of Hytner's professed aims, as stated in an interview in August 1987 – to make classical drama accessible:

> Hytner's burning aim is to wipe out the stuffy and elitist-only appeal of the great classic drama and grand operas

and open them up to be enjoyed by everyday people. He explains: 'I want to stop them being a minority sport. There should be no distinction between art and showbiz. I want to popularize them.'[112]

One of the ways in which Hytner achieved this contemporaneity in these early productions was in his use of an eclectic blend of historical and modern dress in classical plays, giving a sense of timelessness. *Edward II* mixed 'armour' with 'pinstripe', Renaissance and 'punky'[113] modern dress, a decision that Hytner partly justified by asserting that 'that's how Marlowe did it. He was writing about a period that was centuries before his own time but he used a mixture of contemporary and antique costume.'[114] Similarly, *The Country Wife* was set 'in a time capsule which combines the sleazy cocksureness of the Restoration decades with the unashamed chutzpah of the 1980s'.[115]

Hytner's desire not to distinguish between high and low art, but to create what is above all entertainment, is one of the reasons for his varied career – incorporating Shakespeare and grand opera but also pantomime and popular musicals. Hytner was, however, quick to temper his statement with the assertion that he didn't want 'to betray Shakespeare or Schiller or Mozart by messing around with them and not being true to them'.[116] The question of what constitutes 'being true' to Shakespeare is obviously a complex and to some extent unanswerable one, and is in danger of invoking the much-maligned issue of authorial intention. Certainly one of the most notable features of Hytner's first Shakespeare production – *As You Like It* – is that, in terms of fidelity to the text, it certainly does not 'mess around' with Shakespeare. Indeed, the prompt script shows remarkably few cuts to the text – a line or a couple of lines here and there (the most substantial being the frequently cut 4.2 killing of the deer) and, in terms of changes, the relocation of one scene – 3.1 – to between 2.6 and 2.7 and the alteration of four words, mostly, it seems, to make sense of features of the production, for example, the alteration of 'browner' as a descriptor of Celia at 4.3.88 to 'fairer', Suzanne Burden (Celia) being of lighter colouring than Janet McTeer (Rosalind). The killing of the deer scene he claims to have cut because he 'couldn't work out how to do it', but also remarks of the scene's opening question – 'Which is he that killed the deer?' (4.2.1) – 'the answer is "Who gives a fuck?"'.[117]

As You Like It

As You Like It opened at the Royal Exchange on 9 January 1986, the company having begun rehearsals on 25 November 1985. This was the first time, since university, that Hytner had directed a Shakespeare play; indeed it was his first professional production of a classical play, his repertoire at Exeter and Leeds having been mostly twentieth century. However, Hytner has never perceived a particular distinction between directing classical and modern work, his main focus being on making a production speak to a contemporary audience, irrespective of its period of writing. As he explained in an interview in the programme supplement for the tour:

> The only difference between approaching a classical play and a new play is that the writer is dead and not around to be spoken to. As a director, the first job is to bring the play to life on stage for an audience NOW. With an old play there's obviously a fairly delicate relationship to be judged and explored between the audience for which it was written, in this case about 1599, and the audience in 1986. I'm just the chairman, if you like, or the head of a team of people, who are attempting to bring it to life. Any expectations we make of an audience in terms of what they should bring with them of the last 400 years has got, in the end, to relate to where we are now in 1986.[118]

With *As You Like It*, in order to make this connection between '[Shakespeare's] world and our world',[119] one of the first decisions made by Hytner and his team was that 'to try and recreate 1599 in England or in France or wherever ... would convey very little'. Although for Nicholas Shrimpton the 'setting appeared to be Russia in the years after the revolution',[120] Hytner stated that he and Seymour were concerned not to try 'to make any specific modern historical parallels' and to avoid saying specifically 'where Duke Frederick's court was'. The play was to be interpreted rather 'as a contemporary fable'.[121] Hytner's decision not to seek a specific contemporary analogue for the court of Duke Frederick is something that remains characteristic of his Shakespearean productions, a number of which have been set in non-specific, modern-day settings; however, he has become increasingly assiduous about defining a world for each production, moving away from a fabulistic concept of the plays to a more socially realist one – as is evident in his twenty-first century productions of *Henry V, Hamlet, Othello* and *Timon of Athens*.

In addition to epitomizing Hytner's aim of making classical plays relevant, his statement also exemplifies his conception of the role of the director as a collaborator, something that is reiterated by Hytner and other members of the company in their discussions of this production and in accounts of his rehearsal practice throughout his career. As with most of Hytner's Shakespeare productions, the starting point for *As You Like It* was the leading actor – Janet McTeer. McTeer had already played a number of roles at Manchester Royal Exchange and Hytner does not recall whether it was he or another of the associate directors who said 'She should play Rosalind.'[122] Either way, she seemed obvious casting for the role – not least because of her height (just over 6 ft or 1.85m), given Rosalind's own assertion about being 'more than common tall' (1.3.112). The centrality of the actor remains one of Hytner's main concerns – his thinking in relation to a play starts, he asserts, with the question 'Is there someone to whom I might go who might provide that kind of alchemy between part and actor that I think is essential.'[123]

The creation of a strong collaborative relationship with the production team is of equal importance and has often led to Hytner working regularly with the same designers, lighting designers and composers, enabling him to 'develop a shorthand'.[124] Unusually, perhaps, for a Shakespeare production, the collaborative production team at the centre of *As You Like It* was comprised of the director, designer and composer – Hytner, Seymour and Sams. For Hytner, doubtless partly influenced by his wealth of experience in directing opera, the aural was as important as the visual in evoking the locations and atmosphere of Arden. Sams speaks of the idea as being 'to use music like a landscape',[125] a sentiment echoed by Seymour in her description of the 'transformation' at the beginning of the second half of the production, from a wintry Arden to one in Spring, as being 'an absolute fusion' between what was 'happening on the set and what Jeremy [was] doing to the ear'.[126]

With five songs occurring in the forest scenes – 'Under the Greenwood Tree' (2.5), 'Blow, Blow, Thou Winter Wind' (2.7), 'What Shall he Have That Killed the Deer?' (4.2 – cut in Hytner's production), 'It Was a Lover and his Lass' (5.3) and 'Wedding is Great Juno's Crown' (5.4) – music became a particular feature of Arden. Each song was given a distinct quality, the common factor being that all emerged from the company and the situation in which the characters found themselves. Amiens became the 'lead singer', the 'composer in the forest' who has taught the songs to the others using the resources available – the trees or bamboo. This led to the use of panpipes, fashioned 'quite simply by cutting up lengths of bamboo and sticking them together'. 'Under the Greenwood Tree' became a work song; 'Blow, Blow, Thou Winter Wind' a campfire song; and 'A Lover and his Lass' a community song, written by the company themselves. As Sams explains, *As You Like It* often ends 'with a sort of hoe-down or knees-up', but neither he, Seymour nor Hytner felt that this struck the right tone for the end of the play, in which, he asserts, 'there is definitely something magical happening in the forest'.[127] 'A Lover and His Lass' thus filled this gap, creating an opportunity for a lively company song just before the last scene, rather than during it.

For both Seymour and Sams there was 'this marvellous sense that there was a trio of particular kind of mind working together'[128], that this was 'very much a team effort';[129] 'a very mutually rich working process'.[130] Sams and Seymour had both worked with Hytner before *As You Like It* – Sams on *Scarlet Pimpernel* and *Jumpers* and Seymour on *Tom Jones* and *Alice* – and it is clear from Hytner's own comments that he recognized the way in which his strengths and theirs complemented one another. Discussing the directorial/design process, he describes Seymour as having 'a very strong visual response', whilst he had 'a very strong intellectual and emotional response',[131] the two augmenting each other.

In addition to stressing the importance of a strong sense of collaboration within the production team and the company, 'the boss', for Hytner, is the text. For him, the best way for a director or an actor to begin working on a Shakespeare play is 'to mine the text for what the text contains', to declare their 'fidelity to ... the idea of playing at the play'. However, he is keen to point out that fidelity to the text and a desire not to 'betray Shakespeare' is not the same thing as attempting to locate Shakespeare's 'original intention' – 'What Shakespeare would think of it is an irrelevant and rather sentimental question.' The important thing for Hytner was to work out what the text meant then and, more specifically, what it meant 'now'.[132]

Centring on the text, Hytner's rehearsal period began, as is often the case, with 'a very detailed examination and discussion' of the language, characters and situations. Key for Hytner was finding a way of interpreting each moment that felt 'emotionally real'.[133] Duncan Bell, who played Orlando, explains that the impulse for the romantic relationships in the play came from discussions about 'personal experience':

'what kinds of experience have you had of falling in love; do you believe in love at first sight – and so on'.[134] It was, perhaps, this emphasis on finding an emotional truth behind the comic confusions of the play that led to Bell's Orlando, as well as McTeer's Rosalind, seeming 'genuinely tormented and eaten up by ... love'.[135]

In spite of his acknowledgement that one cannot make a Shakespeare play 'seem more like a modern play', Hytner felt that the company could bring 'a set of contemporary psychological responses' to the play, exploring, for example, the relationship between two young women 'in the face of adversity',[136] or the embarrassing situation of 'two guys making friends in the company of the sister of one of them' (3.2).[137] This is something to which Hytner continues to be committed, believing that 'all Shakespeare's plays are steeped in the mess of real life'.[138] In Hytner's view, all scenes in Shakespeare serve a function of driving the story and the characters forwards and 'if at the end of a scene, a character cannot say how the scene has changed him or her, then a solution hasn't been found'.[139] Whilst also accepting that with a play like *As You Like It* 'there is no point pretending that it is contemporary language', Hytner felt that it was possible to get actors to the point 'where the words that Shakespeare uses seem to be the only right words to say at the time'. In his view, in 1986, 'the only problem of Shakespeare's verse speaking' was that of the actors having confidence and 'taking delight in speaking as elaborately or as vividly as Shakespeare asks them to speak'.[140] Speaking in 2013, Hytner's view of Shakespearean verse speaking seemed no less complex. He continues to value actors 'who speak Shakespeare as if it is their first language' and asserts that, quite simply, '99 per cent of the time, the actor's job is to master the text and to speak it as clearly as possible. Nowadays, that's what we mean by good verse speaking.'[141] What Hytner's later assertions make apparent is that the onus is on the actor and that he is most likely to cast in a Shakespeare play those actors to whom Shakespearean verse speaking comes naturally or who have learnt certain techniques in training or other professional work. In *As You Like It*, a number of the actors had, in the view of the critics, not yet mastered such skills. John Peter found 'the verse speaking ... flat, sometimes almost inert', worrying that the production illustrated 'the growing problem that the younger generation of actors are losing touch with Shakespearean technique'.[142] For Michael Schmidt, McTeer in particular did not speak the verse 'with much authority'[143] and Michael Ratcliffe identified a tendency 'to breathe the ends of lines away on an affected dying fall'.[144] Nevertheless the psychological realism found by the actors was noted by critics, particularly in McTeer's performance. Her Rosalind was notable in managing to combine intense passion and vulnerability, a feat most vividly described by Robin Thornber as combining 'the fragile vulnerability of a startled gazelle with the tensile strength of steel mantrap'.[145] For John Barber she was 'ardent' and 'sensitive',[146] for Ratcliffe, 'ardent' and 'insecure'[147] and for Michael Coveney revealing both 'confidence' and 'tenderness'.[148]

Seymour conceived the production in similar terms to Hytner, explaining that the design came both from the text – 'the play as it comes to you' with ideas derived in the first instance from the poetic imagery – and from a desire to 'find whatever the quality is that makes you say I want to do this now, rather than five years ago or five years ahead in the future'.[149] The poetic imagery relating to the locations in the text became the starting point for the design. Like many of Shakespeare's comedies, *As You Like It* revolves around the contrast between the everyday world – as represented by the court – and a festive location emblematic of escape and transformation – as embodied in the forest of Arden. Clear contrasts are established between the two worlds: the court is a corrupt, hierarchical place, an 'envious' place of 'peril' and 'painted pomp' (2.1.3–4), whilst the forest is a place of freedom, a natural environment in which the Duke's former subjects become his 'co-mates and brothers' (2.1.1). However, close examination of the text reveals that the distinction is not as clear-cut as some critics and productions have suggested. In spite of Charles the Wrestler's evocation of Arden as a place where Duke Senior and his men 'live like the old Robin Hood of England' and 'fleet the time carelessly as they did in the golden world' (1.1.113–15), when we first encounter the exiled lords in 2.1, there are allusions to the harsh weather – the 'icy fang / And churlish chiding of the winter's wind' (2.1.6–7). The forest is not without 'peril': Rosalind and Celia fear 'thieves' (1.3.107) and 'assailants' (1.3.111) and Orlando describes it as 'uncouth' (2.6.6), a 'desert inaccessible' (2.7.110) in which the 'bleak air' (2.6.14) threatens to destroy Old Adam. Forests in the Elizabethan periods were still 'synonymous with wildness and danger', the Middle English word 'savage' deriving from the Latin *silva* (a wood).[150] It is not until Act 3 that the environment of Arden seems to become more spring-like and hospitable, the characters more comfortable in the natural environment and the atmosphere of the play more like a comedy than a tragedy. Hytner and Seymour were highly conscious of the contrast between the two environments but also of these early references to the cold, barren nature of the forest. As a result three 'sets' were designed for the production: a bleak, grey court, a wintry forest and a spring glade. The transformation from winter to spring, from peril to freedom, was then emphasized by the placing of the interval after 2.7 and the moving of 3.1 to after 2.6, meaning that the world of the court was entirely left behind after the first half.

Although not set in any particular period of history or location, the court in this production was seen by critics as alluding to a fascistic society, with its grey, hard environment, off-stage sounds of marching and characters clad in grey, high-buttoned uniforms.[151] Such a design concept was not particularly new. Ratcliffe, writing in the *Observer*, suggested that Seymour was 'follow[ing] current practice' in her design for Duke Frederick's court.[152] In fact, as early as 1967, in Clifford Williams's production at the Old Vic, Duke Frederick had been depicted as a 'fascist'[153] and Buzz Goodbody's court, at Stratford-upon-Avon in 1973, had 'the touchy atmosphere of Hitler's bunker'.[154]

As Mike Hubbard (prop-maker for the production) explained, Seymour 'wanted a grey, tarmaccy feel for the court scenes', something achieved by mixing Arditex (a floor levelling compound) with latex to create a dark textured surface.[155] For Seymour the key was to create a cold, harsh environment, giving 'the feeling that winter could kill' even within the walls of the court.[156] The sparse set included a gun rack, with guns and dead animals on display, a further emblem of the court's violence and antagonism towards the natural world.[157] In keeping with Hytner's dual focus on the visual and the aural in creating the play's environments, the court scenes were accompanied by a soundtrack, with the 'disturbing' sounds of marching armies[158] and 'instructors from some distant parade-ground-cum-gymnasium' reverberating off the theatre walls[159] and a continuous barking of dogs, adding to the atmosphere of violent state control.

The initial transformation from Arden to the winter forest was performed in full view of the audience, with the fourteen floor sections being simply turned over, the grey court floor changing piece by piece into the dark green forest. Seymour and Hytner took the song 'Blow, blow thou winter wind' at face value, the 'patchwork overcoats' of Duke Senior and his exiled lords 'immediately imply[ing] Arctic conditions',[160] only ameliorated by the warmth of their campfire. As Seymour explained, this 'strong emphasis ... on the seasons', was 'not entirely of the play' – the lords could be singing and speaking about 'another time' and indeed the song's lyrics may be seen as metaphorical rather than literal – however, she 'felt very passionately that [she] wanted to enact those images, so that people were standing, frozen cold, when they were singing about it'.[161] The inspiration for this scene came, in part, from Hytner's own recollections of school camping trips – 'incredibly demanding and uncomfortable' but with 'a sense of comradeship and excitement' born out of 'great adversity'.[162]

For most of the production's reviewers, the most striking moment came at the start of the second half. Initially the idea had been to change the set from dark forest to spring clearing during the interval. However, the Royal Exchange being a theatre-in-the-round, it is not possible to perform a set change behind a curtain and then reveal it to an audience. Thus, in order to achieve such a moment of revelation, the decision was made to change the set to the mossy glade and then cover it with white snow-like parachute silk, which could be whisked away at the beginning of the second half to reveal 'instant spring'.[163] Hanging willows descended from the flies in what Schmidt and Alan Hulme described as a 'coup de théâtre'[164] and Hytner himself remembers as 'being very beautiful'.[165] This was the moment at which the play moved into another world, taking on 'an air of magic'.[166]

The choice of parachute silk was an interesting one, given the proximity of the production to Adrian Noble's, which opened at the RSC in April 1985, with an Arden swathed in white fabric. Radcliffe interpreted Seymour and Hytner's choice as 'a designer's allusive joke' – a deliberate reference to the Noble production, mercifully whisked away almost as soon as it appeared.[167] However, Hytner denies this, asserting that he used parachute silk because 'that's what I had done in the *Scarlet Pimpernel* and it had worked so well'.[168]

The Arden of the play's second half was a world of physical as well as moral and political freedom, Act 3 beginning with Duncan Bell's Orlando sliding down a rope onto the stage. Seymour was 'very anxious that in Arden the actors should feel they could just tumble over backwards',[169] creating a series of spongy, mossy green mounds onto which the characters could fling themselves – in Michael Billington and Schmidt's view rather too often.[170] This creation of a floor which enabled the actors to perform lying down, stemmed partly from Hytner's growing understanding of the demands and possibilities of the Royal Exchange theatre, which, with its balconies looking down on the action, meant that the actors could perform whole sections 'on their backs, almost as if they were on a bed'.[171]

FIGURE 1 As You Like It, *directed by Nicholas Hytner, the Royal Exchange Theatre, Manchester 1986. Photograph by Kevin Cummins*

For Seymour the costumes to an extent 'grew out of the floor', the different textures and colours of the set dictating the colours and textures of the fabrics.[172] The court costumes were, like the floor, predominantly grey, with silks and 'tropical business suitings' creating 'a metallic feel'; those of the winter forest were dark green, such that the lords 'almost fused into the background'; and those of the spring glade white – emerging partly from 'the classic English image of white cricketers on a village green'.[173] The costumes were also heavily influenced by Hytner's conception of the play as a fable, a sort of modern fairy tale, 'a synthesis of the most contemporary and the most ancient'.[174] Thus, initially Seymour drew two designs for each costume – one fully contemporary and the other more traditional, the final designs combining elements of both. This type of synthesis of periods was a feature of a number of Hytner's early productions of the plays of Shakespeare and his contemporaries, inspired by the sense that Shakespeare himself was writing simultaneously about the world of the play and his own society. The court uniforms were deliberately non-period, with no medals that might seem to allude to a particular country or conflict. The costumes also worked with the set to move the characters from a sense of restriction to one of freedom. Rosalind and Celia were clad in the court in extremely tight grey dresses, in which they could barely move their arms. Once in Arden their costumes afforded them a 'wonderful physical release',[175] the characters shedding layers as the play progressed, such that Rosalind, having entered the forest in cropped trousers, a man's coat, socks and boots, moved to wearing trousers, a white shirt, white waistcoat and plimsolls, and ended up with bare feet in only the waistcoat and trousers. Although Coveney quipped 'is this underwear, or is it the latest male spring fashion?',[176] the production depended, like the play, on the audience suspending disbelief, accepting that Rosalind is in male disguise, and that others see her as a boy, even when, with her bare arms and ankles and long hair falling out of its restraint, she looked extremely feminine.

Reviews of the production were mixed. Coveney described the production as 'irresistible ... brimful of vim and vigour', adding that this is what 'we now expect of this gifted young director'.[177] However, for Schmidt this was 'one of the few disappointments I've had at the Royal Exchange ... a very pleasant evening' but not one 'which one will remember forever'.[178] Particular praise was levelled at the visual and aural design of the production, notably in the second half, Thornber writing that although the production took 'time to come to life' it was 'consistently thrilling in its titillation of the ear and eye'.[179] For Patrick O'Neil, this was a 'stylishly atmospheric woodland romance full of music, mischief, light and energy'.[180] Clearly Hytner's opera directing skills came into play in his marshalling of a large cast in the challenging space of the Exchange, something picked up on by Barber, who, in praising the visual and musical dimensions of the production, added 'Mr Hytner is not an opera director for nothing.'[181] This invoking of Hytner's opera training was one of a number of aspects of the reviews that was to become customary in critical responses to Hytner's productions, particularly during the 1980s and 1990s. Another was praise for Hytner's ability to make a classical play seem new. For Hulme, the text in this production 'sparkle[d] with new-minted freshness'.[182]

The more problematic aspect of the production in the eyes of some of the critics was its sentimentality and lack of darkness. In spite of many of the reviews pointing up the evocation of love as pain in the performances of McTeer and Bell, the production did not, in Peter's view, manage to find the 'moments of darkness' in the excitement of the second half.[183] The reviewer writing in the *Yorkshire Post* similarly 'missed the sense of near anguish in the various lovers and of serious threat from the Duke Frederick's court, by which Shakespeare wisely reminds us that tragedy can always be glimpsed through the bright fabric of happiness'.[184] In an interview a year later, having tackled *Edward II* and *Don Carlos,* Hytner admitted that he had directed *As You Like It* 'very sentimentally', but added the justification that 'there's something true and valuable in optimistic romanticism'.[185]

2

Hytner and
The RSC – 1987–1991

Richard Eyre, then artistic director of the NT, recalls in his diaries that he met with Hytner on 16 April 1987 when Hytner was still working at the Manchester Royal Exchange, describing his impressions of the young director:

> He has a face like a mime – Barrault from *Les Enfants du Paradis* – oval face, arching eyebrows, animated, almost *over*-animated. Flights of ideas and gossip, riffs of enthusiasm, indignation, then repose; latent violence, subverted by a childlike smile. He's prodigiously talented, has a great facility for staging and a great appetite for work. He's from a completely different constituency from me and thinks I should work with new people.[1]

Eyre's comments confirm the fact that by 1987 Hytner had become known for his ability to handle big plays with flair and precision. Over the next few years he was to further enhance this reputation, specializing in large-scale pieces of theatre with huge casts and elaborate sets, establishing this as his theatrical métier. Eyre's statement also explains why, nearly two years after their lunch, at which Eyre invited Hytner to become an Associate of the National,[2] Eyre was to trust him, as his first production at the NT, with *Ghetto*

– a large-scale musical drama with nearly fifty characters, on the theatre's largest stage, the Olivier (the theatre that has now become Hytner's space of choice for his Shakespeare productions at the NT).

Before he was to make his debut at the NT, however, Hytner was invited in late 1987 to direct *Measure for Measure* for the country's other major national theatre company, the RSC. The production opened in November 1987 at the Royal Shakespeare Theatre (RST) in Stratford-upon-Avon, before transferring to the Barbican theatre in London in October 1988. By this time Hytner's second production for the company, *The Tempest*, had opened in Stratford in July 1988, later transferring to the Barbican in May 1989.

Measure for Measure and *The Tempest* at the RSC

Hytner had, he states, always wanted to work at the RSC, 'more than I'd wanted to work at the National, partly because I didn't go to the National as a child'. Having been taken to Stratford by his school and his parents, the RST felt to him 'the most exciting place' and the work of the RSC in the seventies and early eighties 'the most exciting stuff that was available'.[3] Hytner was invited to come to the RSC by its Artistic Director, Terry Hands, who had seen his work at the Manchester Royal Exchange and was reviving the company by inviting new young directors to join its ranks:

> The RSC, then, felt impossible to break into if you hadn't come at it as an assistant director ... That first season I worked at Stratford a whole lot of new directors came.[4]

Hytner was given a free choice of play and chose *Measure for Measure*, a choice which he now describes, ironically, as 'typical of a young director, wanting to start a long

Shakespeare journey'.[5] His subsequent choices of *The Tempest* and *King Lear* were entirely led by a desire to work with actor John Wood, who played both Prospero and Lear.[6]

Measure for Measure

Hytner's *Measure for Measure*, designed by his long-term colleague Mark Thompson, opened with the bases of two large gilded classical pillars dominating the stage, 'elegant reminders', in the words of Peter Kemp 'of the play's concerns: the foundations of authority, the deceptiveness of surface appearance' (*Independent*, 1988).[7] As Escalus and Angelo left the stage at the end of the first scene, the pillars revolved and part of the forestage sank down to reveal a completely different environment – a darkly lascivious but lively under-world with an underground public lavatory inhabited by punkish rent boys. These contrasting locations succeeded in highlighting the dichotomy between the formal court and the permissive streets, between Angelo's stern semblance of morality and the lax morals of the populace under the Duke's regime. As Roger Allam (The Duke) explained, these two separate worlds of the play – the court and the street – were, in Hytner's view 'irreconcilable',[8] an opposition marked by the costumes as well as the set – the 'grey cut-away coats and knee-breeches of the court' which gave way to 'outra-geous cycling shorts and Doc Marten boots'[9] – as if, Michael Billington wrote, 'a society of rigid, ossified formality had been confronted with the milieu of *A Clockwork Orange*'.[10] Hytner describes the costumes as coming from 'an entirely invented theatrical period', but with a 'real post-punk element to the street life'.[11]

These two sections of society, the rulers and the ruled, has 'grown disastrously apart' (Michael Billington, *Guardian*, 1987), the parallels to the contemporary society of Thatcher's Britain painfully evident to many of the reviewers. However, while the leaders might have lost touch with the people,

Hytner's production also succeeded in exposing the pervasive nature of moral and sexual corruption, providing a wider context for Angelo's licentiousness. In 1.2, a besuited businessman, 'identifiable in the following scene as a court official',[12] descended into the lavatory with one of the rent boys, exposing the fact that while the ruling classes were legislating on the lives of the common man, they were themselves indulging in seedy sexual behaviour and drug taking.

A further rotation of the set, after 2.2, revealed the inside of the jail into which grilled walls descended. The set moved seamlessly between these various positions (and other more minor locations), with traps, stage left and stage right, sinking and rising to deliver desks, chairs and tables. The locations may have been clearly differentiated but each possessed a sense of bleakness and brutality. Only in the final scene did the sense of darkness and claustrophobia abate as the middle of the back wall flew up to create a giant concrete arch with a blue, sunlit skyscape behind. However, even here, the hint of the possibility of freedom and escape was compromised by the militaristic presence emphasizing a culture of control.

Atonal music, at times plaintive, at others jazzy, and the sound effects of clanging doors and echoing footsteps, helped to establish the atmosphere in each of the locations, along with the lighting – a cold white for the court room, a bluish tint for the nighttime underworld, near-darkness for the meeting of the Duke and Friar and a warm light for the outside of the nunnery. That the direction, design, lighting and music worked so harmoniously in creating the worlds of the play, was partly due to the reuniting of 'the impressive young Royal Exchange Manchester team' (Michael Coveney, *FT*, 1987), Hytner and Thompson, with Mark Henderson's lighting design (as for *Jumpers, Mumbo Jumbo* and *Edward II*) and Jeremy Sams composing the music (as he had done for *Jumpers, As You Like It, Edward II, The Country Wife* and *Don Carlos*).

FIGURE 2 Measure for Measure *directed by Nicholas Hytner, the Royal Shakespeare Company, 1987. Joe Cocks Studio Collection.* © *Shakespeare Birthplace Trust*

Robert Smallwood suggests that with this production 'a whole critical (and to some extent theatrical) tradition of examining the play in the light of sixteenth-century Christian theology, with Vincentio as a sort of Christian figure, seemed to go out of the window'.[13] Hytner did not focus on the religious aspects of the play but instead directed it 'as an entirely secular drama of politics and sex',[14] a choice which, Brian Gibbons asserts, epitomized a growing trend for productions of the play that bore 'witness to the sociological and political concerns of many modern directors'.[15] Hytner had studied *Measure* for A-level. Then, it had seemed to him 'a statement of sexual liberation':[16] 'From the point of view of the sexual revolution of the early 1970s it was very clear that several characters had sexual hang-ups, that the Duke was a quasi-fascist and that the people who had lots of sex were the heroes.'[17] By the time he came to direct it in Stratford, its meaning had changed. It had become 'a completely different play',[18] 'a play about how individuals relate to government as well as to each other'.[19]

The production struck many critics as extremely apposite, a comment on Thatcher's 'eagerly-predicted thoughts on the New Morality' and a 'timely and vivid account of the hazards of putting such mighty matters into the hands of fallible instruments of government' (Jack Tinker, *Daily Mail*, 1988). However, like Hytner's previous productions of classical plays, the setting of the production was non-specific: a sort of '20th century no man's land' (Nicholas de Jongh, *Guardian*, 1988), with allusions to the Renaissance, the nineteenth century and the 1980s, creating a topographical uncertainty, which permitted multiple associations in the minds of critics and audiences. Some saw allusions to the Nazis (de Jongh, 1988; Martin Hoyle, *FT*, 1988; Jim Hiley, *The Listener*, 1988), others to a Central European communist state (de Jongh, 1988). Allam wholeheartedly approved of this loose twentieth-century setting, asserting that 'If you shift the period of a classical play, the danger is that the production can become about how clever you are in your recreation of the detail of that period, rather than releasing the meanings of the play itself.'[20] Hytner himself is less sure, in retrospect, about the decision, asserting that, influenced by German theatre, the production was 'very operatic ... probably rather over-blown visually; maybe even over-blown conceptually'.[21]

Most of the critics approved of the choice of setting. However, a few felt that in transplanting the action of the play into the twentieth century, elements became 'contrived and unconvincing' (Charles Osborne, *Telegraph*, 1988), making an already difficult play less plausible (Eric Shorter, *Telegraph*, 1987) and that Isabella's 'pious self-righteousness' in valuing her chastity over her brother was more difficult for audiences to accept within a modern-day context (Milton Shulman, *Evening Standard*, 1988). However, Hytner defends this, stating that 'the only degree to which Josette [Simon's] ethnic background [being of Antiguan descent] had any proper impact on the play' was in this respect:

> that being black, because of the piety of so many contemporary black Britons, you believed her decision to become a nun very easily, and you believed, and were sympathetic to her priorities when demands are made on her by Angelo. You didn't find them offensive. You didn't find them eccentric.[22]

Once again, Hytner was praised for his inventiveness, his intelligence,[23] his theatricality[24] and the pace of the production, in which one scene flowed seamlessly into another.[25] Billington, prone to referencing Hytner's opera-directing career in his reviews, did not doubt that the production would be described as 'operatic', but added that he viewed this a compliment 'at a time when opera often has an excitement lacking in straight drama' (Billington, 1987). Whilst Hytner now believes opera to have had a detrimental influence on *Measure for Measure* (see Chapter 1), in 1989 he was drawing positive parallels between the two genres, asserting that he wanted *Measure for Measure* to be 'a big experience',[26] citing opera as a genre that 'insists that you drop everything and share huge passions, emotions of extreme abandon, intimations of harmony and perfection' and asserting that 'one should try to make it like that in the spoken theatre'.[27]

One of the most praised elements of the production was Allam's Duke, both in terms of Allam's performance and in terms of the way in which Hytner's production established him as the central figure of the play – a position often inhabited by Angelo or Isabella but one, for Hytner, that belongs to the Duke.[28] For John Peter, writing in the *Sunday Times*, Hytner's production, in making the Duke 'the centre of the action', restored him to 'his rightful place' and revealed the play, not only 'at long last' as a 'political play' but as 'the most scorchingly modern drama of its time' (John Peter, *Sunday Times*, 1987). Most significantly, rather than playing the Duke as was typical, as a Christ-like figure or 'a surrogate playwright manipulating the plot',[29] Allam found the character's humanity and vulnerability – this was a man 'in the midst of a deep personal crisis',[30] driven from the court by 'fear of government'.[31] As Hytner explains, Allam's Duke 'had had a breakdown before the play started and was totally immobilized; almost literally physically paralyzed at the start of the play, and starting from that was really productive and really interesting'.[32] In acknowledging that the Duke 'is as fallible as everyone else', Hytner and Allam gave the play, in the eyes of critic Irving Wardle, its necessary and often missing 'coherence' (Irving Wardle, *The Times*, 1987).

Allam, as the Duke, was at the centre of the production from its conception. As his account of playing the role in *Players of Shakespeare 3* details, Hytner, having cast him, invited him to be involved in early design discussions and in Hytner and Thompson's research (including a visit to Pentonville prison), something which, Allam stresses, no director had ever invited him to do before and which indicates not only Hytner's view of the Duke as central to the play but also his inclusive and collaborative working methods.[33]

Allam's was not the only reinvention and re-interrogation of character. As Andrew Rissik remarked, the acting as a whole seemed 'new-minted' and 'free of Shakespearean cliché', comments that anticipate critical reactions to many of Hytner's subsequent Shakespeare productions. Alex Jennings's Lucio was not a spirited spiv, as is often the case, but a rather smug yuppie with a laid-back air of 'languid sophistication' (de Jongh, 1988). Unlike in his other ventures with Hytner thus far, however, Jennings's performance divided the critics. While some of them found his contemptuous, suave interpretation effective and amusing (Kemp, 1988; Tony Dunn, *The Tribune*, 1988), others found it 'affected' (Matt Wolf,

City Limits, 1988), 'overdone' and not entirely coherent (Hoyle, 1988). Phil Daniels's Pompey was similarly original in conception: a streetwise, sleazy, unpleasant wide boy, accompanied by his threatening acolytes. In Billington's view, the scene in which he appeared before Escalus in court was particularly effective in being played for more than the usual 'lewd comedy', conveying, through the 'evil' behaviour of this Pompey, 'running intellectual rings round the Bench to volleys of applause from his thugs in the back row', a 'potent image of a disintegrating society' (Billington, 1987).

For some reviewers these characters of the comic subplot (along with David Pullan as Froth and George Raistrick as Elbow) were in danger of stealing the show, something that has been a recurrent feature of Hytner's productions of Shakespeare's Comedies – in particular *The Tempest* (1988) and *Twelfth Night* (1998). Deemed rather less effective were the scenes between Isabella, Angelo and Claudio. Although Josette Simon's Isabella was seen as poised and touchingly vulnerable, many critics felt that her performance was under-powered and lacking in emotional intensity. Also problematic for some critics was Hytner's casting of black actors as both Isabella and Claudio. By casting a black Claudio as well as a black Isabella, Hytner seemed to make a point about the colour of these characters' skin (rather than engaging in racial-blind casting). Jim Hiley and Patrick Marmion both viewed the decision as hinting at racial victimization in the state of Vienna, something about which Hiley had his 'doubts' (*The Listener*, 1988), while Marmion felt that the implications of this choice were not 'followed through' and that 'the issues remain[ed] confused' (*What's On*, 1988). As Smallwood suggests, when in 2.4 Angelo brutally assaulted Isabella, one could not help but see a 'corrupt white male in authority, tyrannizing over the defenseless black woman in subser-vience'.[34] This was an extremely violent depiction of 2.4, in which Angelo seemed to come close to raping Isabella, flinging her onto the floor and sitting astride her. Hytner, however, denies any attempt to make a racial point in his casting of the roles. His casting of Simon was, to all intents and purposes, 'colour-blind', although he resents the implications of the term, stating:

> Why should you be blind to Josette Simon's colour? She's not blind to her own colour. You just say – great, how great, Josette Simon's a great actress, let the fact that she's black either mean something or not mean something, and both are totally legitimate ways of going.

Having cast a black Isabella, he then decided to cast a black Claudio (Hakeem Kae-Kazim) because of his leanings towards 'social realism' and a desire to make Isabella and Claudio clearly 'biologically related',[35] a form of realism that he now regards as unnecessary, asserting that:

> The only thing that seems important to me is that a theatre committed to the classical repertoire, particularly the Renaissance repertoire, which is not of itself socially realistic, must be committed to including the entire theatrical community in its performance. There can hardly be any argument about that.

If the critics were less than complimentary about the portrayal of Isabella, Angelo (played by Sean Baker in Stratford and John Shrapnel in London) and Claudio in the central scenes of the play, they were entirely won over by the production's ending. The final scene of *Measure for Measure* is one that defines the tone of the production. Ever since, in 1970, Estelle Kohler's Isabella, in John Barton's production of the play (which Hytner recalls having seen as a child), 'shocked audiences by silently refusing to acquiesce to the Duke's offer of marriage at the end of the play',[36] the issue of whether Isabella chooses to accept the Duke's proposal has been a key focus of any production. For Charles Osborne, Hytner's ending was 'the most satisfactorily staged that I have seen' (1988), retaining 'a sense of ominous ambiguity' (Jack Tinker, *Daily Mail*, 1988).

When Allam's Duke uttered his fateful words, 'Give me your hand and say you will be mine' (5.1.489), Simon's Isabella backed away, the Duke's subsequent 'But fitter time for that' (5.1.490) eliciting an awkward laugh from the audience. His second attempt, some forty lines later, 'Dear Isabel... what is yours is mine' (5.1.530–3) was once again met with no response, Isabella remaining motionless. As the rest of the company exited, leaving the Duke and Isabella on stage, Isabella, watched by the Duke, moved to the upstage arch, as if contemplating leaving. However, in the final moments she turned to face him, her expression inscrutable, as the lights faded. Hytner knew from the outset that he wanted to create this sort of ambiguous ending: 'I like ambiguous endings and I've done a lot of them'. In having Isabella turn back in the final moments, he wanted the audience 'not to know what she was going to do after the lights came down, because that's how you feel when you read the play'.[37]

The Tempest

Like many of Hytner's productions, one of the notable features of his RSC *Tempest* was its freshness and originality, both in terms of style and interpretation. For Michael Coveney, the production entirely released the play 'from RSC antiquarianism', bringing to it a fresh 'new style' (*FT*, 1988),[38] whilst Sheridan Morley praised 'a totally fresh reading of a familiar text', each line 'rethought and reconsidered' (*Herald Tribune*, 1989). As with *Measure for Measure*, Hytner did not follow some of the more traditional routes in his interpretation of the play, treating it 'neither as Jacobean Masque, lecture on exploitation nor metaphor for theatre' (Michael Billington, *Guardian*, 1989). John Wood's Prospero was 'not an omniscient magus' nor 'a Renaissance prince', but 'an ordinary everyman', 'compellingly human'[39] in his vulnerability and self-doubt. As Hytner explained in a question and answer session at the International Shakespeare Conference in 1988, he viewed Prospero as acting unselfishly, 'on behalf of Miranda'. This Prospero might have been 'quite content to stay on the island' but needed to 'compensate his daughter' for her lost years spent in isolation. He was not comfortable with the role of a ruler, but forced himself to accept it for the sake of Miranda's future.[40] Equally, this Prospero was torn in his enactment of retribution, his 'desire for revenge ... coupled with a Hamlet-like awareness of its final futility' (Billington, *Guardian*, 1989). For Michael Ratcliffe, 'in this age of psychotic, bitter, colonialist Prosperos' this was 'a radical revising of the role' and one 'which only a classical actor of exceptional gifts, discipline and wit could have accomplished' (*Observer*, 1989).

Unusual too in an age of post-colonial readings of the play, was Prospero's relationship with Caliban – a relationship characterized more by guilt than by an assertion of superiority or desire for dominance. From the outset, Wood's Prospero appeared 'suitably shamefaced about the fact that Caliban "serves in offices that profit us"' (Billington, *Guardian*, 1989), uttering these lines (1.2.313–14) stiffly, with an air of embarrassment. In the final scene, Caliban flung himself prostrate at Prospero's feet, fearing that he would be 'pinched to death' (5.1.277). Instead, Wood's Prospero reached down and gently touched his head, uttering his lines with a genuine note of forgiveness to a truly penitent Caliban.

John Kane's Caliban was, perhaps, equally unconventional, in a period when, since Jonathan Miller's seminal 1970 production, multi-racial casting had become standard practice.[41] He was 'not at all the victim of a violent colonialism', but a 'savage with a soft heart, acted by a white man' (Dominic Gray, *What's On*, 1989). Hytner himself was less interested at the time in post-colonial theories than in Jungian archetypes of air, earth, fire and water, wanting to characterize Caliban as 'earth': 'I wanted him literally to erupt from the earth and what we managed was a big boulder that he came out of.'[42]

Certainly this was a relatively sympathetic portrait of a character described in the First Folio dramatis personae as a 'deformed salvage'. Kane's Caliban, though covered in blotches and speaking in a dark, rasping voice, was perceived by the critics as 'a piteous monster' (Rhoda Koenig, *Punch*, 1989), a 'hopeless freedom-fighter' (Dan Jones, *Sunday Telegraph*, 1989), an 'endearing simpleton' (Milton Shulman, *Evening Standard*, 1989), 'a victim more to be pitied than scorned' (Clive Hirschhorn, *Sunday Express*, 1989). As Alden T. Vaughan and Virginia Mason Vaughan elucidate:

> his monster did not aspire to freedom or to hegemony over the island. Rather, he wanted a master who would love him. He wanted to return to the golden age before he was cast out from the family circle; he hoped through Stephano and Trinculo to re-create that golden world. He would be happy as a servant if only he were not pinched. And he loved the island, which, in some mysterious sense, spoke through him.[43]

Sounding not unlike Wood's Prospero in his vowels and intonation, here was a Caliban who had absorbed his master's influence rather than rejected it.

The other roles that seemed notably re-defined by Hytner's productions were those of Trinculo and Stephano – parts often unremarkable in performance. The performances were highly inventive: Desmond Barrit's Trinculo a round, camp, fastidious fool and Campbell Morrison's Stephano a grumpy Glaswegian. Free from the clumsy clowning so often associated with the character, these performances were hailed by many of the critics as the funniest incarnations of the characters they had seen.[44] It is worth recalling that Hytner himself had received accolades for his student performance as Trinculo, at Cambridge.

Virginia Mason Vaughan remarks on two other features of characterization that differed from those of many other productions, most notably Prospero's overtly affectionate relationship with Miranda, a relationship 'highlighted more fully than in many other productions',[45] such that Kate

Kellaway felt moved to describe him as 'more maternal than fatherly', practising 'not a "rough" but a gentle magic' (*Observer*, 1988). In contrast to his obsessively gentle, tactile behaviour towards his daughter, Prospero's treatment of Ariel was unemotional and at times aggressive – a 'much less complex relationship' than that depicted by many of 'his predecessors'.[46] In 1.2 he moved between shouting at Ariel (so that he cowered on the ground) and patronizing him – delivering 'Thou best know'st / What torment I did find thee in' (1.2.286–7) slowly as if to a small child, while in 4.1 his speech to Ariel, 'Thou and thy meaner fellows your last service / Did worthily perform, and I must use you / In such another trick' (4.1.35–7), was not spoken with any gratitude but barked impatiently.

One of the most original elements of this production was its opening moments, the storm sequence. During the eighteenth and nineteenth centuries, the words of this scene were habitually cut in favour of sound effects and music. Indeed, Christine Dymkowski suggests that with the exception of some dialogue in David Garrick's 1757 text and William Burton's 1854 production, 'none of Shakespeare's opening scene was heard on stage until the beginning of the twentieth century'.[47] Even when the words have been spoken on stage, they have frequently been drowned out by the sounds of wind, rain and thunder. Hytner's production began with a raging storm but, as the lights came on with the final flash of lightning, revealing the mariners on deck and the Master in a basket high above the deck, everything went quiet, with the exception of an eerie hum. Only intermittently, as a 'wave' (as detailed in the prompt book)[48] hit the deck, was there a loud crack of noise and flash of light, flinging the mariners to the deck. The critics picked up on two key effects of this strangely quiet storm: firstly its evocation of a sense of 'magic' (Christopher Edwards, *The Spectator*, 1989), the sailors appearing 'to be sleepwalking, as if hypnotized' (Jones, 1989) and secondly, the fact that, unusually, it allowed the lines of this scene to be heard – 'the boatswain whispering his instructions instead of out-roaring the elements' (Billington, 1989). Hytner remains particularly pleased with the reactions to this opening sequence, which was only devised in this way in previews:

> The first preview of *The Tempest* there was a meticulously tech-ed bang, crash, wallop storm. You couldn't hear a fucking word. So we got rid of it. We dealt with it. I think we probably dealt with it [at the] second preview. That's how it happened. It was good because it was absolutely essential to deal with something that wasn't working, and what we chose to make it work immediately seemed to make sense.

This event epitomizes Hytner's view that 'theatre is a compromise' and that 'things are good, not to the extent that the compromise is close to the original idea but that the compromise itself is good'.[49]

The restraint and clarity of the storm were characteristic of the production as a whole. Although Dan Jones felt that the production might 'disappoint at first', the 'storm-tossed ship and Prospero's Island' both seeming too 'bare' and 'artificial' (*Sunday Telegraph*, 1989), many critics praised the 'spectacular elegance and simplicity' (Ratcliffe, *Observer*, 1989) of the set, the 'neutral setting' permitting, in Stanley Wells's eyes, 'full play to the text's symbolic resonances'.[50] Hytner admits that the simplicity and symbolism of the design was not in his 'comfort zone' but, like the conception of Caliban, puts the decision down to an obsession at the time with Jung:

> God knows how or why I decided to do it that way, going for Jungian archetypes. I can't even remember how I applied Jung to the play, but I remember being very taken with Jung at the time. I think I'd gone to see a Jungian analyst for only a matter of weeks, because he was expensive and whatever problem I was having I thought – 'That's all fine now; he's solved that; my head's all better', but I got very into Jung.[51]

Interestingly, none of the critics picked up on this strand of influence, although Hytner's 1998 production of *Twelfth Night* was described by some as Jungian,[52] something that Hytner thinks might have been a 'hangover' from this 'phase'.[53]

The set for *The Tempest* consisted of a raked white circular disc, with a central cave and a single rock stage left (the rock into which Caliban is 'confined' (1.2.361). This was backed by a blue gauze topped with grey curtains, which could be ruched up to create clouds or dropped down to create a dark background and two mirrored panels downstage right and left, all neatly capturing, in the words of Rhoda Koenig, 'the mixture of fantasy and brutality in this strange play' (*Punch*, 1989). Lighting was used to enhance this atmosphere, 'darkening faces into shadow-lands where you really don't want to go' (Dominic Gray, *What's On*, 1989) and giving the scenes with Ariel an eerie bluish tinge. This 'economy of staging' contributed, in Peter Kemp's view, to the 'atmosphere of beautiful lucidity' (*Independent*, 1989), something which a number of critics picked up on. As with many of Hytner's productions, this *Tempest* stood out from others for its 'clarity' (Tinker, 1989; and Martin Hoyle, *FT*, 1989), creating the impression felt Billington, that 'we were listening to it for the first rather than the fiftieth time' (*Guardian*, 1989).

While the set for the production was simple and economical, this did not preclude the inclusion of the sorts of lavish visuals for which Hytner had become known. Maureen Paton looked forward to *Miss Saigon* in her description of the production as a 'ravishing spectacle' (*Daily Express*, 1989) and Eric Shorter and Billington both invoked Hytner's operatic work. Billington compared the production to Hytner's *The Magic Flute* at the ENO, in both his 1988 Stratford and 1989 London reviews, while Shorter praised the 'visual and musical sensibilities' which Hytner brought from his operatic career (*Telegraph*, 1988).

These visual and musical sensibilities were enhanced, once again, by Hytner's collaboration with Sams as musical director and Henderson as lighting designer. Indeed, Billington found the much of the play's magic resided in Sams's music and 'the rapid tonal shifts to arctic-blue in Mark Henderson's lighting' (*Guardian*, 1988). A few critics invoked Caliban's speech about the island in 3.2, in describing Sams's music as full of 'sounds and sweet airs' (Tinker, 1989; Hoyle, 1989) played by 'a thousand twangling instruments' (Tinker, 1989; Paton, 1989), but most stressed its capacity for evoking the odd and mysterious atmosphere of the island.[54] There was, however, a lack of consensus as to whether the large set magical pieces – notably the disappearing banquet with Ariel's appearance as a harpy in 3.3 and the betrothal masque in 4.1 – were 'truly magical' (Hoyle, 1989) or unintentionally 'funny' (Gray, 1989); 'stunning' (Coveney, 1988) or 'kitsch' (Kellaway, 1988).

The disappearing banquet sequence was staged to eerie, discordant music. True to the Folio's stage directions, with Prospero standing, 'invisible', observing everything, the 'strange shapes' entered, 'bringing in a banquet'. This banquet was contained within six glass globes which the shapes laid out in a large circle, 'inviting the King, &c to eat', before exiting. These were, as Gonzalo describes them, figures 'of monstrous shape'; strange creatures with blue monkey-like faces moving in contorted postures. On Alonso's line 'Stand to and do as we', as the lords moved towards the globes, trying to find their way in to taste the food, Ariel, having descended largely unnoticed, suddenly unfurled his wings and with a crash of sound and flash of light the banquet food turned to sand. While Coveney spoke slightly disparagingly of the 'reversible plastic seafood displays' (1988), Anne Donaldson felt that the scene had 'real magic – jardinières of fruit turned to dust while the eye is diverted' (*Herald*, Scotland, 1989).

The next magical sequence, the masque of 4.1, is one of the most difficult to stage in the Shakespearean canon, partly, David Lindley argues, because 'the masque as a literary genre is so deeply embedded in the culture of the early seventeenth century that subsequent productions have had great difficulty in finding a theatrical vocabulary capable of suggesting to an audience its full significance'.[55] One might imagine that with his operatic background Hytner would be particularly adept at staging the masque sequence, with its demands for singing and dancing and indeed, in the eyes of some, he was. For Clive Hirschhorn this usually 'tedious' sequence was transformed into an 'enchanting vision' (*Sunday Express*, 1989). However, Shorter found it 'frankly and impossibly operatic' (1988).

In fact, less of the masque was sung than is sometimes the case, Iris and Ceres both speaking their lines, with only Juno's lines and the Choruses set to music. The whole masque, which Coveney dubbed 'a rainbow-encased Martha Graham ballet' (1988) was accompanied by discordant music to which the goddesses performed simple, stylized, balletic movements, while Ariel floated half way up the proscenium arch, observing. The goddesses appeared in turn, Iris from the rear of the stage, Ceres rising from the back stage centre lift (as if emerging from the earth) and finally Juno, descending from the flies and floating above the stage, each accompanied by a child, who frequently mirrored their actions.

On the line 'Juno does command' (4.1.131), the grey fabric at the back of the stage ruched up, once again, into a cloud-like formation, revealing a golden cornfield, dotted with poppies, in which the reapers and nymphs were seen, performing a country dance. For Hoyle, this was magically reminiscent of 'a Millet canvas' (1989); for Shorter it resembled 'Oklahoma' (1988). As this bucolic vision was abruptly terminated by Prospero on his recollection of 'Caliban and his confederates' (4.1.140) – 'Well done! Avoid; no more!' (4.1.142) – the grey material instantly descended over the gauze again, obscuring the dancers and causing the goddesses to melt away. The 'well-done', much like Prospero's disingenuous expression of thanks to Ariel earlier in the scene, was less a genuine congratulation and more an irritated and dismissive snap, revealing his self-absorbedness and self-centredness.

As Holland's lucid programme note explored, Prospero and his interpretation are central to any production of the play: 'his place at the centre of *The Tempest* – and few of Shakespeare's plays are so completely dominated by a single character – is just as surely significant for the effect of the action on him'.[56] Wood's 'neurotic, tortured, vengeful' (Hirschhorn, 1989) Prospero was, for the most part, hailed by the critics as succeeding in combining vulnerability with power, humour with fury. This was, in Coveney's view, the finest Prospero that he had seen – variously described as 'spell-binding' (Coveney, 1988), 'remarkable' (Dan Jones, *Sunday Telegraph*, 1989), 'thrilling' (Ratcliffe, 1989). Charles Spencer was one of the few who took exception to what he described as an 'exhibitionist' performance which drew 'attention to its own range and versatility while paying scant regard to either the spirit of the play or the precise meaning of the lines' (*Telegraph*, 1989). Certainly Wood's delivery was the area over which critics were most divided, with almost all commenting on his tendency to stress the lines in odd ways, adding unusual pauses and emphases.[57] For some, Wood's habit of painting the words – roaring the word 'roared': 'To cry to th'sea that roared to us' (1.2.149) and darkly growling the word 'dark': 'dark backward and abysm of time' (1.2.50) – was virtuosic and impressive.[58] Morley asserted that 'not since John Gielgud ... have we had a Prospero with an entire orchestra in his voice, nor one so willing to use the full range of its music' (*Herald Tribune*, 1989). For others it was 'annoyingly patronizing' in its spelling out of meaning: less Gielgud-like than 'a cross between ... Brian Redhead and a Blue Peter presenter' (Jane Edwardes, *Time Out*, 1989). Certainly the RSC archive recording of the production reveals Wood's strange howling on 'wolves howl' (1.2.288) engendering titters of laughter in some audience members. In Ratcliffe's view this was 'one of the best spoken Shakespeare performances seen in the capital for years' (1989); in Hoyle's, the whole production was dogged by 'over-emphatic speech ... Everything is *italicized,* stressed, underlined, interpreted almost out of existence' (1989). Hytner himself felt that Wood's use of his voice was completely appropriate to the figure of 'a magus': 'I loved what John did because I love originality and quirkiness and the foundation was pain always ... He used his voice, and he used his intellect and his quirkiness to illuminate things that you hadn't noticed before.'[59]

As a result of working with him on *The Tempest*, Hytner forged a close working relationship with Wood, later casting him as King Lear at the RSC and then as Justice Shallow in *Henry IV Part 2* at the NT some fifteen years later. Wood's appeal, for Hytner, was his inventiveness, vulnerability and volatility – factors that made his work gripping and sometimes unpredictable. Hytner cites what he describes as 'a brilliant moment during a preview in the Barbican', a moment other directors might have found frustrating or infuriating:

> There were a lot of kids in the audience and they were coughing a lot, and in the middle of Act 1 in his story to Miranda he got fed up and turned and shouted 'Will you please stop coughing' and then immediately said 'I'm sorry, I'm sorry', which is so John – lashes out and then realizes I so should not have lashed out. And as a result he killed the show. They were terrified. And Des [Barrit] did his big silent slow walk up the spiral at the back and before he started he went 'ahem' [and then immediately put his hand over his mouth] and they roared with laughter and everything was fine again. But the rest of the cast was furious with poor John – they were furious with him because you know what actors are like. But that was so like John; he would get furious and lash out and then he would lash himself for days about it.[60]

This anecdote epitomizes Hytner's understanding of and sensitivity towards actors and his capacity, as a director, to turn such character-traits to the benefit of a production. Wood's tendency to lash out and then regret his actions perfectly describes one of the main features of his later performance as King Lear.

The ending of this production had something in common

with the final scene of Hytner's *Measure for Measure*, in its exploitation of silence and ambiguity and anticipates Hytner's later productions of Shakespeare Comedies – *Twelfth Night* and *The Winter's Tale*. Although emphasizing the themes of forgiveness and repentance – particularly in the exchange between Prospero and Caliban – the lack of explicit remorse shown by Antonio in this final scene was made explicit. Perhaps influenced by Holland's views, as expressed in the programme note, that 'silence fascinates Shakespeare' and that 'there is nothing in Antonio's few brief comments in the last scene to suggest that he is in the least the "penitent" Prospero assumes or hopes all the King's party have become',[61] the production ended with a notable lack of reconciliation between the brothers. Initially Prospero seemed on the attack. On his line 'For you, most wicked sir ...' (5.1.131), he moved angrily towards Antonio, but in the middle of the speech, suddenly broke down in tears, flinging his arms around Antonio's neck – 'I do forgive / Thy rankest fault' (5.1.132–3). However, Antonio made no reciprocal move, remaining stiff against the embrace and clearly resistant. Following Prospero's invitation to his 'cell' (5.1.303), the lords processed down the cave trap, Antonio bringing up the rear. As he passed Prospero he looked over his shoulder at him, his gaze ambiguously set between repentance and revenge.

Hytner's recollections of his production of *The Tempest* are similar to those of *Measure for Measure*: broadly critical. He candidly states that he doesn't think that the production 'was very good', although he describes Wood, Bell and Barrit as all being 'wonderful'.[62] The critics, in general, felt otherwise, the production being variously described as 'inspired' (Edwardes, 1989), 'enchanting' (Kemp, 1989 and Jones, 1989), 'stylish' (Shulman, 1989), 'elegant' (Christopher Edwards, *The Spectator*, 1989), 'moving' and 'beautiful' (Ratcliffe, 1989), with Hirschhorn going 'as far as to say that if you see a better production than the RSC's *The Tempest* (Barbican) during what remains of this century, it would have to be directed by Shakespeare himself' (1989).

Although these productions were praised by critics and audiences, Hytner has only directed one further production for the RSC in a theatre-directing career that has spanned nearly twenty-five years: *King Lear* in 1990/91. This is, perhaps, surprising given that in 1988, after *Measure for Measure* and *The Tempest* had played in Stratford, he was, according to Morley, already being 'tipped as a prospective future leader of the RSC'.[63] However, when Terry Hands announced in 1989 that he would step down as artistic director two years later, Hytner was approached to put himself forward as his successor (he stresses that he was 'absolutely not' offered the job and was one of many who were sounded out for the role).[64] However, he felt that he was 'too young'[65] for the job. He later stated that he felt no more than a 'welcome visitor' at the RSC, whereas at the NT he immediately felt at home.[66]

Ghetto to *Wind in the Willows* – the Start of a National Theatre Career

According to Hytner, the reason that he was not 'daunted' by the prospect of directing *Ghetto* (1989) on the Olivier stage was his experience in opera.[67] This experience, which he felt may have negatively affected his Shakespeare productions at the RSC, making them representational rather than real (see Chapter 1), was undoubtedly vital in helping him to manage the cast of thirty-eight actors and the musical content of the show.

Set in the Vilna Jewish ghetto in Lithuania between January 1942 and September 1943, the play centres on the Jewish residents' formation of a theatre troupe as a means of survival and consolation and includes songs ranging from traditional Jewish songs to jazz numbers, many of which were written in the ghetto at Vilna (Michael Billington, *Guardian*).[68] For the music, Hytner collaborated once again with Sams, with whom he had now worked on eight theatre productions, including *As*

You Like It, *Measure for Measure* and *The Tempest*. Hytner's team also included other familiar colleagues including designer Bob Crowley, who had designed *The Magic Flute* (ENO 1988) and was to go on to become one of Hytner's most frequent collaborators, working with him at the NT on *The Madness of George III*, *Carousel* and *The History Boys*. Alex Jennings, who had by now done three shows (*Scarlet Pimpernel*, *The Country Wife* and *Measure for Measure*) with Hytner, was cast as Kittel, the sadistic and capricious SS officer in charge of the ghetto. The play was praised as a true 'ensemble' piece (Lydia Conway, *What's On*) with a 'superb cast' (John Nathan, *Jewish Chronicle*), Jennings, Linda Kerr Scott as Djigan, John Woodvine as Gens, chief of the Jewish police and Maria Friedman as Hayyah, a former professional singer, all garnering rave reviews.

Friedman credits the production, and Hytner's direction, as marking a turning point in her career, a point at which she became 'passionate' about theatre and, having worked with Hytner, came to the realization 'that being an actor wasn't just singing, dancing and entertaining, that you could really communicate something to people', making them think.[69] The desire to make a play speak to a contemporary audience is something that has characterized Hytner's work at Manchester and at the RSC, from new plays to Shakespeare and the classics, and it was something that was of prime importance to him in accepting this NT commission. According to Daniel Rosenthal, Hytner was 'initially anxious that *Ghetto* … might be perceived as "Holocaust entertainment"', but made the decision to accept the production on the basis that it had something important and pertinent to say about 'how the shadow of the Holocaust was still affecting Israeli politics, and through Israeli politics, all of us'.[70]

The production opened on 27 April 1989 in a version by David Lan (adapted from Joshua Sobol's Hebrew play via a literal translation). Although this London opening followed productions of the play in 'a dozen cities from Berlin to Los Angeles' (Sheridan Morley, *Herald Tribune*), Hytner's was the 'first English language [sic] production' (Paul Anderson, *Tribune*) – effectively another 'premiere' for Hytner in the mould of *Don Carlos*, the British premiere of an eighteenth-century play (see Chapter 1).

In addition to maintaining Hytner's track record for socio-political immediacy, the reviews of *Ghetto* demonstrate that the production also cemented his reputation for exuberant and spectacular staging, the critics describing it as 'epic' (Morley), 'compelling' (Paul Taylor, *Independent*), 'remarkable' (Clive Hirshhorn, *Sunday Express*) and 'spectacular' (Maureen Paton, *Daily Express*); 'thrillingly' (Charles Spencer, *Telegraph*) and 'magnificently' (Kenneth Hurren, *Mail on Sunday*) staged by Hytner, with his trademark qualities of 'invention' (Jim Hiley, *The Listener*) and imagination (Michael Coveney, *FT*). Eyre's diaries also indicate that although he may have had some reservations about the play, the production confirmed his expectations of Hytner in terms of its staging: 'It's a triumph for Nick [*Hytner*] and Bob [*Crowley*] ... They've staged it brilliantly.'[71] This was the beginning of Hytner's NT career, which was to culminate fourteen years later, with his succeeding Eyre's successor, Trevor Nunn, as Artistic Director.

Hytner followed *Ghetto* with an even bigger and more ambitious project: Claude-Michel Schönberg and Alain Boublil's *Miss Saigon,* a through-sung, operatic musical, inspired by Puccini's *Madame Butterfly* with a cast of forty-one actors, singers and dancers. The production bore some similarity to *Ghetto,* being, once again, an elaborate musical production that tackled a difficult, brutal subject – in this case the Vietnam War. However, this production was on a much larger scale than *Ghetto* and remains the largest budget that Hytner has handled in his career, thus far.

Hytner declares that he has always 'loved musicals'[72] and leapt at the opportunity to direct a West End show. The production met, for the most part, with glowing reviews; a few critics found the score unmemorable and the politics rather insipid, but almost all praised Hytner's production and John Napier's design. Eyre wrote about the production in his diaries, again praising Hytner's staging as 'dazzling' but struggling with the manipulative use of filmed footage of Vietnamese orphans (during the number 'Bui Doi') in order 'to make us feel that the show is authentic'.[73] Other critics noted the use of 'stunning … theatrical effects' (John Gross, *Telegraph*),[74] Hytner's deft handling of 'the scale' of the production (Michael Ratcliffe, *Observer*) and the 'sheer theatrical bravura' of some of the effects, such as the descending helicopter, the thirty-foot statue of Ho Chi Minh and the almost 'cinematic' techniques of staging (Douglas Kennedy, *New Statesman and Society*). Billington once again compared the production to Hytner's work in opera, as he had done with *Scarlet Pimpernel*, *Measure for Measure* and *The Tempest*, praising 'its sharp-edged clarity and its emphasis on narrative values' (Michael Billington, *Guardian*). Hytner was still working in opera alongside his theatre work, directing at major venues such as the Grand Théâtre de Genève (*Le Nozze di Figaro*, 1989) and Glyndebourne (*La Clemenza di Tito*, 1991).

Miss Saigon and *Ghetto* marked the first major nominations and awards in Hytner's career. He was nominated for Best Director at the Olivier awards in 1989 and Best Director of a Musical at the Tony awards in 1991 and was awarded the 1989 *Evening Standard* Theatre Award and the 1989 London Critics Circle Theatre Award for Best Director for both *Miss Saigon* and *Ghetto*. *Miss Saigon* transferred to The Broadway Theatre in New York from March 1991 to January 2001, marking Hytner's Broadway debut. It played in both London and New York for almost ten years, becoming Broadway's twelfth longest running show, and toured to twenty-five countries around the world. According to Rosenthal, it 'gave Hytner financial security for life'.[75] It also cemented Hytner's view that 'we are at our best in the British theatre when we find a way of reconciling art and showbiz', something that has characterized his time at the National Theatre and, indeed, his work since Cambridge.[76]

Hytner's next production was on a much smaller scale: a substantially cut-down version of Ben Jonson's *Volpone* at the intimate 300-seat Almeida Theatre in London, the total production budget of which was less than the cost of the helicopter in *Miss Saigon*. The production, which opened on 3 April 1990, reunited Hytner with Ian McDiarmid (in the title role), with whom he had worked at Manchester on *Edward II, The Country Wife* and *Don Carlos,* and Mike Burnside, who was in Hytner's first four professional theatre productions at Exeter, returning Hytner to more familiar territory than with *Miss Saigon*, the cast and production team of which had largely comprised people with whom Hytner had not worked before.

On *Volpone*, Hytner was also reunited with designer Thompson in their eighth theatre production together, the production concept bearing the mark of their previous collaborations *The Country Wife* and *Measure for Measure*, in having an eclectic design which avoided rooting the play in a particular period but alluded both to the period of writing and to the present day – here the contemporary London of the late Thatcher era. Hytner and Thompson's setting made apparent, in the eyes of the critics, the 'enduring' and 'timely' qualities of the play (Clive Hirschhorn, *Sunday Express*)[77] without falling into the trap of trying to make the play 'a pure tract for our times' (Paul Taylor, *Independent*), something that Hytner had also achieved with *Edward II* and *Measure for Measure*. The set was surrounded by water, giving a suggestion of Venetian canals, but this water was murky and filled with rubbish, indicative of the polluted nature of this world. The carrion bird characters – Voltore (the Vulture), Corbaccio (The Raven) and Corvino (The Crow) – were clad in bowler hats with bright yellow boots alluding to their characters' avian origins, McDiarmid's Volpone wore 'plausibly Jacobean fur and breeches', Dennis Lawson as Mosca was clad as 'an uncanny toyboy in black plastic trousers and green bomber jacket' and Marc Warren's Bonario appeared dressed as a cricketer, carrying a tennis racket in one hand and a dagger in the other. Cate Hamer's Celia seemed a modern figure not only in her attire of a 'sequined sheath-dress' (Tony Dunn, *Tribune*) but also in her demeanour, playing the role not 'as the usual virtuously bland innocent', but as 'an indignant spitfire of a girl'.[78]

The reviews were mostly outstanding. Billington's comments sum up many of the by now recognizable tropes of a Hytner production at its finest: 'fast, funny, visually inventive and very well acted' (Michael Billington, *Guardian*). Other critics commented on the inventiveness of the production as well as citing other features of the production characteristic of Hytner's best work: 'strikingly pictorial' (Hugo Williams, *Sunday Correspondent*), 'vigorous and alive' (Matt Wolf, *City Limits*), 'strikingly intelligent' (Taylor), 'ingeniously clarified and directed', 'tight' and 'taut' (Michael Coveney, *Observer*), 'shockingly' (Charles Spencer, *Telegraph*) and 'savagely' funny (Taylor) and a true ensemble piece, with 'not a dud in the cast' (Annalena McAfee, *Evening Standard*).

Part of the clarity and pace of the production came from the fact that Hytner, in keeping with theatrical tradition[79] cut the play's comic sub-plot with Sir Politic Would-Be, 'that tedious Englishman abroad' (Spencer). He asserts that this decision was partly motivated by the fact that 'it was the Almeida, and in those days the benches were very hard, and I thought that it was too long and not that funny' and partly because of 'a desperate memory of going with such expectations to see Peter Hall's production at the National in the early days (1977) with Scofield and Gielgud: Scofield was mesmerising, as he always was, but poor old Gielgud in a tortoise shell – it was tragic'.[80]

This decision to cut a Renaissance play in order to make it work for a modern audience, recalls Hytner's rather rash excision of the final lines of *Love's Labour's Lost* back at university and has informed much of his work on what he feels are the more challenging plays in the Renaissance repertoire, *The Alchemist* and *Timon of Athens*, for example: 'I'm pretty cavalier. I kind of think there's always next time.'[81]

In this case, most reviewers welcomed the cuts, Paul Taylor arguing that the removal of the sub-plot brought the play 'more into line with modern tastes', making it 'a swifter, darker, bleaker experience' (*Independent*). Billington was one of the few who bemoaned the fact that 'in excising the whole sub-plot of Sir Politic Would-Be, Mr Hytner undercuts Jonson's exposure of human folly and diminishes the play's epic, inordinate grandeur' (*Guardian*). Hytner maintains that in order to engage modern audiences with the Classics – Jonson, Marlowe and Shakespeare, it is sometimes necessary to cut material. Indeed, he now maintains that he feels 'more and more' that 'there are occasions when to be true to Shakespeare you have to rewrite him, or at the very least cut the incomprehensible bits'.[82]

At the end of 1990, on the back of the success of *Ghetto*, Hytner returned to the NT to direct their Christmas production: *The Wind in the Willows*. This time, confident of his track record, Hytner approached Eyre with the suggestion of an adaptation of Kenneth Grahame's book. Eyre had already approached Alan Bennett to write a play based on Grahame's life and suggested that Hytner should meet with him, a meeting which began a collaboration that was to prove one of the most fruitful of Hytner's career. The production reunited Hytner with two friends from his Cambridge University days: his regular collaborator Sams and Griff Rhys Jones, who had directed Hytner in the Footlights' Revue, *Tag*.

Hytner had relished playing Toad in A. A. Milne's adaptation of Grahame's book (*Toad of Toad Hall*), at school, but felt that the play was now dated. Billington praised Hytner and Bennett for having 'rescued the story from the anthropomorphic jauntiness of the ... Milne adaptation', giving the production, with the help of Sams's music, 'a pervasive undertow of English melancholy' (Michael Billington, *Guardian*).[83] Bennett's adaptation was deliberately topical, finding, in Grahame's book, 'a deeper parable for the way we live now' (Sheridan Morley, *Herald Tribune*).

Hytner treated this children's classic much like his work

on classical plays, succeeding in combining elements of an Edwardian nostalgia with nods to the present day. Ratty, Mole, Toad and Badger might have stepped out of E. H. Sheppard's 1930s illustrations with their tweed suits, flat caps and motoring goggles. However, the 'Wild Wood' creatures added a more contemporary dimension, presented 'as spivs with tarty girls who want to develop Toad Hall as a leisure complex' (Tony Dunn, *Tribune*).

Hytner seemed to be on a roll as far as the critics were concerned. Few sought to criticize the adaptation or Hytner's direction of it, which was described by Lynne Truss as 'masterly' (*Independent on Sunday*) in terms of its organization of a huge cast of thirty-four actors, by Kenneth Hurren as 'ingenious' (*Mail on Sunday*) and by John Gross as handled with 'great panache' (*Sunday Telegraph*). Following *Ghetto*, and doubtless influenced by his work on *Miss Saigon*, Hytner had developed a greater confidence with the Olivier stage and he and Thompson made full use of the theatre's hydraulics and revolve. Alastair Macaulay, writing in the *Financial Times*, declared that he had 'never seen the Olivier stage accomplish greater marvels' (*FT*), while Benedict Nightingale asserted that Hytner and Thompson had 'made ampler and more inventive use of the great Olivier stage than anyone so far' (*The Times*). Only a few critics seemed concerned about the scale of the design, which Billington felt was in danger of overwhelming the story (*Guardian*). Hytner's elaborate and varied use of the Olivier stage is something for which he has now become well known, sometimes accused of excess, but more often praised for the ease with which he handles, transforms and even strips back the space.

Wind in the Willows ran for 101 performances between December 1990 and June 1991.[84] During this time, Hytner's production of *Miss Saigon* was running in London and opened on Broadway in April 1991. When Hytner's production of *King Lear* transferred from the RSC to London in May 1991, Hytner had two other productions playing in London and one on Broadway.

King Lear, Royal Shakespeare Theatre, Stratford-Upon-Avon

Having directed *Measure for Measure* and *The Tempest* for the RSC, *King Lear* seemed a natural progression for Hytner: 'a continuing body of work that seems to develop Shakespeare's treatment of authority and the authority figure'.[85] The production reunited Hytner with designer David Fielding and leading actor John Wood, both of whom had worked on *The Tempest*, and, as Hytner commented, 'it was inevitable that the same system of perception and a common aesthetic would be brought to bear upon it'[86] – notably in the form of an abstract, ahistorical setting.

In common with most of Hytner's Renaissance productions up until this point, the play's setting was deliberately anachronistic, 'making visual references to the present as well as the past'[87] and reflecting the fact that Shakespeare often 'specifically avoids a real historical framework'.[88] This is certainly the case with *King Lear*, a play ostensibly set in the pre-Christian world of the eighth century BC – the setting of the historical source – but, as Hytner recognized, quite clearly 'about contemporary [Jacobean] concerns'.[89] The decision to use a mixture of modern and Renaissance costume within an abstract setting was motivated by an attempt to reflect this ahistorical aspect of the play and to highlight simultaneously, as Shakespeare had done, the play's relevance to both the past and the present. Billington, in particular, praised the production's ability to find 'in Shakespeare an echo of the perplexing moral confusion of the world we inhabit', dubbing it 'a *Lear* for the Nineties' (Michael Billington, *Guardian*, 1991).[90]

Like Fielding's set for *The Tempest*, the set for *Lear* was simple, uncluttered and abstract, its centrepiece a large revolving cube, upstage centre. As with Thompson's set for *Measure for Measure* each revolution of the cube enabled a new setting: an enclosed space within the cube or a metal wall against which some scenes were played. Thus, after 1.1

with Lear's throne and much of the action set within the cube, the set revolved to reveal Edmund lying against a wall, suggesting an outside location, but also bringing the scene further downstage and in closer proximity to the audience, appropriate to Edmund's soliloquies in this scene. A further rotation after 1.2 then revealed the inside of Albany's palace within the cube, with a dining table being laid for dinner, the enclosed space giving the impression of being overcrowded by the entry of Lear and his knights at the start of 1.4, although they numbered, in fact, no more than eight.

The cube was not only functional, enabling a smooth transition from one scene to the next, from domestic interior to outside space or dark room, but also served a symbolic purpose – in the words of Carol Chillington Rutter, 'both a display cabinet and a child-scientist's outsized bug box for scrutinizing animal behavior – that began to spin out of control'.[91] Michael Quinn saw in the structure allusions 'to the metaphorical images of Shakespeare's self-referential notion of the world being but a "stage of fools" and fortune's wheel being in constant, unstoppable motion' (*What's On*, 1991), an image which appeared particularly potent with the constant spinning of the cube during the storm sequence.

However, not all critics found the set effective, feeling that it sometimes overwhelmed or distracted from the action, as well as obscuring sight-lines from some seats (Carl Miller, *City Limits*, 1991; Benedict Nightingale, *The Times*, 1991). For Charles Spencer, it was reminiscent 'of the kind of installation art one might be unlucky enough to encounter at the Whitechapel Art Gallery' (*Telegraph*, 1991). Even Holland, otherwise extremely complimentary about the production, felt that the set 'proved inordinately constricting' in the storm scene, rendering it 'notably banal'.[92] Lear and the Fool were both inside the cube, which intermittently spun. However, although backed by a square of revolving grey sky, there was little sense of an actual storm. Indeed, the general quietness of the storm (accented with intermittent flashes of lightning and thunder) resembled that of Hytner's *Tempest*, suggesting that it may have been more a symbolic expression of Lear's mental state than a genuine storm. Hytner describes the set of *Lear* as his 'last hurrah with that kind of abstract design', his subsequent Shakespeare having been 'more rooted and more specific and further along towards the socially realistic end of the spectrum'.[93]

Although, for the most part, stark and minimalist, the cube was transformed in Act 4 into a field of corn, 'a bizarre vision of a perfect English summer, an arcadian idyll which made the characters' pain all the more acute'.[94] It was, Holland

FIGURE 3 *John Wood in* King Lear *directed by Nicholas Hytner, the Royal Shakespeare Company, 1990. Joe Cocks Studio Collection.* © *Shakespeare Birthplace Trust*

remarked, the first time in his experience that a designer had taken 'Cordelia's description of her landscape as an accurate basis for the set: Lear has been seen 'Crowned with ... / ... all the idle weeds that grow / In our sustaining corn' and is to be found in 'the high-grown field' (4.3.3–7)'.[95]

Holland pointed out another 'first' for Hytner's production: 'for the first time in England a major production of *Lear* took full account of recent textual scholarship'.[96] Holland refers here to the fact that Hytner's production chose as its basis the First Folio text of *King Lear*, rather than the usual conflation of Folio and Quarto, a decision doubtless influenced by the separate printing of the two texts in the *Oxford Complete Works* in 1986 for the first time, based on the editors' conviction that 'there are two distinct plays of *King Lear*, not merely two different texts of the same play'.[97] As Hytner's former supervisor, Holland offered advice on this aspect of the production.

King Lear survives in two distinct texts – the First Quarto of 1608, published as *The History of King Lear* and the version printed in the First Folio of 1623, entitled *The Tragedy of King Lear*. Scholarship suggests that the Quarto (Q) represents a version of the play close to the authorial copy, while the Folio text (F) is thought to derive from a revised theatrical text (printed with reference to quarto copy). The two texts of *Lear* differ substantially from one another. Q has about 300 lines that are not in F and lacks around 100 that are.[98] While some of these differences can be attributed to error, others have a more profound influence on the tone and pace of the play. There are a number of significant omissions in F, including the mock trial (3.6.17–55) and Edgar's soliloquy (3.6.100–13) in 3.6, the exchange between Gloucester's servants at the end of 3.7 (98–106), the scene between Kent and a Gentleman (4.3) and the exchange between Albany and Edgar in 5.3 (203–20), as well as the transferral of the play's final lines from Albany in Q to Edgar in F. Many argue that the changes improve the play theatrically and are likely to represent Shakespeare's own revisions, made on the basis of theatrical experience – indeed,

Wells asserts that 'most of us who have studied the two versions of *King Lear* in detail are agreed that the latter is the better play'.[99] Certainly Hytner was of this opinion. In an article for *The Times*, which begins with a playful imaginary conversation in which Burbage asks Shakespeare about Lear's madness and urges him to rewrite Lear's first speech, Hytner explains that scholarship has confirmed that 'Shakespeare revised his plays' and asserts that the Folio seems 'to offer Shakespeare's second thoughts'. Hytner goes on to cite a number of differences between Q and F that proved significant during his rehearsal process. He argues, for example, that Goneril's line in F following 'You see how full of changes his age is' – 'The observation we have made of it hath been little', as opposed to Q's, 'The observation we have made of it hath not been little' – 'changes everything', implying that the daughters have not spent much time with Lear and that his rash actions come as a complete surprise to them.[100] While it is possible that this is a deliberate change, it may be an example of a director reading too much into a textual variant in order to support his case. R. A. Foakes, in his Arden 3 edition states quite simply that 'not' was 'no doubt omitted from F by oversight'.[101] However, Lesley Kordecki and Karla Koskinen argue, along similar lines to Hytner, that Goneril may be 'truly saying they have taken too little care of curbing or at least noting Lear's irrationality', suggesting her 'sense of duty'.[102]

For Holland, 'the use of the Folio text was entirely convincing, providing … a slightly leaner, more purposive form than the conflated text allows for',[103] although the production still ran at nearly four hours. However, Robert Clare, making a case for a conflated text, is at pains to point out that, in spite of both Hytner and Holland's advocation of the Folio text, 'not even Nicholas Hytner could convince his actors that the supposed cuts in 3.6 are viable'.[104] Both Hytner and Wood felt that the mock trial in Q was essential to the scene, arguing that its omission in F may not have been one of design but of censorship.[105] As both Holland and Clare expound, the scene became 'pivotal' to the production, the staging designed to create 'a nightmarish reworking of the opening', echoing the configuration and gestures of the first scene.[106] Lear sat on a covered chair, placed precisely where the throne had been in 1.1, while two stools and a chair were placed on the forestage where the chairs for Lear's daughters had been set at the opening. With a similar echoing used in the final scene, with the placement of the bodies 'again made carefully to echo the opening scene', this scene became the mid-point in a cyclical journey.[107]

The Folio text is not only tighter but also bleaker than its quarto counterpart. The removal of the servants who tend to the blinded Gloucester at the end of 3.7, for example, makes the end of this scene particularly dark, with Gloucester 'thrust … out at gates' (3.7.92) to wander alone. As has become common, the interval in Hytner's production came after this scene. However, unlike Peter Brook who used this placing of the interval to place focus on the blinded Gloucester, cutting the servants and bringing up the house lights as Gloucester stumbled off stage, the focus in Hytner's production was on Regan. Rather than directing her line 'How is't my lord?' (3.7.92–3) to Cornwall, to whose cries she was seemingly indifferent, Regan spoke the line to Gloucester, in a moment which suggested genuine concern and tenderness but also derangement, the question being a painfully inappropriate one to a man whose eyeballs have just been torn out at her instigation. The audience was thus left at the interval, with an uneasy sense of a deterioration of relationships, morals and mental stability.

The play's first scene is key in establishing the world of the play, the relationships between characters – in particularly Lear and his three daughters – and the character of Lear himself. Describing rehearsals for the production, Hytner commented that one of the discoveries of the play's first scene was that, in spite of the subsequent behaviour of many of the characters in the play, 'very few people in the play set out to do evil – in fact, a lot of them set out to act well'.[108] In Hytner's view, Lear's behaviour in the first scene was not that of a mad, stupid or capricious man: 'Lear is setting out to divide his kingdom because he thinks that is the best thing to do.'[109] In the absence of any grandsons and in the interests of avoiding civil war, he has little alternative but to divide his kingdom between his three daughters. The problem lies in the way in which he chooses to do this.

Neither the F nor Q text provides an indication of the setting of the first scene. It is clear that Kent, Gloucester, Lear, Albany, Cornwall and Lear's three daughters are present and both texts list 'attendants' (F) or 'followers' (Q). However, there is no suggestion how many members of the court might be in attendance or what the environment might be.[110] If this scene takes place in a domestic environment, then the emphasis is on Lear's personal relationship with his daughters and sons-in-law, and his private distress at Cordelia's failure to declare her love. If it takes place in a public arena, it is rather on Lear's pride and reputation, his desire to have his daughters make public declarations of their love for him and his humiliation and anger when Cordelia fails to do so. Although the first scene of Hytner's production was clearly a formal occasion, Lear's entrance being heralded, as the F and Q stage directions suggests, by a 'Sennet', Malcolm Rutherford described this production as presenting *Lear* 'as a domestic drama' (*FT*, 1991). In spite of the additional lords present, there was an atmosphere of intimacy, partly effected by Wood's quite informal tone and lack of magisterial bearing and partly by the lack of grandeur in the setting, the set for the first scene consisting of a single chandelier and fabric-covered chair (Lear's throne) in the otherwise unadorned cube and three chairs on the forestage. Hytner describes his interpretation of this first scene as 'domestic and archetypal' – a continuation of his interest in Jung – something that he claims he would no longer be able to do, viewing the political dimension of the play as vital: 'I would love to see a convincingly political Lear, a Lear with a real social context'. However, he still maintains that one of the play's chief themes is that of the parent/child relationship:

It's impossible to be a parent, and it's impossible to be a child. What it seems to be saying is that any expectation that the parent or child derives from this relationship is doomed to disappointment.[111]

A further question arises as to Lear's intentions in the play's first scene: whether he has decided before the scene begins to make a trial of his daughters' loves or whether it is a spur of the moment impulse. If the former, Lear seems more calculating and manipulative. If the latter, he may appear merely to have a brief flash of madness or momentary lapse of judgement. Hytner's production chose the second of these options, Hytner speaking in interview of Lear's 'sudden decision to ask his daughters which one loves him the most'.[112] This was made clear by Wood's insertion of a long pause before 'Tell me, my daughters' (1.1.48), as if he was thinking up the love trial in that moment.

An audience's impression of Lear's actions in the first scene is, of course, partly dependent on the theatrical decision as to when he begins to display hints of insanity. Wood himself liked 'the idea that Lear is in some senses mad before the play starts. He's certainly reached a point where he wanders in and out of reality.' For him this was the key to the first scene: 'that's what the first scene is about'.[113] The critics seemed divided as to the extent of this Lear's madness in the opening scene. Rutherford found Wood 'a pretty nondescript monarch at the beginning' (1991); however, Carl Miller described him as 'leaner and a little dottier than usual from the outset' (*City Limits*, 1991). Certainly Wood's Lear seemed to swing from one emotional extreme to another – one minute indulging and almost smothering Cordelia with affection and the next exploding with anger. There were also moments when he seemed to forget his status as a king, physically lashing out at Kent in an almost petulant rage on 'O vassal! miscreant!' (1.1.162), pushing him to the floor. For Milton Shulman, the level of anger displayed by Wood in the first scene left him little room for development:

> John Wood, as Lear, takes on these domestic matters with
> such apoplectic rage that it is difficult to fathom how much
> angrier he can get when on the blasted heath he becomes a
> metaphor representing not just a kingly mind overthrown
> but the collapse of universal order. (*Evening Standard*,
> 1991)

In fact, Wood's Lear became less angry and forceful as his
madness began to take hold and for Shulman it was in this
descent that, 'this Lear acquire[d] a stature that justifies our
pity' (1991).

As Holland details, Wood's Lear's state of mind became
unbearably moving from as early as 2.2, 'the most intense'
scene of the production.[114] When Goneril arrived at the castle,
she was accompanied by two nurses, pushing a wheelchair,
clearly 'certifying him as insane in modern terms'.[115] When
Lear saw her, he clutched desperately at Regan, determined
not to look at Goneril. What, in Holland's view was heartbreaking, was that 'He knew — and the awareness was
excruciatingly painful, frightening and humiliating — that
she probably was, for all her harshness, right.'[116] 'I prithee,
daughter, do not make me mad' (2.2.410), was not a cry of
anger, but a quiet plea not to label him as insane. Wood's
portrayal of madness was nuanced, moving from pain to a
sense of release, switching 'in a second from intemperate rage
to sweet tenderness', but also, in Billington's view, finding an
element which he had not seen before – an 'insatiable intellectual curiosity', a 'heightened awareness' (1991). By the end
of the play Lear had moved from an 'unpredictable person-
ality' to a 'straightforwardly moving one' (Nightingale, 1991),
finding a simplicity and 'directness' that in Spencer's view,
finally 'brings us to the heart of this magnificent play' (1991).

Once again, Wood came in for criticism from some critics,
who, as with his Prospero, felt that his vocal delivery was
distracting and indulgent. Spencer bemoaned his tendency
to move 'again and again, in the course of a single line ...
from quavery croak to rumbling roar', feeling that this was

'a technique that shows off the actor's virtuosity rather than illuminating the role' (1991). As in *The Tempest* Wood displayed a tendency to paint the words – deepening his voice on 'darker' and drawing out the word 'long'. However, for Quinn, Wood succeeded in achieving 'a credible description of the character' (Quinn, 1991), and Eyre, who records his feelings about the production in his diaries, states that he 'marvell[ed] at the detail of John Wood's performance'.[117]

Certainly Wood presented a complex figure, and as Nightingale remarked, there was much in the performance that helped 'to explain the elder sisters' behavior and justify the rebelliousness of Alex Kingston's Cordelia' (1991). Goneril and Regan were, from the outset, 'clearly long-term victims of paternal rashness' (Billington, 1991), while Cordelia seemed to have been smothered and infantilized. For Wood this 'overwhelmingly possessive love' for Cordelia, was key to his characterization.[118] In the first scene, far from displaying anger at her declaration of 'Nothing' (1.1.87), he smiled as if indulging a small child. When Cordelia, kneeling beside him, uttered the words, 'Obey you, love you, and most honour you' (1.1.98), he grabbed her face and kissed her, apparently hearing only the positive interpretation of her words. It was not until 'Let it be so. Thy truth then be thy dower' (1.1.109) that he suddenly lost his temper, storming around the stage shouting and then, in a fit of pique at having to divide the kingdom into two rather than three, gabbled his lines at Cornwall and Albany before tossing the crown into the air for them to catch.

This quickness of temper was a feature of Lear's behaviour from the outset, his behaviour towards all three of his daughters switching between affection and fury.

His treatment of Goneril in 1.4 was irrational and unreasonable and it was clear that he was already losing his mind. On her entrance into 1.4, Goneril clearly tried to reason with him over his knights, stating her case clearly and, asking him quite patiently, 'A little to disquantity your train' (1.4.240). When Lear became upset, she knelt by him and tried to comfort him. However, he soon lost his temper and began railing, hitting himself repeatedly on the head on 'Lear, Lear, Lear' (1.4.262) and then pulling Goneril down onto the floor on 'Hear, Nature, hear!' (1.4.267), cursing her with such intensity that by the time he let go of her she fell, howling and sobbing to the floor. Moments later he rushed on, fired a gun into the air, then ran to embrace her, before throwing her to the floor on 'father's curse' (1.4.292).

His behaviour towards Regan was similarly erratic and hurtful. In 2.2, encountering Regan at Gloucester's castle, he kissed and embraced her, clasping hold of her all through his invective against Goneril. Like Goneril, Regan tried to calmly discuss his behaviour with him, only to be screamed at. Both daughters displayed a genuine sense of frustration and distress as it became clear that their father could not be reasoned with, that he was irrational and might become verbally and physically aggressive at the slightest provocation. Indeed, after his exit from 2.2, their exchange – 'This house is little ... ' (2.2.480) – was not angry but pained, both seemingly trying to justify their behaviour to themselves and each other.

One of the features of this production on which a number of critics remarked was the more human and 'complex' (James Christopher, *Time Out*, 1991) treatment of the two elder sisters. As Holland commented:

> If we have grown used to seeing Regan and Goneril as fairytale characters out of, say, *Cinderella*, Hytner argued for a different approach.[119]

Hytner states that he is 'absolutely on their side. I mean not where they go to, but I'm on their side.'[120] The production avoided demonizing Goneril and Regan by making apparent the motivation for their actions. Nightingale cited this as 'the friendliest picture of the "ugly" sisters to date', both 'frustrated, exhausted and, indeed pushed towards breakdown by John Wood's maddeningly mercurial Lear'. In Nightingale's view, Estelle Kohler's Goneril, in particular, did 'her best to be the dutiful daughter' for much of the early part of the play, but occasionally snapped, clearly reaching 'the end of her tether when the Fool mimed urinating on her'[121] in 1.4, prompting her invective against Lear's retinue: 'Not only, sir, this your all-licensed fool / But other of your insolent retinue' (1.4.191–2).

Regan was more unstable and volatile than Goneril – her behaviour recalling in some respects that of her father in her sudden bursts of extreme anger mixed with moments of unexpected affection. Her behaviour towards Gloucester seemed particularly erratic. In 2.1, when encountering Gloucester at his castle, Regan displayed concern and affection for him, embracing him in sympathy when hearing of Edgar's supposed plot against him. In the following scene she was 'tenderly solicitous', wrapping him in a blanket after he was roused from bed by Kent and Oswald's fight. Holland suggests that 'Gloucester was clearly her substitute father, another example of the displaced affect, the excess of a love that cannot be offered to the right object, that need to love that marks the production.'[122] And yet, her behaviour for most of 4.1 was vicious and vengeful in the extreme.

Over the centuries many critics have cited Goneril and Regan as the 'embodiment ... of evil'.[123] Samuel Taylor Coleridge referred to them as 'utter monsters',[124] Maynard Mack called them 'paradigms of evil'[125] and they appear alongside Edmund in a chapter in Maurice Charney's *Shakespeare's Villains,* characterized as the 'evil older sisters'.[126] Although Hytner challenged the notion of the sisters as inherently malevolent, asserting that the company had 'found that it was a play about how these two girls were trying to love their father', he nevertheless used the term 'evil' in relation to the pair and the play, arguing that 'evil ... is accepted as a concept and is present in the play' and that 'Regan and Goneril stumble into embracing evil'.[127] As Nightingale noted, while making apparent the motivations for Goneril and Regan's actions, Hytner did not fall 'into the contemporary trap of sentimentalizing them' (1991). Indeed, Spencer, while commenting that the actors stressed 'the psychological damage their father has inflicted on them at the expense of a sense of innate evil', found what he described as 'Miss Dexter's frantic sexual excitement during the blinding of Gloucester ... horrible to behold' (1991). Having curled up on the floor in a fetal position while Gloucester berated her, she rose up screaming in apparent delight as his first eye was plucked out, frenziedly urging Cornwall on to tear out the other eye.

If Goneril and Regan have habitually been viewed as the evil sisters, then Cordelia has been deemed the Cinderella figure: 'The daughters become a binary equation', with 'Cordelia as the completely laudatory woman'.[128] Hytner's production sought to avoid this binary. Although the physical appearances of the sisters might initially have suggested an adherence to a more traditional mode of presentation, Regan and Goneril both having dark hair, cropped short (Goneril) or tied back (Regan) in the first scene, while Alex Kingston's Cordelia's Pre-Raphaelite strawberry blond hair hung loose, their bearing and behaviour suggested less of a contrast, all three sisters attempting to reason with their father before losing their tempers with him.

In spite of some critical commentary that suggested that Kingston's Cordelia was little more than 'a cypher' (Rutherford, 1991), 'too good to be true' (Quinn, 1991), her performance imbued the character with a degree of strength and rebelliousness from the outset. Far from pandering to her father, when Lear kissed her after 'most honour you', she reacted by angrily standing up and shouting her next lines at him. Her response to Burgundy's rejection of her showed a similar strength of character – sarcastic and dismissive in tone. On her return from France in 4.4 her demeanour was, for the most part, pleasantly assertive and indicative of genuine concern for her father. However, Spencer's description of her as 'oddly unendearing ... more priggish head prefect than devoted daughter', might be said to ring true of her manner in 'prescrib[ing]' to her sisters their 'duty' (1991) and her rather smug, self-satisfied delivery of the lines ''Tis known before.

Our preparation stands / In expectation of them' (4.4.22–23), when informed of the imminent arrival of the British powers. This element of the interpretation was perhaps influenced by Hytner's own dislike of the character:

> I don't like Cordelia. I think she's cold and proud at the beginning of the play. I find it difficult to cope with the fact that someone who is cold and proud and certain comes back and allows herself to be put in that birdcage.[129]

There is no doubt, that with Wood in the title role, the production's focus was on Lear and his daughters. However, the critics praised most of the performances: David Troughton's Kent, 'a bumptious parody of the old retainer' (Billington, 1991), but one whose reaction to Lear's final demise was 'heart-rending' (Louise Kingsley, *Independent*, 1991); Norman Rodway's 'fine, noble Gloucester' (Quinn, 1991); Linus Roache's 'rational Edgar' (Shulman, 1991); and Ralph Fiennes's 'charismatic Edmund' (Kingsley, 1991). As Holland acknowledged, 'the only major mistake was Linda Kerr Scott as Fool'.[130] Following her critically acclaimed performance in *Ghetto*, Hytner cast Kerr Scott, believing that it would be 'amazing to have this tiny scrap of humanity; the kind of person that you could imagine being a fool'. However, he admits that it is extremely difficult to make the Fool work in a contemporary context:

> of course the Fool is one of the reasons that the play, in the way that I think about Shakespeare now, is impossible to do because who the hell is the Fool? A professional fool – there is no contemporary equivalent at all.[131]

Kerr Scott asserted in interview that she intended to play the role as 'a union of male and female which is as young as a 12-year old boy and as old as a very old man'.[132] Certainly the Fool is an ambiguous character – often played as Lear's contemporary, but possibly, as is suggested by Lear's references to him as 'boy', conceived as a much younger figure. Since Alois Brandl suggested, in 1894, that the roles of the Fool and Cordelia may have been doubled on the Renaissance stage,[133] critics have continued to point out not only the convenience of the two characters sharing no stage time but also the thematic links between the two, a theory which may have influenced theatrical practice. Hytner was by no means unusual in casting a female Fool. Ever since Priscilla Horton played the role in Charles Macready's 1838 production, a series of 'young and pretty actresses' have been cast in the role, providing, Foakes argues, 'a visual link with Cordelia'.[134] The Renaissance Theatre Company's production of *Lear*, which ran concurrently with Hytner's, also featured a female fool, played by Emma Thompson; however both Thompson and Kerr Scott, in Foakes' view, provided different but 'much tougher' images of the character than had become typical from female performers.[135] Hytner's casting of Kerr Scott was, he asserts, 'gender blind': 'I didn't care what sex she was'.[136]

There was no visual link in Hytner's production between the Fool and Cordelia. Kerr Scott's fool was a strange little androgynous Scottish figure, described by Billington as 'a capering Scottish Olive Oyl' (1991). Highly physical, she clambered about the set, leaping up on the table in Goneril's house and sitting affectionately on Lear's lap. If much of the comedy inherent in the language was lost, some was gained through an exploitation of her size and physicality. In 1.4, her singing of 'Fools had ne'er less grace in a year', was accompanied by a dance in which she contorted her body to humorous effect, eliciting laughter from the assembled knights and the audience. When she began singing 'The hedge-sparrow fed the cuckoo so long' (1.4.206), two of the servants simply picked her up and hung her on a hook on the wall, leaving her dangling there for most of the rest of the scene until taken down by Goneril on 'You, sir, more knave than fool' (1.4.307). However, in the view of most of the critics, Kerr Scott was unable to match her physical agility with a vocal one, her voice high and weak and difficult to hear against the prevailing thunder. As well as lacking in vocal power and verbal dexterity, for some critics, the non-human aspects of the characterization of the Fool (more a 'spindly puppet' (Nightingale, 1991) or 'androgynous sprite' (Kingsley, 1991) than a man or boy) affected the character's 'rapport' with Lear (Nightingale, 1991). Clive Hirschhorn was alone among the critics in feeling that the scenes between the Fool and Lear worked 'beautifully' (*Sunday Express*, 1991), although Spencer agreed with Hirschhorn in finding Kerr Scott's Fool 'touching', if 'bizarre' (1991).

Much of the critical commentary on Hytner's *Lear* was reminiscent of that for his other Shakespeare productions in its references to the operatic,[137] highly theatrical[138] style, but also to the fresh[139] and intellectual[140] aspects of the production. For Coveney, this was 'the most original, illuminating and kinetic production of the play' he had experienced (Michael Coveney, *Observer*, 1991). Some critics felt that the spectacle of the production was in danger of undermining its emotional impact: 'Nicholas Hytner's juggernaut of a production ... threatens to crush the pagan heart of the play under layers of sumptuous craft' (Christopher, 1991). However, in Billington's view this was effectively remedied with the production's transfer to the Barbican in May 1991:

> Something quite astonishing has happened to the Nicholas Hytner-John Wood *King Lear* on the journey from Stratford to London. By the Avon, it was everything except moving. Now it combines emotional reality with intellectual brilliance to make it the best Lear seen in Britain since Peter Brook's 30 years ago. (1991)

In spite of the relative success of the production, Hytner claims that he 'won't return to *Lear*' and that he doesn't enjoy it as a play:

> I find *Lear* now a play that I don't look forward to, because I find myself not galvanized by anybody. I think it's a very

difficult play – a very difficult world to enter in to … I find spending four hours with that horrible old man really, really difficult and I find it really difficult to feel sorry for him. The play doesn't work for me.[141]

Indeed, *King Lear* (2013–14) is one of the few National Theatre Shakespeare productions during Hytner's tenure as Artistic Director that he did not direct himself, having done six Shakespeare productions in ten years.

3

1991–2001

Hytner in the 1990s

Following the success of *Ghetto* and *Wind in the Willows*, Hytner was invited back to the NT a number of times during the 1990s, directing *The Madness of George III* (1991–2), *The Recruiting Officer* (1992), *Carousel* (1992) and *The Cripple of Inishmaan* (1997). These productions are widely representative of Hytner's commitment to a varied repertoire – new writing, established classics and musicals – a commitment that has characterized his work from his student days at Cambridge to the present day. They also continued to cement his reputation for work that combines intellectual rigour with theatricality. In 1992 Stephen Fay, writing a profile of Hytner for the *Independent on Sunday*, was clear that one of the reasons for Hytner's success was 'the uncanny way he regularly identifies what he calls the "centre" of a play or opera, making the work intellectually clear and wildly theatrical', one of his trademarks being 'visual boldness'.[1]

When *The Madness of George III* opened to rave reviews in the Lyttleton, *Wind in the Willows* was playing once again in the Olivier, furthering Hytner's relationship with Bennett and his status as an established NT director. The run of *George III* was extended to 147 performances in the Lyttleton, before going on tour in the UK – 'one of the most commercially successful regional tours in NT history'[2] – and the US. By the time it returned to the NT in 1993, Hytner had mounted two more productions at the theatre. Stephen Fay's article, entitled 'Hunting the Hit-Man', pointed out that, as *The Recruiting Officer*, the first of these, was going into previews, four of Hytner's shows were already running in London – 'all ... among the hottest tickets in town' – *Miss Saigon, Xerxes* (in a revival at the ENO), *Wind in the Willows* and *The Madness of George III*.[3] *The Recruiting Officer* was a reasonable critical, though not financial, success; however, *Carousel*, his next production at the National, was another critical and commercial triumph, playing for 130 performances at 98 per cent box office sales.[4]

As would become typical of Hytner's time at the NT, the production proved controversial, in this case due to his casting of black actor Clive Rowe as Mr Snow, a move criticized by some journalists who variously interpreted it as either 'flabbergastingly racist'[5] or inappropriately 'politically correct'.[6] The press coverage of this casting addressed, argues Rosenthal, 'one of the most important issues to have emerged since the NT was established': the fact that the theatre 'stood at the heart of by far the most ethnically diverse city in Britain'[7] – something which, as a national theatre, it had a responsibility to reflect in its casting and choice of repertoire. Hytner was, of course, already well known for his multiracial casting, particularly in his Shakespeare productions: Josette Simon and Hakeem Kae-Kazim having played Isabella and Claudio in *Measure for Measure* (see above) and Patterson Joseph having played Oswald in *King Lear* (as well as Worthy in *The Recruiting Officer*). He was to make an even more profound statement, by casting Adrian Lester as the first black Henry V in the play's history, at the NT in 2003.

Characteristically, Hytner refused to be cowed, either by press criticism or by the Richard Rogers estate, with whom he had battled over the casting of Rowe, threatening to cancel the production rather than to recast the role. He tackled the press head on, writing an article in the *Independent* which pointed out that plays and in particular musicals, are not illustrative of real life and thereby making the objections to Rowe's casting seem utterly ridiculous:

> They seemed unconcerned by the constant presence of a 30-piece orchestra, and by the odd propensity of these particular New Englanders to break into song at the drop of a hat, or to employ ballet as a regular means of discourse. It didn't bother them that the sea was represented by blue lino, the shore by a green carpet. But a black man representing a herring fisherman – hold the front page.[8]

Hytner invokes Shakespeare on a number of occasions in the article, asserting that colour-blind casting has become widely accepted 'in Stratford', where 'the appearance of non-white actors caused a frisson 20 years ago'.[9] This is an interesting assertion given his comment in an interview of 1987, in which he predicted that the casting of Josette Simon as Isabella in *Measure for Measure* would cause 'a big fuss', arguing 'you go on doing it so that in the end no fuss is made'.[10] Presciently, given that he was to cast Adrian Lester in the role, Hytner cites *Henry V* in his *Independent* articles as exemplifying the need for 'imaginative conspiracy between actor and audience', adding, 'If he is good enough, he becomes Henry V by telling you he is: he doesn't have to look like him, particularly if he speaks blank verse, which the real one presumably didn't.'[11]

Hytner won Best Director of a musical for *Carousel* at the Olivier Awards and the production won Best Musical Revival. It transferred to the Shaftesbury Theatre in 1993, where it ran for a year and then to The Lincoln Center, New York in 1994, where it played for eleven months, winning 'plaudits for being the first mixed-race production to appear on Broadway'.[12] This was to prove significant in terms of developing Hytner's career in the United States, following on from the success of *Miss Saigon*. Hytner was appointed an associate director of the Lincoln Center, to which he was to return in 1998 to direct Shakespeare's *Twelfth Night*.

Twelfth Night at the Lincoln Center

Following *King Lear*, *Twelfth Night* (July–August 1998) was the only other Shakespeare play that Hytner directed during the 1990s. Although collaborating on the project with designer Bob Crowley, with whom he had worked on *Carousel*, and with actor Paul Rudd from his film *The Object of My Affection* (as Orsino), Hytner found himself, unusually, working with a cast and crew with whom he was largely unfamiliar, a mixture of experienced older classical actors and young film and television stars, including Helen Hunt (who had just won an Oscar) as Viola and Kyra Sedgwick as Olivia, an experience that he cites as 'extremely enjoyable'.[13]

It was also the first time that he had directed a production specifically for the Vivian Beaumont Theatre at the Lincoln Centre, *Carousel* having transferred there. In fact the Beaumont proved an ideal space for staging Shakespeare – similar in shape and size to the Chichester Festival Theatre and Festival Theatre at Stratford Ontario, with the audience arranged on three sides around a pentagon-shaped stage. Interviewing Philip Bosco who played Malvolio in the production, Patricia Lennox comments on the auditorium being 'something like the kind of theater Shakespeare wrote for'.[14] Bosco himself responds to this assertion somewhat cynically: 'With that enormous amount of water on stage?'.[15] What Bosco refers to are the pools of water as part of the set, 'more than 10,000 gallons at every performance',[16] turning 'the upstage portion of the Beaumont playing space into a vast lagoon traversed by curving walkways'.[17] In Bosco's view, this was 'a terrible mistake. They spent a fortune just to put that bloody water on stage and then they were stuck with it. And they had to do something with it.'[18] However, for many of the reviewers this aspect of the design was wonderfully effective – 'enchanting',[19] 'stupendously lovely'[20] – and firmly rooted in the imagery of the play. Hytner himself felt that the water was 'well used', citing as particularly effective, 'from a technical, comic point

water imagery

of view' the keeping back of 'the comic ducking' of Sir Andrew until late in the play,[21] in 4.1, during his fight with Sebastian.

For Joanna Coles, writing in the *Guardian*, the onstage pools cleverly 'reflect[ed] the obsession with water and drowning in the text'.[22] Water as an overriding theme in the design seemed to make sense not only of the shipwreck that begins the play but also of the proliferation of water images in its language, especially in the references to the sea ('That, notwithstanding thy capacity/ Receiveth as the sea' [1.1.10–11]; 'But mine is all as hungry as the sea' [2.4.101]); the metaphor of drowning ('*Olivia:* What is a drunken man like fool? *Clown:* Like a drowned man, a fool, and a mad man' [1.5.127–8]; 'She is drowned already, sir, with salt water, though I seem to drown her remembrance again with more' [2.1.29–30]); the images of tears ('she will veiled walk / And water once a day her chamber round / With eye-offending brine' (1.1.29–30); 'with adorations, fertile tears' [1.5.249]); and direct references to water ('So went he suited to his watery tomb' [5.1.230]). Elizabeth Story Donno cites the production as an instance of the 'continuing relevance of Jungian theory', which associates water with the unconscious and the emotions, to the play 'with its symbolic pools of water for shipwreck, reflection and ritual cleansing'.[23] Although Hytner does not specifically recall the Jungian influence on this production, he remembers being particularly interested in Jung throughout his time at the RSC when working on *Measure for Measure*, *The Tempest* and *Lear*, citing all three as 'archetypal'.[24]

For designer Bob Crowley, the water, with its reflective surface, was particularly emblematic, firstly, of 'the narcissism of the characters, constantly looking at their own reflections',[25] brought out to comic effect in 2.4, when Orsino, uttering the words 'Unstaid and skittish in all motions else / Save in the constant image of the creature / That is beloved' (2.4.18–19), rolled onto his stomach and gazed longingly at his own reflection in one of the pools and, secondly, of the theme of 'twinning'. In a platform talk at the Beaumont theatre, Crowley cited as his main inspiration for the design, 'the play's use of twins as a metaphor for the self-knowledge that comes from true reflection'.[26] The sexual associations of water imagery were also brought to the fore in the production, with both Orsino and Sebastian stripping off and immersing themselves in the water, Sebastian pulling the fully clothed Olivia in after him for an embrace in 4.3, so that her clothes became clinging and partially transparent.

Much like Hytner's other Shakespeare productions up until this point, the setting was modern but abstract, 'suspended somewhere between colonial India and an imaginary Middle East',[27] the stage swathed in silk hangings with a 'design taken from Persian carpets and embellished with patterns inspired by Indian illuminated manuscripts'.[28] Indeed, Crowley's research for the design drew on 'two exhibitions at the Metropolitan Museum of Art: one of Oriental carpets, the other of illustrated pages from an Indian manuscript'.[29] As Hytner explained in an interview in the *New York Times,* Shakespeare's 'stage world … is typically crammed with inconsistencies and anachronisms' and 'the provision of a solid social context is often illuminating, but always to some degree confines the plays to a place much narrower than Shakespeare's imagination'.[30] This statement may seem in direct conflict with Hytner's later productions of *Henry V, Hamlet, Othello* and *Timon of Athens*, all of which seemed rooted in recognizable contemporary settings. However, this is, in part, due to his perception of a clear difference between the demands of Shakespeare's romantic comedies and his tragedies:

There are plays that sink under the weight of too literal a response to the world they purport to represent. Have you ever seen *The Tempest* set on a real desert island? It's like *Treasure Island* without the parrot.

Meanwhile, in many of the romantic comedies, Shakespeare plays with the idea that the experience of love re-makes reality; that the lover, like the lunatic and the poet, shapes the world according to the dictates of his own fantasy. Unfold yourself to a play like *A Midsummer*

Night's Dream or *Twelfth Night*, and you're very quickly imagining on stage a high fantastical world shaped by fancy.[31]

However, for Hytner, 'the political plays – the great tragedies in particular ... work best when rooted in a coherent world'.[32]

The Eastern setting 'heightened the play's atmosphere of fantasy'[33] and established Illyria as an other-worldly environment: 'not here, not now, somewhere different, a world where romantic impossibilities are made possible'.[34] As Hytner explained, the 'kind of worlds' he and Crowley liked to create were those 'of imagination'[35] – a poetic rather than literal response to the play. For Crowley, the generically Eastern environment enhanced 'the play's fabulistic side', the non-specific nature of the setting allowing 'people's desire and dreams – and the language – room to breathe'.[36]

The production's costumes, designed by Catherine Zuber, were equally eclectic, mixing Middle Eastern robes with 'Japanese-style umbrellas',[37] the dishevelled suits of Sir Toby and Sir Andrew with an Edwardian tailcoat and waistcoat for Viola. Rudd's Orsino went from richly-coloured harem wear, exposing his bare chest in the first scene, to tight trousers and gold boots in the last, in an image resonant, for Charles Isherwood, of 'Adam Ant at the height of his '80s pirate look'.[38] Key to the costume design as described by Crowley, was 'the idea of disguise, that it's only a layer of clothing, a thin piece of fabric, protecting somebody from being discovered'.[39] That characters were always within close proximity of discovery, was also suggested through the use of the curved walkways, which permitted entrances and exits to overlap, sometimes to comic effect. At the end of 2.1, as Sebastian left the stage up stage right, Malvolio entered, shouting after him, only for Viola to enter (as Cesario) down stage left, so that for a moment Malvolio saw both twins.

In addition to adding a degree of exoticism, the Eastern ambience also helped to bring out the play's sexual imagery, the production beginning with Orsino and his servants sprawled on stage, bare-chested. Don Shewey asserts that, while Hytner acknowledged 'in interviews that his production of ... *Twelfth Night* ... continues the theme of unrequited love he explored in his film *The Object of My Affection*', he was 'shyer about saying ... that the production also investigates the same slipperiness of sexual identity that figured heavily in the film'.[40] This is, perhaps, because it seems to go without saying: Shakespeare's *Twelfth Night* is clearly engaged with the ambiguities of gender identity and disruption of sexual difference. The emergence of queer theory, has resulted in a number of readings of the play that stress the themes of bisexuality and homosexuality, principally through the figure of the cross-dressing Viola, but also in the relationship between Sebastian and Antonio. Janet Adelman describes Antonio's love for Sebastian, as 'the strongest and most direct expression of homoerotic feeling in Shakespeare's plays',[41] while Stephen Orgel refers to them as an 'overtly homosexual couple'.[42] In Hytner's production, Julio Monge's swarthy Antonio was clearly besotted with Rick Stear's Sebastian, clasping his hands and embracing him for just a moment too long in 2.1, loth to let him leave for Orsino's court.

The gender confusion brought about by Viola's disguise was used to comic effect throughout the production: in 1.4 when Viola's first task, as Orsino's new favourite, was to remove his gown and sarong, stripping him to his tight-fitting underpants for bathing – a task which she carried out with surreptitious glances at his groin; in the 3.1 encounter between Cesario and Olivia, when Olivia, having declared that 'Love sought is good, but given unsought is better' (3.1.157), flung herself at Viola, giving her a lengthy kiss on the lips before wrestling her to the ground; and in 5.1, when Orsino mistakenly clasped Sebastian's face to deliver the line 'Be not amaz'd' (5.1.260), forcing him to repeat the words again to Viola. Although these moments met with laughter from the audience, Don Shewey praises Hytner for not milking the cross-dressing 'for laughs', but playing it 'for maximum emotional disorientation', particularly in Viola's reactions towards Orsino's madness + unrequited love   _marriage(s)

affectionate behaviour.[43] In 2.4, Orsino, conversing with Viola
as Cesario on the subject of love, began slowly undoing her
neck tie and top shirt buttons, while she was clearly pained by
her inability to show her true feelings for him, tears coming
into her eyes as she listened to Feste's song 'Come away, come
away death' (2.4.51–66).

As a whole, Hytner's production acknowledged the play's
darker aspects: 'the themes of madness and unrequited love
hang[ing] like a heavy rain cloud'.[44] Equally, the so-called
comic subplots of Malvolio's gulling and Sir Toby's drunken
exploits had their own tragic elements. Malvolio's treatment
was far from a light-hearted trick, the filthy, blood-encrusted
steward reduced to pitiful sobbing, while Brian Murray's Sir
Toby was clearly a troubled alcoholic, frequently staggering
around the stage with his clothes in disarray, his words slurred.
The production also exploited the unresolved elements of the
play's ending, with Feste's final song accompanied by a series
of departures – most notably those of the solitary Sir Andrew
Aguecheek and Antonio, the latter looking regretfully at the
four lovers dancing together at the back of the stage, epitomizing Hytner's feeling that it is 'a desperately sad play'.[45]

For Dewey the ending was particularly effective in
questioning the suitability and happiness of the marriages
with which the play ends:

> Maria's hitched to Sir Toby, a prime candidate for detox.
> Settling down with Viola's twin Sebastian, Olivia has
> blithely exchanged her Cesario doll for one with working
> male parts. And with Viola, Orsino faces the prospect of a
> heterosexuality that has never been more than theoretical
> for him. Knowing everything we know, it's hard to believe
> that all's well that ends well.[46]

For some, the overriding mood of 'erotically-charged languor'
led to a rather slow, and 'listless' evening.[47] For others, the
production was attractive and funny in equal measure, 'with
sight gags and jokes rendered in clear and accessible terms'.[48]

The production's mood and its design were fully enhanced by its eclectic music, composed by Jeanine Tesori and mixing 'ethnic music, modal folk songs, driving dances, segments that might be from Morocco, Broadway riffs, pop licks, chamber music and coloristic sound effects'.[49] As with the set and costume designs, Hytner and Tesori felt that the fantastical nature of the play, 'the timelessness of the locale and the gender-bending confusions of the characters called for music that was equally ambiguous: elemental yet mystical, familiar and exotic, simple yet ethereal'.[50] According to Anthony Tommasini, 'Tesori went to a downtown percussion store' and asked them to show her 'all the instruments that nobody else ever rents, the more exotic the better'. These included 'metallic Tibetan temple bowls that are played by rubbing a wooden stick around the rim', 'gongs, wooden blocks, chimes and bells as well as unorthodox newer creations like the daxophone, a German-made instrument of bowed wood with a convex finger board that is used for a wide range of sound effects, like bird-calls and ocean waves'.[51] Hytner's ideas for the music recall those for *As You Like It* at the Manchester Royal Exchange in 1986, in particular the notion that the music should be 'natural',[52] played live and seem to emerge from the characters and the situation rather than appear as incidental music.

Unlike with *As You Like It*, *Measure for Measure* or *King Lear*, this production showed a greater willingness on Hytner's part to alter the Shakespearean text in order to make it more readily intelligible to his audiences. This is something which Hytner has become increasingly inclined to do, feeling 'more and more ... that there are occasions when to be true to Shakespeare you have to rewrite him, or at the very least cut the incomprehensible bits'.[53] Hytner's production of *Twelfth Night* is cited by Alan C. Dessen in *Re-scripting Shakespeare* as an example of a production in which directors 'fearful of losing their auditors and not getting them back, regularly cut or simplify syntactically complex passage or otherwise streamline long speeches'. As he goes on to note, the production 'provided an unusually large number of such changes: for example, *sink-a-pace* became *hornpipe* (1.3.130–1), *con* became *learn* (1.5.174), *revolve* became *consider* (2.5.143), *chev'ril* became *kid* (3.1.12), *pilchers* became *sardines* (3.1.34), and *barricadoes* became *stone walls* (4.2.37).[54] In an article 'Teaching What's Not There' Dessen again cites this production, noting Hytner's decision to cut Malvolio's line in 2.5, when, having read the letter, seemingly from Olivia, he remarks 'She did commend my yellow stockings of late, she did praise my leg being cross-garter'd'. As Dessen explains:

> the director's rationale is clear, for later in this scene Maria tells the other conspirators that "He will come to her in yellow stockings, and 'tis a color she abhors, and cross-garter'd, a fashion she detests" (2.5.198–200). To omit Malvolio's supposed "memory" is therefore to eliminate an anomaly, a possible source of confusion.[55]

This is something that Hytner is always anxious to do, feeling that sometimes 'in order to be true to Shakespeare, we have to change him'.[56]

Although the concept, direction, design, music and lighting were all highly praised, the main criticisms of the production surrounded its casting. Most critics felt, with Vincent Canby, writing in the *New York Times*, that Helen Hunt (as Viola), Paul Rudd (as Orsino) and Kyra Sedgwick (as Olivia) were 'not quite ready for their star roles', lacking 'the vocal technique, the stage presence or the innate personas that would give character to some of the loveliest, wittiest romantic language in the canon'.[57] Hunt's delivery was criticized for being 'mechanical',[58] Rudd's for being 'florid'[59] and Sedgwick's 'obvious and exaggerated'.[60] For Bosco, an experienced Shakespearean actor, this was a fundamental problem with the production:

> Some of the people in the company had very little experience

doing Shakespeare. And it shows. You cannot make up experience when you don't have it.[61]

Bosco describes the read-through, done in the glass lobby of the theatre with views of New York, in which 'some of the people were not reading very well'.[62] He recalls thinking 'here we have people who have never done a Shakespearean play before in their lives. And it struck me, what is wrong with this imbalance? It's unthinkable for anyone to play professionally at the Met or the Philharmonic who hasn't done the groundwork, the beginning levels, the apprenticeship, all of that.'[63] Hytner disagrees with Bosco, asserting that Kyra Sedgwick as Olivia was 'fantastic' and Paul Rudd as Orsino was 'great'.[64]

Nevertheless, for many critics, the production was 'more than usually dependent on its comic characters',[65] a criticism previously levelled by some critics at both *Measure for Measure* and *The Tempest* and perhaps symptomatic of Hytner's evident facility for comedy, stemming back to University. The performances of Brian Murray as Sir Toby Belch, Max Wright as Sir Andrew Aguecheek and Philip Bosco as Malvolio were roundly praised. For Ben Brantley writing in the *New York Times*, Murray and Wright's performances were 'blissful vaudeville as rich in psychological detail as ... hilarious shtick'.[66] In addition to using their 'consummate technique' to 'make each comic exchange ... gut-wrenchingly funny',[67] Wright and Murray managed to achieve poignancy, effectively conveying 'the subliminal sadness and anxiety' inherent in the play.[68]

Bosco's Malvolio achieved a similar balance between humour and pathos, although for some the latter outweighed the former. 'Bosco isn't the funniest Malvolio I've ever seen, but he may be the most pitiable; his humiliation comes close to being truly tragic', wrote Clifford A. Ridley.[69] This is something which Hytner fought hard to achieve, persuading an initially sceptical Bosco, who felt that Malvolio was 'outlandish, comic', to see him as 'a serious man' who 'is cruelly, cruelly treated' and, in the play's final moments, extremely 'angry'.[70] This does not mean that the performance as a whole lacked humour. Lennox describes the letter scene as 'hysterical', generating 'two rounds of applause' from the audience: 'The first when you thank Jove, and you're humble about it in this curious way' and the second after 'the smile', when Bosco skipped off the stage.[71]

On the whole, the critical reception was mixed. For Brantley, 'it promise[d] … more than much of the cast [could] deliver'.[72] However, for Coles reviewing the production for the *Guardian*, it was 'in a class of its own', demonstrating Hytner's 'flair and range'.[73] The production was broadcast on PBS (The Public Broadcasting Service) as part of their series 'Live from the Lincoln Center', being only the second time that the series had presented a live theatrical performance.

Hytner's Film Career

Although it was just over four years between the opening of *Carousel* at the NT and the opening of Hytner's next NT production – *The Cripple of Inishmaan* in January 1997 – Hytner's connection with the theatre continued throughout this period: *Wind in the Willows* was revived for Christmas 1993 (playing through to June 1994) and 1994 (playing until the end of February), *Carousel* played in the West End and on Broadway and *The Madness of George III* was remounted at the National and played internationally, before being made into a film, *The Madness of King George,* marking Hytner's debut as a film director and the first of his National Theatre productions to be re-made for cinema, winning the BAFTA for Best British Film and Best Film at the *Evening Standard* British Film Awards in 1995. Unlike some of his contemporaries, like Sam Mendes and Stephen Daldry, who have moved easily between the genres of theatre and film, Hytner has made only a couple of forays into film directing. In an interview with Andrew Dickson in 2010, he admitted that although he had wanted a career in the movies, this was not to be.[74] Most of Hytner's films have been adaptations of his theatrical successes: *The Madness of King George, The History Boys* and *The Lady in the Van.*

Buoyed by the success of *The Madness of King George*, Hytner spent much of the late 1990s in New York, attempting, in part, to build his film career. In 1996 he directed Arthur Miller's own film adaptation of his 1953 play, *The Crucible*. What is striking about accounts of the film is that they show similar commitments from Hytner to those characteristic of much of his theatre work: a desire to make a classic play relevant to contemporary society, to find a universality in a play, ostensibly about the Salem witch trials of the late seventeenth century but clearly alluding to McCarthyism and the political climate of 1950s America. Hytner claimed that he wanted to make the film because he found the story 'universally truthful' and 'alarming[ly] topical', speaking 'directly about the bigotry of religious fundamentalists across the globe, about communities torn apart by accusations of child abuse, about the rigid intellectual orthodoxies of college campuses'.[75] Hytner's account of the film's setting is also reminiscent of his attitude towards theatrical classics, his aim being not to precisely reproduce the historical setting but to find a world in which all the actors can believe and invest: 'Ultimately, what you do is create a world for a purpose, which is to give the people about whom your movie revolves some kind of concrete existence.'[76] However, as Jonathan Coe pointed out, theatre permits a different level of historical flexibility and symbolism from film, with its inevitable 'pseudo-verisimilitude'. In his view, the necessarily historically specific settings and real locations in *The Crucible* resulted in a loss of 'universality'.[77] The film was reasonably well received, attracting a number of award nominations for Miller, and awards for Joan Allen (Elizabeth Proctor) and Paul Scofield (Judge Thomas Danforth).

Hytner followed *The Crucible* with two American-set movies: *The Object of My Affection* (1998) and *Center Stage*

(2000), the first a romantic comedy about a pregnant social worker who falls for her gay best friend and the second a teen drama about dancers at the fictitious American Ballet Academy in New York. While *The Object of My Affection* did reasonably well at the Box Office and received a mixed critical response, *Center Stage* received largely negative reviews. Although, at the time of *The Crucible*'s release, Hytner expressed his 'love' of 'making movies', asserting that 'you get a huge buzz, and you feel more creative',[78] he has since stated that the only film of this era of which he is proud is *The Madness of King George*, because, as he commented in an interview in 2012, 'I don't instinctively think through the camera.'[79]

During the 1990s Hytner also continued to direct theatre and opera elsewhere, productions including Verdi's *The Force of Destiny* (ENO, 1992), Oscar Wilde's *The Importance of Being Earnest* (Aldwych Theatre, London, 1993), Mozart's *Don Giovanni* (Bavarian State Opera, 1994), Janáček's *The Cunning Little Vixen* (Théâtre du Châtelet, Paris, 1995) and Alan Bennett's *The Lady in the Van* (Queen's Theatre, London, 1999). These productions continued Hytner's close association with Alex Jennings, who appeared as Ernest in *The Importance of Being Earnest*, and Alan Bennett, author of *The Lady in the Van*, and initiated a working relationship with Maggie Smith, who played both Lady Bracknell in *The Importance* and Miss Shepherd in *The Lady in the Van*, a role that she was to reprise some fifteen years later in Hytner's film production of the play, with Jennings as Alan Bennett.

Hytner's production of *The Importance of Being Earnest* was to have been a radical queering of the text, with Jack and Algernon clearly gay (a reading of the play encouraged by the frequent assertion that the word 'earnest' was slang for homosexual), but this was dropped during rehearsals. As it was, some vestige of this initial idea remained in the relationship between the two men, namely in their greeting of one another with a kiss,[80] but not in the overt manner originally intended. Although Kenneth Hurren referred to

the 'gay touch' (*Mail on Sunday*)[81] evident in the two performances and Sheridan Morley to the pair as 'a couple of
lip-kissing gay young things' (*The Spectator*), most reviewers
appeared either not to notice or to find the relationship
unremarkable.

It is interesting to note that a hint of a gay relationship
between characters had also been observed by some critics
in Hytner's *Wind in the Willows* (1990), most notably by
Michael Billington, who wrote 'there are fleeting moments
when it seems to be a story of two closet gays (Rat and
Badger) fighting over the affections of a young boy (Mole)'
(*Guardian*), and Rhoda Koenig, who described it as 'a
complacent tale of boy animals together, evading work,
adulthood and heterosexuality' (*Punch*).

Although Hytner's own homosexuality has not been a
dominant feature in his choice of new plays or in his interpretations of classical works, the abandoned interpretation
of Wilde's play precedes a period where gay relationships
came to the fore in his work: in the film *The Object of my
Affection* (1998), in the explicitly homoerotic elements of his
production of *Twelfth Night* (1998) and in his production of
Mark Ravenhill's *Mother Clap's Molly House* (NT, 2001).

The Twenty-first Century

Hytner began the twenty-first century with two more London
Theatre productions: *Orpheus Descending* by Tennessee
Williams at the Donmar Warehouse (2000), starring Helen
Mirren, and *Cressida* by Nicholas Wright, a play about boy
players in the 1630s, at the Albery (2000), starring Michael
Gambon. In 2001, he returned to the NT to direct his first
Shakespeare production for three years and his first in Britain
for eleven years: *The Winter's Tale* in the Olivier.

The Winter's Tale

Working with designer Ashley Martin-Davies, Hytner's *Winter's Tale* was set firmly in the present day – a departure from his previous Shakespeare productions, which had tended towards eclectic or abstract settings. The court of Sicilia was a grey, minimalist penthouse apartment, backed by a view of city skyscrapers and containing a concert piano. In 2.1 the scene moved to a games room with a table-tennis table and darts board. More than one critic quipped that the characters appeared to have emerged from the pages of *Hello!* magazine (Sheridan Morley, *The Spectator*; Roger Foss, *What's On*),[82] Leontes strolling in wearing stone linen trousers, brogues and a blue cable knit sailing jumper, the courtiers in 'sharp suits' (Charles Spencer, *Telegraph*) and sipping champagne. Although Ashley Martin-Davis asserted that he and Hytner had wanted to create 'a kind of euro-modern world, rather than any specific city like London or Paris',[83] Benedict Nightingale felt that the location was firmly 'your and my England' (*The Times*). Certainly some reviewers identified allusions to the British Royal family, Michael Dobson commenting that Alex Jennings's appearance as Leontes, in the play's final act, 'seemed deliberately to suggest another royal guiltily overshadowed by a dead wife, Prince Charles'.[84] Bohemia was immediately dubbed 'Glastonbury' by almost all the critics: a hippy rock festival, where Phil Daniel's Autolycus, likened in a number of reviews to Ali G (Michael Coveney, *Daily Mail*; Spencer; Foss; Georgina Brown, *Mail on Sunday*), played electric guitar, as Florizel and Perdita shared a joint, giving Florizel's line 'These your unusual weeds' (4.4.1) a humorous twist.

Reviewers seemed diametrically opposed as to the success of this modernization. Roger Foss, Nicholas de Jongh and Susannah Clapp (Foss; Clapp, *Observer*; de Jongh) found the contemporary references inventive and refreshing, creating a production 'compellingly in tune with our own times' (Foss). Other critics were sceptical about the motivations. Both

Charles Spencer and John Gross commented that, 'far from' making the play seem 'relevant', the modernization felt jarring and made the poetry seem stilted (Spencer; Gross). One of the main objections was that modern dress seemed unsuited to a Romance with its 'fantastical' (Kate Bassett, *Independent on Sunday*), 'wonder-working', (Gross), 'old-fashioned' (Spencer) qualities. Equally difficult to accept, was the notion that a modern-day prince would send his attendants to seek judgement from the Delphic Oracle. It was, however, the modernization of Bohemia that caused the strongest objections from the production's dissenters, Gross describing it as 'a total disaster' and Spencer declaring, in horror, that he could 'scarcely believe it'.

In Shakespeare's play, Bohemia is a festive, pastoral realm, part of a classical literary tradition in which the simplicity of the country is contrasted with the complexities of urban life. Perdita is dressed as Flora, the Roman goddess of flowers, while Florizel is disguised as a shepherd. It is a place of innocence and unsophistication, of singing, dancing and jollity. As A. D. Nuttall suggests, even Autolycus the trickster 'is as free from real *sophistication* as his victims'.[85] Nevertheless, Bohemia does not provide a straightforward contrast in mood to Sicilia. Philip M. Weinstein has noted that within the Bohemian scenes, 'there still remains considerable conflict', 'images of death or diminution' and ultimately a lack of resolution.[86] Many productions of *The Winter's Tale* have struggled to capture these complexities, 'to make Act 4 work'.[87] This becomes particularly difficult when a production is in modern-dress. While finding a contemporary analogue for the court of Sicilia can seem reasonably straightforward, directors attempting to find a modern equivalent to Bohemia's sheep-shearing festival, have attempted a 'free-ranging, *Hair*-type musical'[88] (Trevor Nunn in 1969), a 1950s village fete (Adrian Noble, 1992) and a Southern American hoe-down complete with audience participation (Matthew Warchus in 2002).

Hytner's rock music festival may have captured some of the fun and comedy of Bohemia but, in overshadowing the

location with Autolycus, with his songs and raps, paraphrased
lines and adlibs, it lost the poignancy and innocence of the
scenes. It was, as Jane Edwardes commented, as though 'one
ha[d] wandered into an entirely different play' (*Time Out*).
For Michael Billington, for whom Hytner's production went
'oddly adrift in the rural revels', what this Bohemia also lost
was its engagement with 'the nature versus nurture debate'
(*Guardian*). Billington refers, presumably, to the convention
embedded in the play that Perdita, in spite of her upbringing
as the daughter of a shepherd, whose son can barely read,
has emerged as an educated, poised young woman, whose
language (both in her vocabulary and use of verse) is that of a
noble woman rather than a shepherdess. Melanie Clark Pullen,
wearing a pale cheesecloth shirt and skirt, was, in Alastair
Macaulay's words, 'ignoble' (*FT*), far from the 'personification
of virtuous charm, grace, and beauty'[89] described by J. H. P.
Pafford in the Arden edition of the play. In Matt Wolf's view,
she and Florizel seemed 'like two incipient potheads eager to
"get down"' (*Variety*). By contrast, the modern-dress setting
for Sicilia seemed to Billington to act as 'a vital counter-
point to the story's inherent romance' (*Guardian*) even if,
as Susannah Clapp commented, one wondered why Leontes
would 'wait days for his messengers to bring news about his
wife's fidelity from Delphi when he could surely have paged
the Oracle'.

This was a production that provoked strong reactions.
Some, including Michael Coveney, Foss and Georgina
Brown,[90] raved about every aspect, in particular the setting
and the acting. Others – Sheridan Morley and Gross included
– were unremittingly negative[91] and Spencer was incandescent
with rage, describing elements as 'downright disgraceful' and
referring to the 'footling inanity' and 'crass vulgarity' of the
production.

What most critics, even Spencer, were agreed on, was that
the production's ending was moving[92] and magical.[93] Most
significantly, it did not try to lead the play to a forced sense of
resolution. Macaulay summed up Hytner's approach, writing:

what makes him so fascinating a Shakespearian is that he ... never tries to tie up Shakespeare's loose ends and make him into a more neat or satisfying playwright than he is.

In the play's final scene, after Hermione's transformation from a statue, she says little. We hear from Polixenes that she 'embraces' Leontes (111) and from Camillo, that she 'hangs about his neck' (112), but when she speaks it is to Perdita and not Leontes. There are no words between the pair, deferring their resolution beyond the play's end. Hytner heightened this, retaining a sense of suspicion in the reunion between Hermione and Leontes. Skinner's Hermione seemed reluctant to embrace Leontes and did so slowly and only briefly. As she explained, 'She embraces him and seems to try for reconciliation but I just think there's so much damage and pain.'[94] Meanwhile, Leontes seemed equally hesitant in expressing his joy at his wife's resurrection. Paulina's invitation to Perdita to 'interpose' seemed partly prompted by the long, awkward silence between husband and wife, who stood opposite one another, unable to speak. Just as Hytner's *Measure for Measure* had ended with an uncomfortable and uncertain moment between the Duke and Isabella and *The Tempest* with a moment of tension between Prospero and Antonio, so Hytner's *Winter's Tale* finished, not with an image of Hermione and Leontes united or with a picture of a newly-happy family but with Hermione and Perdita, who had been clutched in an embrace on the floor since their reunion, left alone on the stage after Leontes and the rest of the court had left. The image was, in the words of Georgina Brown, 'heartbreaking and wonderful', with Hermione's 'sense of waste and loss ... almost unbearable' (Brown) and 'reconciliation ... enclosed by sadness' (Clapp).

Mamillius was a key figure in Hytner's production from the beginning. The evening began not with Camillo and Archidamus in conversation but with Mamillius, dressed as Time, with a scythe, wings and black cloak, reciting Shakespeare's 'Sonnet 12' to a crowd of admiring adults

– 'When I do count the clock that tells the time … '. The moment was clearly designed to be premonitory, the sonnet about the ravages of time and children acting as their parents' legacy, foreshadowing Mamillius's early death. It also established Mamillius as a choric figure. After his death and following the abandonment of the baby Perdita, he appeared again, at the beginning of the second half, dressed once again as Time, to speak the first lines of Time's speech, 'I that please some … To use my wings' (4.1.1–4). As the adult Perdita entered to take up the next section of the speech ('Impute it not … seems to it (4.1.4–15), Mamillius sat down beside the basket containing the baby Perdita, watching over her. When Polixenes, who took up the next lines (4.1.15–23), spoke the words 'I turn my glass', it was Mamillius who turned over the hour glass, as if controlling the shift of fourteen years. Finally, he picked up the baby basket and exited, hand in hand with the Old Shepherd. Mamillius's presence was also felt at the beginning of Act 5, where the walls of the Sicilian court were decked with huge portraits of Hermione and her dead son, while a large black marble slab detailed Leontes's role in their deaths, reminding the audience of the costs of his behaviour.

As well as being moved by the play's ending, most reviewers were also united in their praise of Alex Jennings's performance as Leontes, both Coveney and Macaulay asserting that Jennings is at his best as an actor when working with Hytner.[95] This was their sixth production together. Once again Hytner was back in his comfort zone, casting actors with whom he had worked a number of times, including Julian Wadham and Phil Daniels. Indeed, he cited this friendship group as one of his reasons for tackling the play: 'When you find that you and your friends have passed 40, it's time to do The Winter's Tale. I have known Alex Jennings … Julian Wadham and Phil Daniels for ages. They're all past 40, and the read-through was strangely moving: hearing actors I was young with being referred to as 'ancient Sir'.[96]

It was, in part, the intricacies of Jennings's performance that the critics found so impressive, John Peter describing it as the 'the richest, most complex and most emotionally intelligent thing he has done' (*Sunday Times*). In the early scenes Jennings gave the impression of a man reluctant to grow up – a 'spoilt boy' (Peter) with 'a slightly arrested public-schoolboy quality' (Taylor), tossing around a rugby ball with Polixenes, much (as suggested by a photograph of them in childhood) as they had done as boys. In Hytner's view, 'Leontes is at that time in life where contentment, success, power and wealth have become suffocating and he throws it all away irrationally. His jealousy is a symptom of his need to lash out against a malaise, clearly stated in the play as being no longer young.' Jennings spoke similarly, explaining that Leontes's rage is partly about growing older: 'about that sense of loss, of moving into acceptance that you are on the downward slope'.[97] He perfectly portrayed this nostalgia for youth, fierce jealousy and sudden loss of reason, providing 'a masterly study of a man determined to drag his whole world down with him' (Gross).

Critics were equally glowing in their comments about Deborah Findlay's performance as Paulina, which succeeded in combining absolute integrity with humour, but less so about Claire Skinner's Hermione, a performance which was understated and delicate but perhaps a little under-projected for the Olivier stage. Skinner's performance may have been a casualty of the fact that the production, as a whole, seemed more focused on the men. It is notable that most of Hytner's comments on the production at the time revolved around Leontes and Polixenes and the male mid-life crisis. In this production, both Hermione and Perdita seemed to fade into the background, Hermione overshadowed by Leontes and Perdita by Phil Daniels's exuberant, outrageous Autolycus.

Irrespective of whether the critics enjoyed the production or not, almost all began or ended their reviews with a comment on its implication for Hytner's chances as future artistic director of the theatre. In 2000, Trevor Nunn had announced the end of his tenure as artistic director of the National. Although some favoured Stephen Daldry or Sam

Mendes, both of whom had recently made hugely successful film debuts – Mendes with *American Beauty* and Daldry with *Billy Elliot* – Hytner was firmly in the running to take over the theatre. For Coveney, *The Winter's Tale* 'did his cause no harm at all', for Clapp it 'boost[ed] his chances' and for Billington, it marked him out 'as a likely future director of the National'. Conversely, Spencer asserted that he had 'chosen a terrible time to come a cropper' and Robert Gore-Langton that the production had not 'done his job application any favours'.

Nevertheless, only a few months later, while Hytner was directing *Mother Clap's Molly House* by Mark Ravenhill in the Lyttleton Theatre (2001), it was announced that he was to succeed Trevor Nunn as Artistic Director. Chapter 5 explores Hytner's tenure as Artistic Director, in terms of programming, education work and creative innovations, such as the Travelex seasons and National Theatre Live broadcasts. Chapter 4 looks at his productions during his twelve-year administration, in particular his work on Shakespeare.

4

The National Theatre Years: Hytner as Director

During his tenure as Artistic Director, Hytner directed twenty-seven productions for the NT. As one might expect from his previous work, fourteen of these were new plays: *His Dark Materials*, adapted from Philip Pullman's trilogy by Nicholas Wright (2003), *Stuff Happens* by David Hare (2004), *Southwark Fair* by Samuel Adamson (2006), *Rafta, Rafta ...* by Ayub Khan-Din (2007), *Collaborators* by John Hodge (2011), *Travelling Light* by Nicholas Wright (2012) and *The Hard Problem* by Tom Stoppard; three plays by Richard Bean – *England People Very Nice* (2009), *One Man, Two Guvnors* (2011) and *Great Britain* (2014); and three plays and a pair of short plays by Alan Bennett – *The History Boys* (2004), *The Habit of Art* (2010), *People* (2012) and *Hymn* and *Cocktail Sticks* (2012). Significantly, seven were plays by Shakespeare: *Henry V* (2003), *Henry IV Part 1* and *Part 2* (2005), *Much Ado About Nothing* (2007–8), *Hamlet* (2010–11), *Timon of Athens* (2012) and *Othello* (2013), the most by any single author and an indication of Hytner's talent and passion for directing Shakespeare's writing.

Henry V

When, on 1 April 2003, Hytner began his first official day as Artistic Director of the theatre, he had already begun rehearsing for his first production at its helm: *Henry V*. The production was the focus of much scrutiny and publicity. First, it seemed an interesting choice for a man inheriting the mantle of Laurence Olivier (the first Artistic Director of the National Theatre), whose film of *Henry V* is seen as a landmark in the history of Shakespeare on screen. Second, it was the first time that the play had been performed at the NT. Third, the production marked the beginning of the National Theatre's Travelex scheme, by which two-thirds of tickets were made available at £10 for each performance, encouraging a more diverse audience, particularly of young people. Fourth, Hytner had chosen to cast black actor Adrian Lester as Henry V, a famous white English king; and fifth, most significantly, the start of rehearsals coincided with the launch of British military action in Iraq, providing a startling parallel to the events of Shakespeare's play.

When Hytner chose *Henry V*, a number of months before rehearsals began, he could not have foreseen the advent of this military conflict. Evidently the play was topical, in the context of British military action in Afghanistan following 9/11. However, by the time rehearsals began, a play featuring, as Hytner put it, 'a young charismatic leader sending British troops to war in a cause with dubious legitimacy in international law',[1] seemed even more strikingly resonant. If Hytner had had any doubts as to whether the production would be 'a modern or a classic'[2] in its design, the parallels with contemporary politics made him certain that modern-dress was the most appropriate choice – indeed, in an interview with Billington early in rehearsals, he asserted that 'it would be incredibly irresponsible to do it any other way'.[3] By the time rehearsals commenced, Hytner was clear that the play would be done 'in a totally contemporary context' and would explore 'the way contemporary media spin is involved in the waging of war nowadays'.[4]

However, he was also determined that the production should not be seen to take a simple pro- or anti-war stance, but should explore the moral ambiguity inherent in the play. In doing so, he was actively rejecting the legacy of Olivier, whose film of the play, released in 1944, was unequivocally patriotic and propagandist, removing elements of the play that conflicted with the image of a heroic king and avoiding depicting the 'bloody realities of war' by employing a 'heightened artificiality'.[5] He was also 'passionately' rejecting Gary Taylor's reading of the play as 'an unequivocal endorsement of Anglo-Saxon military omnipotence', citing Henry's 'psychological compulsion' to be always 'shifting responsibility' onto others, as an indication that Shakespeare was deliberately creating a complex character, not a straightforward hero.[6]

Hytner's decision to stage *Henry V* was not exclusively motivated by the political climate but also by one of the aims of his first season, which was to cut back on design costs in the Olivier theatre (cutting the production budget by two-thirds for each play).[7] *Henry V*, with its opening chorus speech, apologizing for the lack of spectacle and encouraging the audience to use their imaginations to 'deck our stage', was 'obviously suited' to such 'stripped-back staging'.[8] Hytner wanted to strip the Olivier stage back to 'its bare architectural form', to create an 'empty space'.[9] However, this did not mean that the production would lack spectacle. Indeed, in creating a realistic image of modern warfare, Hytner not only employed realistic-looking weapons and smoke effects but also real military Land Rovers, driven on and off the stage during the battle scenes, which Kate Bassett felt was actually 'at odds' with the inducements of the Chorus (*Independent on Sunday*).[10]

The parallels with contemporary politics came to the fore in the opening scene, a conflation of 1.1 and 1.2. Men in dark suits gathered around a long black cabinet table, while the Archbishop handed out 'bound documents'.[11] The similarity to Tony Blair's 'dodgy dossier', issued by Alastair Campbell, making the case for the invasion of Iraq on the spurious basis that the Iraqis had weapons of mass destruction, was not lost on the audience. Bassett reported on their 'cynical laughter and simultaneous intake of breath when Henry's advisors – in suits and ties – present us with blatantly questionable, satirically convoluted justifications for an invasion'. For Michael Dobson, the Salic Law speech 'surely, can never have been so electrifying', 'unprecedented' in its 'vividness'.[12] Far from the comic farce of Olivier's film, with Canterbury scattering papers as his speech became more confused, this archbishop was sure of his position, brimming with 'self-satisfaction'.[13]

More than one reviewer saw an explicit parallel between Lester's Henry and Tony Blair. For John Nathan, the parallels were so clear that he 'could've sworn' that Lester's 'voice took on Tony Blair's chopped speech pattern' (*Jewish Chronicle*). Charles Spencer, asserting that 'we could be at a Number 10 Cabinet meeting discussing Security Council resolution 1411 on Iraq', could not resist adding that the Dauphin's scornful gift of tennis balls in this first scene made one think of 'the French president's notorious recent gift of second-best wine' (*Telegraph*). Rumours had circulated, only a week prior to opening night, that bottles of wine that Jacques Chirac had sent to Tony Blair as a birthday present had been of a questionable vintage.[14] However, Lester's Henry was far more than just a satirical portrait of Tony Blair. The characterization was nuanced, in keeping with the ambiguous stance of the production. This was not the heroic, chivalrous King of Olivier's film but a complex ruler, 'determined but also racked with doubt, magnanimous but also revealing flashes of a meaner spirit, deeply religious but also capable of ruthlessness' (Spencer).

Lester's Henry was as much a modern politician as a medieval king. His casting in the role was in marked contrast to Olivier's Henry, who was modelled on the famous late sixteenth-century portrait of the king that appears in the National Portrait Gallery. By casting a black actor as Henry,

Hytner was making both a political and a theatrical point. Clearly Lester was going to look nothing like the real Henry V. Hytner was casting 'the best actor' for the role,[15] irrespective of the colour of his skin, something that David Lister saw as part of a wider policy plan by Hytner 'to show from the start that he is going to bring a more radical approach to casting and choice of productions'.[16] The casting was also in the spirit of the Chorus's demands that the audience should use their imaginations, and of the Elizabethan theatre. When Lester remarked that he wanted the audience to 'look at the character rather than at the person who's playing him',[17] he was asking them to behave much as an Elizabethan audience must have done in accepting a young boy as a woman. Hytner's colour-blind casting extended beyond Lester, with Cecilia Noble cast as both the Hostess and the Queen of France and Faz Singhateh as Westmorland. Pistol was also played by a black actor – Jude Akuwudike – but here the audience were not asked to be blind to his colour but to embrace it, Akuwudike playing the role with a strong Jamaican accent.

Hytner also broke with recent tradition in his casting of the Chorus, casting a woman – Penny Dowie – in the role and thereby 'adding a much-needed female perspective to this oppressively masculine play' (Spencer, *Telegraph*). Hytner felt that this casting provided a way of 'theatricalizing the dialectics between rhetoric and reality', of exposing some of the gaps between what the Chorus tells us that Henry does and what he actually does: 'The Chorus tells us, for instance, that we're going to see Henry moving from tent to tent raising the spirits when in fact he stirs up nothing but trouble.'[18] Recognizing the 'strong sense that the Chorus is ... jingoistic, pro-Henry ...',[19] Hytner and Downie had originally conceived her as 'a gung-ho Fox News kind of war reporter'. However, they 'settled on her interpreting the role "like a lecturer trying to reimagine the play for the audience"'[20] – a historian who had 'almost fallen in love' with her subject[21] and who became 'increasingly disappointed' that he did not live up to her expectations, something which Hytner remembers as being particularly effective: 'I thought that was good. If it's been done before, I haven't seen it.'[22]

The status of the Chorus as 'unreliable narrator' conveniently missing out elements that 'puncture Henry's chivalric narrative',[23] and 'consistently ... whip[ping] up enthusiasm for his *mis*representation of what follows'[24] has long been recognized. Not only does the Chorus provide a misleading account of Henry on the night before Agincourt but misleads in almost every speech. The Act 2 Chorus's declaration – 'Now all the Youth of England are on fire... and Honour's thought/ Reigns solely in the breast of every man' – for example, is followed by a scene set in Eastcheap in which Pistol seems interested only in the spoils he can gain from war. Hytner further accentuated the irony of this moment. As Downie's Chorus spoke these lines, Bardolph and Nym were seen, in a bar, watching television and idly flicking channels from the King's address to the nation (the last 7 lines of 1.2) to snooker, football and a speech by the Archbishop of Canterbury. Hytner also divided this chorus speech, so that the section about the English (lines 1–11) was immediately followed by the Eastcheap scene. This move, common on the nineteenth-century stage,[25] also makes more sense of the latter part of the speech, placing the Chorus's declaration that 'the scene / Is now transported ... to Southampton' immediately before the scene located there (2.2).

The King's address was one of a number of television broadcasts that featured in the production, emphasizing the propagandist role played by the media in times of international conflict. Henry's speech to the citizens of Harfleur was spoken directly to an onstage camera, clearly recording it for public broadcast. However, having delivered the lines 'mowing like grass / Your fresh fair virgins, and your flowering infants' (3.3.13–14), Lester's Henry indicated to the camera operator to stop filming, shrouding the television audience from his further brutal threats and preserving his media image.

One of the most effective uses of one of these television broadcasts was in 3.4. This scene, in which the Princess

Katherine attempts to learn English from her lady in waiting Alice, is often played for its comic value. However, Hytner undercut the comedy, showing the two women watching Henry's televised broadcast from Harfleur, screened with French subtitles. Katherine's request to learn English, far from fanciful, was born of necessity: from a realization that she needed to learn the language of the occupying force and of her likely future husband.

This serious, moving depiction of Katherine and Alice was part of a general attempt in the production to make the often comic French seem a 'credible and a reasonable opposition'.[26] Nicholas de Jongh welcomed a rare exception to the usual representation of the French as 'vain, effete fools' (*Evening Standard*). Indeed, by the end of the play, they were clearly demoralized and Katherine's reaction to Henry's wooing undermined the sense of a straightforward happy ending. Although, as Reynolds and White explain, the inherent comedy in the scene came out more fully once the production was in front of an audience, something to which Lester responded,[27] the final images of the play retained a sense of ambiguity. Katherine was clearly angered by Henry's insistence on kissing her, reacting by shouting aggressively at him 'Laissez, mon seigneur ... indigne serviteur' (5.2.250–3) and her 'reluctance willingly to accept her fate' was indicated 'not only by her lack of enthusiasm in returning the kiss, but also by her refusal to take Henry's hand on the public announcement of their marriage'.[28] The production's final moment – 'an awkward photographic tableau of cross-Channel unity' (Paul Taylor, *Independent*), with the English and the French stiffly drinking champagne, accompanied by the Chorus's bleak look into the future left the production feeling open-ended and lukewarm in its sense of English glory. As Peter remarked, 'it is entirely typical of both Shakespeare and Hytner that the debate is morally charged and inconclusive' (*Sunday Times*). Indeed, one recalls the ambiguous, troubled endings of Hytner's productions of *Measure for Measure*, *The Tempest*, *Twelfth Night* and *The Winter's Tale*.

A further use of the television screens as a means of giving characters a greater humanity came at the start of 2.3, where the screen in the tavern was used to show a home video of Falstaff just prior to the Hostess reporting his death. As has become a common device in film versions of *Henry V* (Kenneth Branagh used flashbacks to scenes from *Henry IV* and Oliver showed Falstaff on his deathbed recalling Henry's rejection of him from *2 Henry IV*), Hytner made use of an extract from *1 Henry IV* (an edited version of 2.4.371–403), showing Falstaff and Hal carousing together in a pub. This not only provided a more poignant context for the reporting of Falstaff's demise but, in its direct juxtaposition with the final lines of 2.2 (185–94), also broadcast and showing an unsmiling Henry in full military uniform, illustrated Henry's dramatic transition from a dread-locked young man, consorting with ordinary men in the pub, to an often cold and principled leader. It also served to make all the more shocking the moment of Bardolph's execution (3.6) – an execution carried out by Henry himself, with a gunshot to the head, drawing 'audible gasps of shock' from the audience.[29] This moment split the critics. Peter found it 'deplor[able]', 'something neither a medieval king nor his modern incarnation would ever do'. Hytner had been advised of this by Richard Smedley, the company's military adviser. However, as one might expect from Hytner's penchant for arresting affects, 'the retention of the coup de théâtre produced by the shock of this action won out over its truthfulness'.[30]

Interviewing Lester in 2013, Julian Curry suggested that in contrast to Olivier's expurgation of 'the most gruesome aspects of war', Hytner might have 'overemphasized them', something that Lester rejected. However, Hytner certainly didn't shy away from moments in the play that display Henry's ruthlessness and 'pettiness',[31] something that he felt comes across particularly strongly in Henry's treatment of Williams in pursuing the challenge made when in disguise – 'Give me any gage of thine, and I will wear it in my bonnet: then, if ever thou darest acknowledge it, I will make it my quarrel' (4.1.205–7). Hytner cites this as indicative not only of a 'phenomenal pettiness' – 'He's just won the greatest victory in English history and the thing that is obsessing him is taking revenge against a poor little grunt, who had the temerity to utter a few insignificant words of criticism against him' – but also of Henry's lack of responsibility:

> the revenge is actually pretty dangerous. It's really dangerous setting pumped-up drunken squaddies against one another. That brawl that he provokes could be really bad news, and that's all done by the 'hero' king – mean-minded, vain and petty.[32]

In order to emphasize this point, Hytner began 4.8 with the soldiers drinking and partying to loud rave music. Pumped up by alcohol and success, the angry exchange between Fluellen and Williams prompted a brawl in which all those onstage joined in, a fight which might have escalated further were it not for Henry's entrance ('How now, what's the matter?' [4.8.19]).

Whereas both Olivier and Branagh had cut Henry's instructions at Agincourt: 'Then every soldier kill his prisoners' (4.6.37), Hytner provided another shocking moment, which undermined any conception of Henry as a straightforward hero. The French prisoners were brought on in a line and forced to the ground, hands on heads, the English soldiers pointing their guns at them. As Peter reports, Henry's order to kill these 'prisoners of war' was 'hideous in its briskness' and even Henry's own soldiers were shown to react in horror to the command. This moment in the production also served to flesh out the character of Fluellen, making an often absurdly comic figure into a more complex character – as is Hytner's wont. Henry having left the stage, Fluellen gave the order to 'Fire', an order ignored by the soldiers, leading Fluellen to take his machine-gun and mow down the prisoners himself in cold blood (a moment that is usually confined to off-stage). As Robert Blythe who played Fluellen noted, having the character carry out the King's orders gave the following scene, 4.7, 'normally played as sort of low comedy ... a different complexion entirely because it's played by a man who's just committed an atrocious act'.[33]

Having the English soldiers mutiny against Henry at this moment was part of Hytner's desire to create an army that seemed real. By the time this scene was rehearsed, Hytner stated that 'the actors had really started to inhabit the notion that they were the contemporary British army'.[34] This had partly come from extensive military training which was designed to make the actors look and feel like soldiers. Some critics found the soldiers 'sympathetic' (Jane Edwardes, *Time Out*); others quite the reverse. What was clear was that Hytner had no desire to sentimentalize them – any more than he had Henry. Rather than heroic cries of support, Henry's 'Once more unto the breech dear friends' (3.1.1), was met with tired groans from a clearly exhausted army and later, in what Peter described as 'among the play's most chilling moments', one of the soldiers looted the pockets of the dead Bardolph, clearly motivated by selfish gains rather than honour.

In creating a believable army, Hytner was open to improvisation from the actors, the soldiers improvising 'off-line naturalistic military asides such as "At ease, men, three minutes" from Exeter to the army and "Fuck off!" from the army to Mountjoy'.[35] In Henry's speech before the gates of Harfleur, the soldiers' angry chanting drowned out several of Henry's lines ('Whiles yet the cool and temperate wind of grace ... spoil and villainy' [3.3.30–2]). Lester explains that early in the rehearsal process, Hytner 'stood up and said he wanted the Shakespeare to sound like modern language, like squaddies and officers on a battlefield'.[36] This is, again, characteristic of Hytner's desire to make Shakespeare relevant and accessible and, if Benedict Nightingale felt that it was 'questionably' Shakespearean, he also found that it made the 'soldiery come to life' (*The Times*).

In addition to allowing some improvisation around the text, Hytner also made some more substantial changes to the text in order to tighten its focus, most notably at the play's opening. Hytner conflated the first two scenes so that they ran into one another, cutting the exit of the two Archbishops and rearranging lines at the start of 1.2 and cutting around 150 lines from the Folio text, including lines 136 to 221, in which Henry discusses the need to defend England against the Scots who are likely to plan an invasion, a section which Hytner felt 'didn't work in a modern context'.[37]

There were a number of other internal cuts made to scenes, for example, the removal of 48 lines from 4.2, resulting in the cutting of the characters Rambures and Grandpré; however, the only other cut on which the critics commented was that of the leek-eating scene at the beginning of Act 5. Hytner cut the first eighty lines of 5.1, placing Pistol's speech (lines 81–90) at the end of Act 4. Nightingale felt that the cutting of the leek-eating somewhat undermined Robert Blythe's performance as Fluellen, by removing some of the comedy. However, in an interview with Rosenthal, Hytner defended the decision, asserting that, in order to make the play 'three hours long, rather than three and three quarters', he had cut 'what I think are the boring bits', adding 'I don't regret not seeing Pistol beaten about the head with a leek by Llewellyn. There may still be people who fall off their seats with laughter at the sight of a man attacking another man with a leek ...'[38] Hytner's assertion, that he finds 'a lot of Shakespeare's comic writing tricky',[39] may seem odd from a man who has been heavily involved in comedy since university and whose productions have often been praised for the slickness of their comic routines. However, in this production he seemed to steer away from trying to make explicitly comic some of the moments more frequently exploited by other productions, for instance the dubious and convoluted justification provided by the archbishops, turned by Olivier into a slapstick routine, the English-learning scene between Katherine and Alice, and the final wooing. Perhaps the close correspondence of the play's events to those of 2003 made it difficult to justify the humour in these scenes.

The accounts of the production in Reynolds and White's Diary, Lester's interview with Julian Curry in *Shakespeare on Stage* and the *Stagework* website all provide some indication of Hytner's methods as a director. Lester describes his rehearsal methods simply as 'straight up on its feet. Books in hand'.[40] He expands by stating that the company 'had a read-through as usual' and that Hytner 'talked a bit about acting Shakespeare' and in particular 'what he didn't like, what he thought was "dead" Shakespeare',[41] Shakespeare that doesn't sound like 'natural speech'.[42] Hytner himself confesses that 'he is "no good at playing games" and thus prefers to get straight on with the play itself'.[43] Thus, after the first read-through, rehearsals followed a straightforward pattern described by Reynolds and White: 'a scene would be read-through, any issues discussed, and a general approach agreed upon before the actors got to their feet to sketch out a staging'.[44] What Reynolds, White and Lester all allude to is the democracy of Hytner's rehearsal room, combined with a strong sense of the directorial aims of the production. Reynolds and White assert that 'it was always clear where the power lay: with Nicholas Hytner'; however, they go on to explain Hytner's methods of working with the large ensemble of actors playing soldiers and cabinet members, describing it as 'skilled and patient', with Hytner spending time speaking to every individual, 'even if they had no words to speak', so that 'they knew why they were in the scene, and what they had to do'.[45] This approach, is, as will become increasingly clear, typical of Hytner: a simple, democratic, no games rehearsal process, in which the creation of the world of the play – and each actor's under-standing of this world – is of prime importance.

Reynolds and White's diary also makes clear that Hytner's democratic approach extends from the cast to the entire crew. They describe the first day of the technical rehearsal on which Hytner 'called all the actors on stage where the stage crew … were already gathered' and asked them all to introduce themselves one by one – 'a symbolic gesture … whose impor-tance was not lost on the crew or the actors'.[46] Although

Hytner has, in the past, had a reputation for sometimes losing his temper (the result, he suggests of an uncharacteristic outburst being caught on camera on the *Making of Miss Saigon* DVD),[47] Reynolds and White suggest that during the technical rehearsal for *Henry V* he remained calm, setting an example followed by the rest of the cast and crew. Perhaps, much like Henry, Hytner's new role as Artistic Director meant that he had to throw off any of the hot-headedness of his youth and assume an air of calm authority.

Only two of the major reviews were negative: John Gross, who found the analogy with the contemporary conflict 'absurd', claiming that it broke down 'at a hundred points' (*Sunday Telegraph*) and Toby Young, who declared himself to have been 'reduced to a spluttering, eye-popping rage' by the production's politics: 'How dare he stage such an unpatriotic production of *Henry V* in the Royal National Theatre ...?' (*The Spectator*). For the most part, the critics were glowing in their praise for the production's immediacy and energy, describing it as 'startlingly up-to-the-minute' (Bassett), 'thrilling' (Spencer) and 'truly victorious' (Roger Foss, *What's On*) and, for Aleks Sierz, 'the most coherent and intelligent production I can remember' (*Tribune*). Dobson went as far as to suggest that the production 'must rank as the most successful attempt to get Shakespeare back into the centre of serious public discourse in England for many years', expressing his hope that Hytner would 'repeat the experiment on another work by this acute political commentator at his earliest opportunity'.[48]

Henry IV Parts 1 and 2

Two years later, Hytner elected to mount Shakespeare's 'prequels' to *Henry V*, *Henry IV Parts 1 and 2*, again with precision timing, however, for Dobson, without the acute political commentary achieved with *Henry V*.[49] The productions opened on the eve of the general election and, in spite of the fact that Hytner did not choose to follow the production style of his *Henry V*, by updating the plays to a modern setting, their topicality was remarked upon by some reviewers. Sheridan Morley asserted that these were 'perfect play[s] for an election week even when seen across six centuries', offering 'a window on our world' (*Daily Express*),[50] while Jane Edwardes commented on the appropriateness of opening 'Shakespeare's state-of-the-nation plays, just as we choose who should run that same nation' (*Time Out*).

Even though the 'contemporary parallels' were not 'hammered home' (Edwardes, *Time Out*), the two plays offered what Michael Billington described as 'explorations of our national psyche and landscape' (*Guardian*), which remain relevant to the political and social climate of the twenty-first century: the relationships between 'church and State, father and son, good and evil, moral and spiritually bankrupt' (Morley) and issues of 'power, nationhood and identity' (Victoria Segal, *Sunday Times*). Only Dobson, writing in *Shakespeare Survey,* was critical of what he perceived as 'a surprisingly missed opportunity', in the week leading up to an election, for the production to say anything explicit 'about the nation whose history it supposedly dramatized'.[51] For Dobson, the chief problem was in the anachronistic, 'non-particularized' setting, a design choice familiar from a number of Hytner's former Shakespeare productions (including *Measure for Measure*, *The Tempest* and *King Lear* at the RSC) but one which Dobson felt was inappropriate for a history play.[52] The design mixed pseudo-Medieval and modern dress, a technique that Hytner considers apposite for a Shakespeare play since it reflects the practices of the Renaissance theatre: 'Very plainly Shakespeare is using the old medieval world to refer to his modern Renaissance world.'[53] He felt that the eclectic design reflected the fact that these plays are 'specifically about the medieval world', while also acknowledging that they 'consist of themes and characters that are completely relevant to a contemporary audience'.[54] Actors wore medieval gowns and jerkins with contemporary jeans and cardigans, lounged on leather armchairs and ate bacon and eggs off china plates, but fought with broadswords, simultaneously alluding to the past while incorporating certain recognizable semiotics of the present. Hytner aimed to achieve a production that 'look[ed] medieval', but felt 'universal'.[55]

As with *Henry V*, this was the first time that the two *Henry IV* plays had been performed at the NT. Once again, they were part of a Travelex £10 season, now in its third year, and were performed in the Olivier theatre, which seemed to Paul Taylor to be their 'rightful home' (*Independent*), allowing the 'epic' quality of the plays to come to the fore while retaining an 'astonishing intimacy' in the more domestic scenes (Charles Spencer, *Telegraph*). As part of the Travelex season, the design budget for the two productions was, as with *Henry V*, curtailed, necessitating a simple set. Mark Thompson created a raked central ramp, backed by a screen on which photographic images appeared, either to indicate location – the court, churches, taverns, forests and fields – or as a form of pathetic fallacy, depicting a cloud-filled, wintry sky.

The ramp was flanked by a desolate battlefield, on which, at the opening of *Part 1*, keening women were seen, mourning over the corpses of their dead husbands and sons, as Henry IV and his court processed down the centre of the stage – an effective image of a war-ravaged reign, which served both as an indication of Henry's precarious state, his inability to unite his country and 'an arresting premonition' (Taylor) of the aftermath of the Battle of Shrewsbury at the end of *Part 1*, after which the image was repeated. For Hytner it was 'crucial to make clear' from the very beginning, with a clear visual image, 'that these plays are occurring in a country which has been ravaged by civil war for many years'.[56]

As in his production of *Henry V*, Hytner was keen to dramatize the 'seriousness' of war in the plays.[57] In a move reminiscent of his provision of a serious context for the often comic exchange between Katherine and Alice in 3.4 *Henry V*, Hytner asserted of the frequently farcical scenes of the recruitment of the ragged army in Gloucestershire that, 'despite their comic names', they should 'not be portrayed as comic characters', but as 'dignified, terrified, sensible rural people, who simply do not want to go to war'.[58] As Bella Merlin outlines, this decision to 'clarify the dramatic function' of these often superficial characters gave the actors playing them 'a good basis of realism from which to work, as a result of which the early shape of the scene immediately became more textured and interesting'.[59] This creation of a concrete environment in which the characters could exist as real people is typical of Hytner's approach to Shakespeare. As he asserts in his essay 'Stand and Unfold Yourself', he believes that 'the power even of the great tragedies springs from their ruthless observation of the ambiguities and indignities of the real world'.[60]

The stage setting was enhanced by the music for the production, which reflected 'the ongoing cocktail of medieval and modern',[61] mixing 'speed garage' with 'medieval ballads and choral pieces'.[62] The music was part of an elaborate soundscape commissioned by Hytner from Conspiracy – a group comprising of Ben and Max Ringham and Andrew Rutland – which mixed live and recorded music with sound effects and rhythm. As well as reflecting the eclectic design, the soundscape also enhanced the key theme of destruction – created, as Max Ringham explained, with 'creaking metal' and 'distant rumblings', 'a crackling, crunching, distressed sound'.[63] Used not only in the transitions between scenes but also during them, the sound effects and music combined with the lighting to add to the wintry atmosphere, amplify the horror of the battle scenes, gently underscore moments of intimacy and heighten key political speeches.

Staff director Samantha Potter suggested that, in addition to mixing a medieval and modern aesthetic in the design and music, Hytner hoped to achieve a sense of universality by drawing 'contemporary-feeling performances' from his actors, wanting 'the verse to be spoken in a very easy-sounding way'.[64] On the first day of rehearsals, much as he had for

Henry V, Hytner told his actors that his 'first priority' was 'clarity' and that they were not to 'worry unduly about the rules of verse-speaking'.[65] This focus on intelligibility above the demands of the metre is one that is characteristic of Hytner's Shakespeare productions, which are often praised for their clarity. However, the reviews for *Henry IV* suggested that some of this clarity was marred by issues with enunciation, particularly in the performances of Michael Gambon (Falstaff) and Matthew Macfadyen (Prince Henry).

When asked about his impulse for staging the two *Henry IV* plays, Hytner was quite clear that the starting point had been Gambon: 'it all started off with Michael ... I suspect that every production of *Henry IV* should start there, because if you don't know who's going to play Falstaff there's no point in doing them'.[66] However, while Gambon's Falstaff was generally regarded as a highly accomplished performance, most agreed that it was somewhat impaired by its inaudibility (Billington; Bill Hagerty, *Sun*; Jane Edwardes, *Time Out*; Benedict Nightingale, *The Times*), something which Hytner admits was probably due to the fact that Gambon 'left it too late, as even he would admit now ... He should have played Falstaff five years earlier'.[67]

Nevertheless, this was a nuanced portrait of Falstaff, which combined humour and attractive impishness with a 'seductive sadness' (Susannah Clapp, *Observer*) and vulnerability (Kate Bassett, *Independent on Sunday*), the character developing from a jocund figure in *Part 1* to a wretched, piteous figure in *Part 2* (Walker). It also avoided sentimentalizing the fat knight, who was clearly out for himself, from the moment at the end of 1.2 in *Part 1* when he grabbed his and Hal's unfinished breakfast, greedily wrapped it in newspaper and took it away with him, to the final image of *Part 1* when, having waited for the others to depart the battlefield, he turned to rob the corpses of Hotspur and Blunt. Benedict Nightingale felt that Gambon's Falstaff was too 'morally ill', lacking in 'charm, fun and ... charisma' (*The Times*). However, most critics felt that he was able to combine the 'troubling disreputable, flawed' elements of the character with a 'lovable' quality (Carole Woddis, *Herald*), capturing 'a growing sense of age, decrepitude and melancholy' (Billington) which made his final rejection by Hal – 'I know thee not, old man' (5.5.47), shouted aggressively at a keenly expectant Falstaff – particularly moving. As a poker-backed Hal warned Falstaff 'on pain of death … Not to come near our person by ten mile' (5.5.63–5), Gambon's Falstaff crumpled under the weight of his grief, sobbing and trying to grasp at Hal's robes and, after Hal's exit, emitted a deep wail. Once again, Hytner had created a closing scene that was imbued with sadness and a lack of resolution. Henry IV was never presented as the hero of the plays, the productions providing a constant reminder of the costs of his regime, and the accession of Hal to the crown was similarly troubling, *Part 2* ending 'in a chilly purposefulness, with the newly crowned Hal, grim and gleaming, advancing with Cromwellian determination, while a huddle of discards, giddy goats and boozers, wastrels, dotards, schemers and scammers look on bewildered as their hopes and histories are swept away' (Clapp).

The cruel rejection of Falstaff by Hal did not come as a great surprise in this production, with the establishment from the outset of a relationship in which 'the love between Falstaff and Hal is all one way' (Billington). Gambon's Falstaff was clearly enamoured of MacFadyen's Hal, his face lighting up whenever Hal appeared. However, MacFadyen's Hal showed little tenderness towards his friend, leading Nicholas de Jongh to comment that, 'his attachment to the drunken old knight' seemed 'so lightly worn I wondered at the point of it' (*Evening Standard*). This Hal was less torn than is often the case in productions between a genuine love for his tavern friends and his plan to 'imitate the sun' (1.2.192), to behave badly in order to make his reformation seem all the greater. Critics saw his attitude towards Falstaff, Poins and the other frequenters of the tavern as full of 'contempt', making it 'almost too easy for him to cast off Falstaff' (Clapp). Nevertheless, at the end of Part 1, seeing Falstaff apparently dead on the battlefield, in spite of his attempts at humour – 'could not all this flesh/ Keep in a little life?' (5.4.101–2) – his voice was choked with tears.

If the relationship between Falstaff and Hal was less pivotal to this production than in many, the relationship between Hal and his father seemed at its core. Billington described the centrality of the father–son relationship as 'the strength of Hytner's production'. This was an intensely pained relationship, with David Bradley's Henry IV clearly despairing of a son who appeared as profligate and irresponsible as that which he had just deposed. For Hytner, 3.2 in *Part 1* became about Henry's 'basic intention', 'to tell Hal that he is now just like Richard II used to be' while 'Hotspur is like I was' – something that is 'incredibly wounding to Hal'.[68]

This came to the fore in 5.1 of *Part 1*, before the battle of Shrewsbury, when following Hal's offer to 'try fortune' with Hotspur 'in a single fight' (5.1.100), Henry kicked his gage aside with contempt, publicly humiliating him. In Susannah Clapp's eyes, the coldness and 'fish-eyed insolence' of Prince Hal were derived from his father's 'frostiness', showing 'that it's not just the crown, but character that passes down the genera-tions' (*Observer*). These moments of rejection and humiliation were those in which Macfadyen's Hal became moving – a son desperate to gain his father's love and his attention. Bradley's Henry was a gaunt, guilt-ravaged man, struggling both with fatherhood and with kingship. The move from 'righteous ruler to a powerless death-bed shadow of his former self' (Roger Foss, *What's On*) was described as 'perfectly judged' (Clapp), this Henry reminding Charles Spencer 'for once' of why the plays are named after him (*Telegraph*).

Although some critics focused on Gambon's performance as being at the heart of the production, for many one of its great merits, as with many Hytner productions, was the quality of the ensemble acting, a feature undoubtedly partly due to Hytner's inclusive and democratic rehearsal process, which involved working 'simply and chronologically, with all the actors involved in a particular scene sitting around in a circle, reading through the text and ensuring that every single line and image was fully understood by all concerned',[69] with 'all ideas gratefully received'.[70]

The ensemble included John Wood (who had played both Prospero and Lear for Hytner) in the relatively minor role of Justice Shallow. This was a piece of inspired casting and Wood was singled out for praise by almost all the critics. Dobson described it as 'a baroque, virtuoso piece of work'.[71] Wood's tendency towards a vocal delivery that spanned registers and indulged in word-painting, which some critics had found distracting in his performances as Lear and Prospero, were here praised, Dobson describing his 'rapidity at shifting tones of voice and registers of feeling' as enlivening,[72] while Clapp asserted that he made 'every line of Justice Shallow sound new-minted'. It was in these Gloucestershire scenes that the humour of the plays came to the fore, creating what was, for many, the high point of the evening, with Wood's Shallow 'bounc[ing] with glee at the memory of his supposed youthful excesses' (Jane Edwardes, *Time Out*), while Adrian Scarborough's Silence continually broke into drunken song. Scarborough was cast as both Silence (conceived in this production as 'Older than God. 99 and three quarter years old')[73] and the young Poins, a doubling which recalls that taken on by Olivier in the same plays in 1945–6, when he doubled the roles of Hotspur and Shallow in order to display his virtuosity. The Gloucestershire scenes (*Part 2, 3.2, 5.1 and 5.3*) are often cut or trimmed in productions of the play. That Hytner did them pretty much in their entirety (with the exception of much of Falstaff's last speech in 5.1), allowing them to take on 'a blissfully leisurely'[74] pace, was a mark of the contrast that he found between 'the hectic, propulsive, action-filled Part One with the elegiac, death-haunted and autumnal Part Two' (Billington).

In the process of his directing of Shakespeare, Hytner has become increasingly comfortable with cutting and altering the Shakespearean text to make it work for a contemporary audience. In this case he was clear that both plays needed 'to run at under three hours', which necessitated the cutting of 'between 300 and 400 lines from each play'.[75] Staff director Samantha Potter described these cuts as 'essentially based on two factors – removing repeated information which doesn't progress the story, and removing sections which are extremely difficult for a modern audience to understand'.[76] These cuts were predominantly made before rehearsals began but, as Merlin notes, in the process of rehearsal, Hytner was 'very open to negotiating which lines might be cut and which words might actually be changed to enable the story to be told with ultimate contemporaneity'.[77] Dessen described the cuts for *1 Henry IV* as much of what he has 'come to expect' – Prince Hal's list of the words learned from the drawers (2.4.15–20), Falstaff's invocation of the camomile (2.4.400–2) and much of Worcester's politic speech to Hotspur (3.1.175–87) – but expressed surprise at 'the omission of Hotspur's pre-battle speech (5.2.81–8) which can be a stirring, charismatic moment that also reinforces the issue of "time"'.[78] Dessen also notes the way in which Hytner dealt with the problem of linking the two parts of *Henry IV*, the movement 'from Prince Hal's triumph in various senses at Shrewsbury at the end of Part One to his backsliding in his next appearance … the "small beer" scene with Poins' in *Part 2* (2.2). In order to remove 'any sense of the "new" Hal in the final moments' of *Part 1*, Hytner rewrote *Part 1* (5.5):

First, the King's opening speech (5.5.1–10) was directed not at two figures, Worcester and Vernon, but at three, for Douglas was included here among those sentenced to death. Prince Hal's subsequent two speeches and Prince John's [Lancaster's] response (17–33) were gone, so that not only the account of Douglas' flight and capture was eliminated but, more significant, so was the example (in John's words) of Hal's 'high courtesy' (32) in awarding the ransom of Douglas and the honours of the day to Prince John in keeping with his earlier praise (5.4.17–20). Rather than publicly giving credit to both his brother and Douglas,

Prince Hal had no role in the closure of this production – and the final image was of the Falstaff Hal had promised to help 'if a lie may do thee grace' (5.4.157) rifling the onstage corpses.[79]

This left the audience with an ambiguous sense of Hal and, in particular, Falstaff at the end of *Part 1*.

For the most part, the reviews were highly complimentary, praising this 'superb new production' (Spencer) with its 'impressive staging' (Georgina Brown, *Mail on Sunday*). A number of reviews picked up on aspects of the production which have become Hytner trademarks: 'a bold, impressive pace' (Nightingale, *The Times*), a fine 'sense of Shakespeare's politics' (Macaulay) and a way of making Shakespeare 'accessible' (Woddis).

The Alchemist

In between *1* and *2 Henry IV* and his next Shakespeare production at the National Theatre – *Much Ado About Nothing* – Hytner tackled another of Ben Jonson's plays: *The Alchemist* (September–November 2006). This was Hytner's second Jonson, following *Volpone* in 1990, and was a play that Hytner states he had 'always loved', adding that he loves all of Jonson's plays.[80] Indeed, when Hytner left the NT in 2015, the gift given to him by the theatre was a facsimile of the Jonson First Folio, a gift selected by Simon Russell Beale.

Hytner acknowledges the difference between doing a Shakespeare play and a Jonson one, namely that Jonson's work seems obscure because 'he isn't performed very often', adding:

the reason the Jacobean and Elizabethan playwrights who aren't Shakespeare seem more obscure than Shakespeare is not because they are or were more obscure than

Shakespeare, it's just because Shakespeare's the one that we've embraced. It's through Shakespeare that our language has been invented. It's because of Shakespeare's plays that our language has evolved the way it's evolved in the last 400 years.[81]

As a result, Hytner made even more changes to the Jonsonian text than he has tended to do with Shakespeare plays, working with playwright Samuel Adamson to cut around 700 lines,[82] and making 'numerous alterations to make what Jonson intended clear to a present-day audience'.[83]

Designed, once again, by Mark Thompson, with whom Hytner had worked on *Edward II, Measure for Measure, Volpone* and *1* and *2 Henry IV*, the concept for the set, arrived at before rehearsals began, was, 'not unlike … the two *Henry IV*s':[84] 'not exactly contemporary nor entirely period'.[85] However, with this production the aim was not to create a synthesis of periods, but to make a decision in the first two weeks of rehearsal about whether the production was to be in period costume or in modern dress. In spite of having directed a series of eclectic productions of Shakespeare and other Renaissance dramatists, Hytner declared that he had 'lost faith in the idea that you can make a synthesis of 1610 and 2006 so that you can get the best of all worlds'.[86] This marked a quite significant moment in terms of Hytner's Shakespearean direction. Prior to this point, he had done five eclectic productions (*Measure for Measure, The Tempest, King Lear, Twelfth Night* and *Henry IV Parts 1* and *2*) and three modern-dress productions (*As You Like It, The Winter's Tale* and *Henry V*). After this, he was to direct another four Shakespeare productions at the NT: one quite firmly rooted in the seventeenth century – *Much Ado About Nothing*; and the others resolutely modern dress – *Hamlet, Timon of Athens* and *Othello*.

As the company rehearsed, they increasingly found that the play felt contemporary. Hytner justified this with the assertion that 'period production is very inauthentic' and that since *The Alchemist* would have been 'a modern dress play', this seemed 'the most direct option' with this or any other Renaissance play.[87] It was also felt that, with Jonson's often obscure syntax, a seventeenth-century setting might further distance a modern audience from the play.[88] The final design was actually more reminiscent of the 1950s than the present day, a rarity for Hytner, who states that he has long 'fallen out of love with' the notion of 'pick a period, any period'. However, with *The Alchemist*, he asserts that 'the references' that the company found 'were Ealing Comedy and English noir', adding 'I think the point about Jonson is it's so particular, it's so specific, it's so urban. It doesn't have the amplitude of Shakespeare. Whatever you do, you have to be very, very sharp about it.'[89]

The Alchemist marked Hytner's seventh production with Alex Jennings (following *Scarlet Pimpernel*, *The Country Wife*, *Measure for Measure*, *The Importance of Being Earnest* and *The Winter's Tale*). It was his first with Simon Russell Beale – the beginning of another fruitful working partnership. It was also the first time that Jennings and Beale had appeared on stage together, something that Hytner had been looking to achieve for 'three and a half years'.[90]

The production received glowing reviews, which praised both the contemporary setting – 'it makes absolute sense since we live in the age of webcons, holiday scams and a burgeoning casino culture' (Michael Billington, *Guardian*)[91] – and the casting, both Benedict Nightingale and Charles Spencer asserting that Beale's and Jennings's performances were the funniest on the London stage (Benedict Nightingale, *The Times*; Charles Spencer, *Telegraph*). The reviews also picked out some by now familiar Hytner tropes: the production's freshness and inventiveness (Paul Taylor, *Independent*), 'verve and imagination' (Christopher Hart, *Sunday Times*) and clarity (Susannah Clapp, *Observer*) along with the excellent comic timing and strong acting ensemble.

Much Ado About Nothing

The following year, Hytner returned to Shakespeare, with another collaboration with Simon Russell Beale – *Much Ado About Nothing* – a production widely praised by the critics for its success in balancing the tragic and comic elements of the play (Michael Billington, *Guardian*; Benedict Nightingale, *The Times*)[92] and in particular, for its investment in psychological realism and emotional truth (Paul Taylor, *Independent*; Claire Allfree, *Metro*; Kate Bassett, *Independent on Sunday*; Georgina Brown, *Mail on Sunday*). Hytner succeeded in 'creating a genuine world on stage', 'occupied by recognizable people' (Billington), something that has become increasingly important in his productions and felt particularly vital here, in a play that seemed to him, 'with the exception of *The Merry Wives of Windsor*', to be that 'most securely set in the real world'[93] and 'always better served by productions as meticulously detailed as the marriage between Beatrice and Benedick'.[94] Such meticulous detail – 'the maids breathe on the cutlery to give it a last polish as the guests arrive for dinner' (Sarah Hemming, *FT*) – was noted by the critics. In spite of staging this play on the Olivier stage, as he had done with all his NT Shakespeare productions, Hytner managed to turn what had been an epic setting for *Henry V* and the *Henry IV* plays into an intimate domestic space.

Setting was once again a key decision for the production: the 'first question you ask'.[95] Unusually for Hytner, this production was set in Messina (Shakespeare's setting) in 1598, the year of its composition. Although, as with the *Henry IV* plays, this setting permitted the incorporation of certain contemporary 'textures',[96] 'unavoidable' when doing a play in the twenty-first century',[97] these were minimal. As Hytner explained, the 1598 setting seemed appropriate for this play, 'a very Catholic play', in which 'the honour code is very important'.[98] In addition to losing the sense of an 'oppressive Catholic honour code', Hytner felt that, with a contemporary setting, one would 'also lose that sense of why they arrive back from war so light hearted': while 'in the Elizabethan imagination you can come back from a quick skirmish and play a comedy', in the twenty-first century war has become such a 'wholly terrifying phenomenon' that such a notion would seem problematic to a modern audience.[99] Although the production was, as Hytner described it, 'knowingly cavalier'[100] about the historical accuracy of its Elizabethan setting, the company undertook historical research in the early stages of rehearsal in order to enrich their understanding of the period, looking at 'Elizabethan law and order, Italian and Elizabethan army life and Italian carnival masque' in order to provide context and inspiration.[101]

The revolving set, designed by Vicki Mortimer, turned regularly to reveal a series of interiors, facades and alleys; the windows, iron balconies and slatted wooden walls proving 'ideal for eavesdropping' (Billington) in a play that revolves around overhearing and overseeing. Indeed, for Hytner, this was one of the most important facets of the play, the non-sexual pun on the play's title, *Much Ado About* 'Noting' as in 'listening'.[102] In addition to permitting moments of overhearing, the revolving set also importantly allowed the action of the play to run without pause, permitting one scene to run into another and allowing a series of different settings to emerge, revealing the inner workings of this Sicilian house. In 1.1, for example, following Don Pedro's line 'Amen, if you love her; for the lady is very well worthy' (1.1.209–10), the set began to revolve as maids entered, some setting up one of the bedrooms, while others cleared the breakfast table, the scene between Benedick, Claudio and Don Pedro continuing throughout as they entered the bedroom. The set also featured a swimming pool, the use of onstage water recalling both Hytner's *Twelfth Night* and *Volpone*.

Rachel Portman's music, played on a guitar, mandolin, brass, wind and percussion, not only helped to conjure the Sicilian setting, but also to enhance the atmosphere of particular scenes, with loud carnivalesque music before 2.1;

slow, sultry music for the first couples' dance, followed by a riotous tarantella at the party (2.1); and a sombre Miserere in 5.3 at the scene at Hero's grave. Music was particularly key for Hytner in this last scene: 'Whenever Shakespeare calls for music, you know that he recognizes its insidious communicative power.'[103] The scene began with a parade of darkly-hooded monks, led by Friar Francis and followed by Claudio, carrying candles and singing, the music fuelling Claudio's misery as he flung himself in tears on Hero's grave: 'Now, music, sound, and sing your solemn hymn' (5.3).

The main focus of reviews of the production was on the characters of Beatrice and Benedick, strictly the sub-plot of the play but usually regarded as the leading roles, with Benedick having the largest speaking part with 17 per cent of the lines. As has become common, the roles of Beatrice and Benedick were cast with leading actors, in this case Beale, who played Benedick as a rotund, 'bookish, bachelor-soldier' (Billington) and Zoë Wanamaker, whose Beatrice was a 'waspish' (Taylor) but vulnerable woman, often seen taking refuge in a bottle of wine. Both performances were praised for combining, like the production itself, the humour and pain inherent in the play, the characters being 'very funny and immensely touching' (Hemming). Wanamaker herself recognized that Beatrice, in particular, has 'a deep sadness'.[104] Christopher Hart felt that while Beale's Benedick seemed 'an amiable uncomplicated figure', frequently 'gloriously funny', Wanamaker's Beatrice was 'a poignant and unhappy sight', eliciting 'considerable sympathy'. This was, he felt, partly to do with our culture, which seems to dictate that 'it is much easier … to laugh at a middle-aged bachelor than at a middle-aged spinster' (*Sunday Times*). It is also, perhaps, because Beatrice's gulling scene is, as Hytner recognized, a great deal darker than Benedick's. For Hytner, the two gulling scenes had a quite 'different texture' – with Beatrice forced to overhear some 'really nasty things' about herself[105] and Wanamaker's Beatrice reacted particularly painfully to Hero's assertion that she 'cannot love' (3.1.54).

Much was made in the reviews of the fact that Wanamaker and Beale were not conventional casting for Beatrice and Benedick, particularly in terms of their age, Beale being nearly forty-seven and Wanamaker in her late fifties.[106] Quentin Letts expressed some doubt about the wisdom of casting older actors in these roles: 'I have always thought of Beatrice and Benedick as handsome late-30s, not crumpled (and in Mr Russell Beale's case spherical) veterans' (*Daily Mail*). Indeed, Wanamaker herself was surprised at having been asked, stating that her first question to Hytner was 'Aren't I a bit old?', but going on to say that it came to make sense: 'Speaking as a woman, when you get to your late thirties you know that the clock is ticking. You also begin to know that your perfect partner ain't going to happen unless you make a compromise of some kind.'[107] For most reviewers the age of the actors added poignancy and 'depth',[108] making all the more touching Beatrice's sadness at having been left on the shelf (Nicholas de Jongh, *Evening Standard*) and highlighting 'the mature depth of their eventual relationship', in contrast with that of Hero and Claudio (Julie Carpenter, *Daily Express*).

Of course, Beale and Wanamaker were by no means the first actors to play these roles in middle age, John Gielgud and Peggy Ashcroft having famously played them in 1950 at The Shakespeare Memorial Theatre aged forty-six and forty-three respectively, and Harriet Walter and Nicholas le Prevost having performed them more recently at the RSC in 2002 aged fifty-one and fifty-five. Since Hytner's production, the roles have even been played as octogenarians by Vanessa Redgrave (seventy-five) and James Earl Jones (eighty-one) at the Old Vic in 2013. As Hytner explained, playing the pair in middle age established them as 'people who have lived, failed, resigned themselves to loneliness and, through a genuine sense of each other in the round ... become capable of the compromise that long-lasting relationships require'.[109]

One element of the relationship that came out particularly clearly in the production was something often missed by audiences: the fact that Beatrice and Benedick have had a previous relationship. Beatrice's assertion in 2.1, that Benedick won her heart before 'with false dice' (2.1.263) is sometimes overlooked, but for Wanamaker it was central to her characterization. As Hytner outlined, it was essential for the actors 'to create a past for Beatrice and Benedick' and they agreed 'on a very specific history – not something that we intended to be legible to the audience, but a foundation for the palpable pain that they cause each other by being in each other's presence'. The assumption made was that 'at some stage Beatrice read their deepening friendship as blossoming love, that she pushed too hard and that Benedick did a runner … And the memory is still raw'.[110] Even if the details of this past relationship was not intended to be read by an audience, most of the critics picked up on the fact that the two had hurt each other in the past (Spencer; Allfree) with not only 'won my heart with false dice', but other lines such as 'I know you of old' (1.1.139–40) heard afresh (Clapp).

If the reviewers spent some time commenting on the evident vulnerability of the characters, they also commented in detail on a key piece of comic business – or rather two pieces – in the two famous gulling scenes (2.3 and 3.1), in which both Beatrice and Benedick ended up fully submerged in an onstage swimming pool (much as Aguecheek had done in the pools of Hytner's *Twelfth Night*). In the case of Benedick this was particularly comic, the character diving into the pool in order to avoid being seen by Don Pedro, Claudio and Leonato and being forced to remain underwater for some time, as the three men gazed down in silence at the pool, only to emerge sodden on Beatrice's arrival, attempting to impress her with a casual, sexy, but ultimately sodden swagger. It seems puzzling that Hytner chose to repeat this business only a scene later. Indeed, Billington felt that the reiteration of this 'gag' was a mistake. However, many reviewers seemed unperturbed by the apparent lack of originality, Paul Taylor finding the variation of the gag 'exquisitely judged' and helpful in explaining why Beatrice in later scenes 'is nursing a bad cold' (*Independent*). Beatrice, keen to overhear Hero, Ursula and Margaret, took up the straw hat and mop of a maid, which had been left by the pool. When the bucket fell into the swimming pool, Beatrice, attempting to retrieve it, fell in after it. The rehearsal diaries provide some indication of how this repetition came about. Annette Vieusseux describes Wanamaker and Beale as competing for 'the "Italian comedic opera" moment of falling in the pool as they each eavesdrop'.[111] Clearly neither won the argument, and in the end both were allowed to take advantage of the idea.

It is, perhaps, indicative of the prominence of the sub-plot in this production that it was these two gulling scenes, as opposed to the usually pivotal marriage scene that was remarked upon in most of the reviews, even though the aborted marriage was the point viewed by Beale as a turning point for Benedick – the moment when, having 'allied himself with the military side, with the boys, with the men, with the hard drinkers, with the casual sex with people he doesn't know … he thinks "I'm going to swap camp"'.[112] An exception to this was Carol Chillington Rutter, for whom 'the real triumph of this production … was the way it interrogated the deeply serious crisis in masculinity this play brings to book', brought to the fore in 4.1, which 'showed men at their ugliest, hanging around the back, egging each other on'. Rutter identified this scene as central to Beale's interpretation of Benedick, the moment when 'you could see the man's knowledge system in ruins': 'Moments earlier this Benedick's world had been staggered by the suggestion that women were faithless. Now it was devastated by the certainty that men were wrong.'[113]

The main plot, revolving around Hero and Claudio as a whole, received far less attention from critics than the Beatrice/ Benedick sub-plot. Most reviewers found Daniel Hawksford's Claudio rather an unattractive figure. For Julie Carpenter, his 'moody Claudio teeter[ed] on the brink of villainy', while Susannah Fielding's Hero bordered 'on the petulant' (*Daily Express*). This non-idealized portrait of the lovers was, perhaps, part of the production's keen focus on psychological realism. These were real and flawed figures, whose error was to fail to 'bother to note each other',[114] to be bound up in their own narcissism, but who ultimately could be seen to have 'changed'.[115] For Hytner, the scene at Hero's grave (5.3) was key to this – to an audience's understanding that, although Claudio has behaved 'abysmally', 'it is possible for him to change', to be genuinely repentant. It was not only important, in Hytner's view, for the audience to see 'the weight of Claudio's repentance' but for Hero to witness this as well, so that she could be deemed to believe that this man 'is worth taking the risk on',[116] creating the possibility of a genuinely celebratory final scene, in which both marriages can be seen to be happy.

Although most of the reviews focused on the performance of Wanamaker and Beale, many commented that one of the strengths of the production, characteristic of a Hytner venture, was the strength of the ensemble and Hytner's ability to transform scenes and characters who are often passed over, in particular Don John, the Watch and Leonato.[117] Oliver Ford-Davies's Leonato was described by a number of critics as Lear-like (Billington, Edwardes, Bassett), particularly in the aborted wedding scene, but also moving in his affection for and agony over the plight of Hero.[118]

The 'watch' scenes in the play are notoriously 'difficult to pull off',[119] with many of the jokes often falling flat for modern audiences. For Hytner the only solution was to 'cast very funny actors and let them get on with it'.[120] He cast Mark Addy as Dogberry and Trevor Peacock as Verges. For many of the critics, this casting choice paid off. What seemed to be most successful about the performances were their adherence to the sort of psychological realism that characterized the production as a whole. Hytner describes one of his main roles as a director as being to 'challenge every actor at every point to behave truthfully, to behave with integrity'.[121] As Rutter remarked, 'Frequently tedious in the extreme, here the Watch scenes were comic gems because these beetle-browed incompetents, who dismantled their activity in the very act of constructing it, took themselves entirely seriously.'[122]

Finding a psychological realism was also key to the

interpretation of Don John. As Hytner noted, Don John is a character with whom 'much is left to the actor',[123] particularly in terms of grounding the character in 'emotional reality'.[124] Hytner revealed that Andrew Woodall, playing Don John, had found a motivation for his hatred of Claudio in deciding that 'Don John had once made a pass at Claudio' that had been rejected, allowing him 'to give emotional flesh where the playwright has provided a functional theatrical skeleton'.[125] Although this decision did not manifest itself in obvious ways for an audience – most critics picking up on the character's depressive, alcoholic traits – many found this Don John to be far more fleshed out, 'interesting' (Edwardes) and psychologically complex[126] than is often the case.[127] Benedick Nightingale described this as 'the best Don John' he had seen, 'pale, sweaty, sullen, world-weary, sick with a sort of exhausted loathing of his fellow creatures' (*The Times*), while other critics compared the character to Edmund in *King Lear* or Iago, resulting in a production that succeeded in treading a fine line between comedy and tragedy – an '*Othello* with laughs and a happy ending' (Nightingale).

The NT's rehearsal diaries for the play indicate a similar process to both *Henry V* and *Henry IV Parts 1* and *2*, with a read-through, followed by a close reading of the play, 'stopping regularly to clarify the text',[128] and then, in the second week, beginning to put the play on its feet. Interestingly the rehearsal diaries indicate Hytner's desire to get the play 'up on its feet', somewhat earlier.[129] As he expressed in interview, 'I think that too much discussion without getting up there, doing it, trying out how it fits, can be a little bit self-defeating.'[130] However, he was persuaded to engage in discussion a little longer by Beale who particularly enjoyed the in-depth analysis and felt that certain things could be lost once the actors were moving around 'because you're always thinking about something physical'.[131] It is indicative of Hytner's respect for his leading actors that he bowed to Beale's suggestion.

John Nathan picked up on certain 'hallmarks of a Hytner production', 'all present' in *Much Ado About Nothing*: 'the utterly seamless movement; the close control of mood through music ... and sudden sublime tenderness that catches you unawares' (*Jewish Chronicle*). It was also characteristic of Hytner that the production was deemed both 'satisfying and thought provoking' and 'accessible' (Tim Walker, *Sunday Telegraph*), always one of Hytner's concerns. As with other Hytner NT Shakespeare productions, this was partly achieved through a relaxed attitude towards amending and cutting the text, Hytner making 'small cuts and suitable word substitutions prior to the beginning of rehearsals'.[132] Wanamaker commented that many of her lines in the first scene were cut, but felt that this was appropriate since 'no matter how much you know or listen, however much you mime it, it's not going to help you. An audience just cuts off. Once you've lost them, there's no point in having it.'[133] This assertion chimes with Hytner's view, that 'to be true to Shakespeare you sometimes have to confront the incomprehensible stuff head-on by cutting it or even re-writing it'.[134]

It was to be a further three years before Hytner was to direct another Shakespeare play at the NT, allowing others to direct the main-stage Shakespeare productions. Thereafter followed three productions in consecutive years: *Hamlet* in 2011, *Timon of Athens* in 2012 and *Othello* in 2013. All three productions were tragedies and all were characterized by a contemporary setting. As Hytner later discussed, this came from his growing conviction that 'the political plays – the great tragedies in particular ... work best when rooted in a coherent world' and more particularly a coherent world, that is recognizable to a modern-day audience.[135]

Hamlet

For Hytner, '*Hamlet* was certainly conceived as an entirely contemporary play', a 'barely disguised image of the system under which those who first watched the play lived'. While this might have created 'an unimpeachable argument for creating on stage a vivid image of the late Elizabethan world from which the play sprang', Hytner felt that 'to do so would rob a contemporary audience of something that Shakespeare's audience took for granted. They came to the theatre as much to watch themselves on stage as they did to watch the downfall of princes greater than themselves.'[136]

There have, of course, been numerous modern-dress *Hamlet*s, dating back to Barry Jackson and H. K. Ayliff's 1925 Birmingham Rep production and, indeed, in the years leading up to Hytner's production, Gregory Doran's production at the RSC (2008–9), Michael Grandage's at the Donmar Warehouse (2009) and Paul Miller's at the Sheffield Crucible (2010) were all in modern dress. However, such modern-dress productions have tended to be divided between those who seek to present the play essentially as a domestic tragedy (Grandage's 2009 production and Sarah Frankcom's 2014 Manchester Royal Exchange production), removing all reference to Fortinbras, and those that seek to emphasize the political context and draw parallels with our own culture of conflict and surveillance. Hytner's was in the latter camp, as was clear from the opening moments in which, as the lights went down, the sound of low-flying fighter jets roared through the theatre, establishing the military context.

For Hytner, the personal and political in *Hamlet* are 'inextricably linked' and thus Hamlet is 'paralysed as much by the barrier the State puts in the way of anyone knowing anyone else, as he is by his desperate search to know what's going on inside himself'.[137] The restrictions of the state thus became vital, taken to extremes in the depiction of a totalitarian court in which everyone was constantly being watched or listened to: 'Everything is observed, everything is suspect'.[138] Polonius, warning Ophelia about her relationship with Hamlet in 1.3, produced CCTV images of them together; in 3.1 Ophelia, forced to return Hamlet's love letters to her, carried a Bible that was bugged; and every corner was covered by surveillance cameras. Claudius's court was policed by security guards

FIGURE 4 *James Laurenson and Rory Kinnear in* Hamlet *directed by Nicholas Hytner at the National Theatre, 2010. © Johan Persson/ ArenaPAL*

with earpieces and microphones, who kept tabs on everyone. Denmark was indeed akin to a 'prison', a place where Hamlet was trapped, never alone and yet completely isolated.

In this contemporary world, the media also had a role to play – not unlike its role in Hytner's *Henry V*. The court was watched not only by its secret police but by the wider world. Claudius's first speech in 1.2 was delivered as much for the benefit of the television cameras as for the assembled court, as were Fortinbras's final words, framing the production with moments in which, as Hytner asserted, 'no social gesture is trustworthy'.[139]

The culture of the police state led to the redefining of certain moments in the play: the return of Laertes to court, where, in spite of his apparent reconcilement with Claudius, his rebel army were taken away, seemingly to be executed, and, in particular, the death of Ophelia. This latter was shown not to be a suicide or accident, as it is often perceived to be, but a murder. Following Horatio's reading of Hamlet's letter (4.6), Ophelia, sitting on the ground, was approached by two of the security force who trapped her and swiftly bundled her out of one of the doors, muffling her shrieks. Clearly the risk of Ophelia strewing 'dangerous conjectures in ill-breeding minds' (4.5.15) was too great to be borne.

This directorial decision added a corresponding twist to Gertrude's 'Willow' speech in 4.7 (166–83). Often discussed as strange for its inference that Gertrude has witnessed the death of Ophelia without making any attempt to save her, this speech became a front. Bridget Escolme describes it as delivered in a 'stilted, self-conscious fashion as if the speech was what she has been instructed to say'.[140] For Billington, it also had beneath it 'a fine coded rage', as if Gertrude were 'at last aware of the depths of her husband's depravity' (*Guardian*).[141] Certainly Gertrude seemed to need a drink in order to get through it, stopping to pour herself one after 'Unto that element' (4.7.179) before sitting down. When, following the speech, Laertes asked 'Alas, then, she is drown'd?' (4.7.183), the first of Gertrude's two 'Drown'd's (4.7.184) was delivered as an ironic and angry question to Claudius; the second, a confirmation to Laertes, an evident lie. These were the sorts of details that, in Carol Chillington Rutter's view, 'made this *Hamlet* a constant revelation'.[142]

Gertrude, in this production, was thus a more complex figure than is often the case, transpiring to be a consummate liar. In a further moment of unusual, though, as Hytner admits, not entirely original interpretation – 'there are few ideas about Shakespeare that someone hasn't already had'[143] – Claire Higgins's Gertrude was shown to be able to see the Ghost of her dead husband in the closet scene but to be pretending otherwise to Hamlet. The reconsideration of this moment in the play is typical of Hytner's approach, a thorough mining of the text and re-evaluation of the evidence:

When you think about it, you're forced to wonder why Gertrude can't see the ghost. Everybody else who comes across him sees him perfectly clearly. Horatio sees him. Even the sentries on the battlements see him. This ghost does not seem to list invisibility amongst his many undoubted talents, which led us to ask: is it possible that Gertrude *does* see the ghost, but cannot bring herself to admit to Hamlet that she can see him? And the answer is: every single line of the scene works just as well if Gertrude is lying.[144]

Gertrude was one of many dissemblers in the court. In another original moment, suffused with 'grim humour',[145] in the final scene of the play Fortinbras entered shaking hands with Osric and one of the security guards, who had clearly been in his paid employment for some time – a further twist in this state of corruption and dissimulation.

Moments such as those described above, helped to remould some of the main characters and to make aspects of the play feel 'freshly minted' (Neil Norman, *Daily Express*) with 'genuine repointings of lines' (Susannah Clapp, *Observer*). For David Lister and Georgina Brown, Higgins succeeded in 'redefin[ing] Gertrude' (Brown, *Mail on Sunday*; Lister, *Independent*), not only in the moments detailed above, but in her rejection of a 'weak, lovestruck, pliable and guilt-ridden mother and wife', in favour of a 'more realistically self-assured woman, who will have a drink when it suits her, is more than capable of barking out orders herself and knows exactly what she wants out of life' (Lister, *Independent*).

Patrick Malahide's Claudius was cold, calculating and uncompassionate: 'utterly convincing as a man who would kill his brother, usurp the crown, and run a state with a mixture of paranoia, steely control, mistrust and snooping that would put Richard Nixon to shame' (Lister, *Independent*). He was compared by a number of reviewers to Vladimir Putin (Christopher Hart, *Sunday Times*; Ian Shuttleworth, *FT*; Bassett, *Independent on Sunday*; Claire Allfree, *Metro*; Caroline McGinn, *Time Out*) but betrayed characteristics of other modern politicians adept at manipulating the media: 'He opens his hands wide to show he has nothing to hide, clasps them to his breast to show the sincerity of his heart: all the scurvy tricks of every democratic wheedler from Clinton to Bush to Blair' (Hart, *Sunday Times*).

David Calder's Polonius was 'not the bumbling fool we sometimes see' (Lister, *Independent*), but far more the spymaster, drawing on interpretations of the character that see Queen Elizabeth I's Secretary of State Francis Walsingham as its model. A number of critics commented on his interpretation of the line 'To thine own self be true' (1.3.78) in his advice to Laertes – both 'ironic' (Libby Purves, *The Times*) and 'poignant',[146] the change in tone and slight pause that followed, betraying his realization that he has not followed this advice. Hytner explains how this moment came about: 'one day in rehearsal, without warning, David Calder ... approached the end of his speech of advice to Laertes and flinched. He seemed to dry. And then, under the heavy weight of what felt like deep personal shame, he said: 'This above all: to thine own self be true' ... From the heart, like many fathers, Polonius wants his son not to make his own mistakes.' Hytner asserts that in this moment, which 'electrified' him, he 'knew immediately that the Calder's Polonius had helped Claudius assassinate the old King, and was tortured by his own treachery'.[147]

Other characters often appearing merely as ciphers also seemed more fully-fleshed out in this production. Ruth Negga's Ophelia was, initially, a 'feisty' (Lister), 'sexy' (Brown), 'streetwise' (Henry Hitchings, *Evening Standard*) figure, making her descent into madness and isolation all the more poignant; James Laurenson's Ghost was singled out in almost every review – a 'calm' (Hart), 'quiet' (Hitching, *Evening Standard*) figure, who seemed to merge into the walls of the palace. Even Osric, usually a foolish foppish figure, had a clear motivation, appearing only too aware of Claudius's plans for the duel and then transpiring to have been an informer.

Although it might seem almost impossible to find new ways of performing some of the most famous speeches in the Shakespearean canon, one of the performances praised most for its new-minted quality was Rory Kinnear's Hamlet who, reviewers remarked, seemed to have delved afresh into every line,[148] making well-worn speeches seem 'coined on the spot' (McGinn). This was a performance praised for its naturalness,[149] its intelligence and clarity[150] and its 'Everyman' quality,[151] a Hamlet who seemed just 'an ordinary bloke' (Spencer) who might provide 'amiable company for a night on the beers' (Quentin Letts, *Daily Mail*).

The casting of the title role was of prime importance to Hytner, who waited two years to find an appropriate and mutually convenient time for him and Kinnear to work together on the play (Lister), having already directed Kinnear in two productions at the NT: *Southwark Fair* and *The Man of Mode*. Kinnear was, perhaps, not obvious casting for the role. Certainly, this was the thirty-something Hamlet of the Second Quarto and First Folio, rather than the eighteen-year-old of the First Quarto. But, although this Hamlet was far from adolescent, he seemed very much a student, wearing a hoodie and trainers, his bedroom a mess of unwashed clothes and dirty wine-glasses. As might have been expected of Kinnear, whose previous roles at the NT had included a 'volatile'[152] Vincentio in *The Revenger's Tragedy*, a hilarious yet 'vulnerable'[153] Sir Fopling Flutter in Hytner's production of *The Man of Mode* and a pained yet comic Pytor in Maxim Gorky's *Philistines*, his interpretation of Hamlet managed to be both funny (McGinn; Hart) and touching, capable of making the audience laugh, but also feel his grief, particularly when referring to his dead father.[154] For Georgina Brown, this was '*the* Hamlet of our times'.

One of the main difficulties for Kinnear was the lack of information given in the text about Hamlet's relationship with other characters – his mother, his father, Ophelia, Claudius, Horatio and Rosencrantz and Guildenstern – prior to his father's death: 'you don't see enough of Hamlet before-hand' and 'the glimpses that you have of the previous relationships … ones that you presume might have been happy relationships, or indeed have an element of loving about them, you don't see them working particularly successfully'. Thus, whenever there was a chance to 'show the light beforehand', the company tried 'to seize it' – in particular at the end of the closet scene, with Gertrude, and in the nunnery scene, when Ophelia returns Hamlet's letters.[155] This last moment was key to fleshing out the relationship between Hamlet and Ophelia, and filling what Hytner perceived as a gap in the text. As Hytner explains, although Hamlet says to Ophelia 'I did love you once' (3.1.115), 'he never says why he's stopped loving her'. Kinnear performed this line in a way that 'made you believe that they were profoundly devoted to each other, that he was heart-broken, maybe by his own mistrust of her, and that he'd pushed her away'.[156] As he took back the love-letters that he had clearly sent her, he was reduced to tears, choked as he said 'I did love you', but delivering 'once' as if angry at both himself and Ophelia.

Hytner and his company also considered the relationship between Hamlet and his father afresh, looking at the evidence in the text. For Hytner, 'one of the most striking things about the scene between Hamlet and his father's ghost is that the ghost utters not one affectionate word toward his son'. This led them to 're-examine the whole nature of their relationship', considering that the old king – 'a brutal warrior' – might have had 'little in common' with his 'graduate student' son, concluding that 'it was the gulf between them, more than the bond between them, that consumed young Hamlet, and made it impossible for him to take immediate action in response to the ghost's demands for revenge'.[157] While this may have led to a relationship that lacked warmth, it provided Kinnear's Hamlet with a powerful reason for his delay.

The production was summed up by Libby Purves as having 'clarity, relevance, courage and detail', all of which descriptors have become epithets for Hytner's best work. In order to ensure clarity, Hytner underwent his by now common process of altering some of the words, in particular those that have changed their meaning significantly since the early modern period: for example, changing the word 'doubt' to 'fear' in Hamlet' s line, 'My father's spirit in arms! I doubt some foul play' (1.2.256) and 'lets' to 'bars' in, 'I'll make a ghost of him that lets me' (1.4.85). As Hytner states:

> [Hamlet] doesn't doubt foul play at all, because in this context, in 1600, *doubt* meant *fear*. He *fears* foul play … so the line means almost exactly the opposite of what a modern audience would hear. So it seems to me that in order to be true to Shakespeare, we have to change him, and we did.[158]

Hytner also made the decision to remove many of the references to 'swords', since clearly modern-day characters would not be armed with such weapons, except when fencing. Hamlet's 'Swear by my sword' (1.5.167) became 'Swear by my hand' and 'Up, sword' (3.3.87) became 'Up, blade'.

This production seemed to cement a style for Hytner's Shakespeare productions. Its successful hallmarks can be seen in those that followed – *Timon* and *Othello* – in the detailed, socially-realistic contemporary setting, freshness of interpretation, reinterpretation of characters and alteration and excision of elements of the text to provide clarity and modernity.

Timon of Athens

Timon of Athens is, according to its Oxford editor John Jowett, 'Shakespeare's least loved play'[159] and one of his most rarely performed. It is known to be a collaboration between Shakespeare and Thomas Middleton and is considered by many to be unfinished, a factor which has, as Jowett observes, 'encouraged theatre practitioners to adapt the text freely'.[160] It is a play that lacks key human relationships, Timon being the only one of Shakespeare's tragic heroes to have no family or dependants; that finishes anti-climactically with the title character's offstage death; and that features the 'apparently untheatrical device', in its second half, of 'having almost a third of its action made up of the single sequence in which Timon, statically dwelling in the woods, is visited by a succession of Athenians'.[161] These are just some of the features that have made *Timon* an unpopular choice for the stage and yet one that has seen some remarkably successful productions in modern times: Peter Brook's 1974 production at the Bouffes du Nord in Paris, Trevor Nunn's 1991 Young Vic production with David Suchet as Timon and Gregory Doran's 1999 production with Michael Pennington in the title role. Michael Billington suggests that its resurgence in popularity has been 'largely because we find its savagely satirical portrait of a wealth-worshipping society based on naked self-interest ever more topical'.[162] Hytner acknowledges this appeal:

> It would have taken a theatrical imagination less opportun-
> istic than mine not to recognize in *Timon*, as many other
> directors have recognized, a mirror of our own world.[163]

Hytner's production, with Simon Russell Beale in the title role, opened at the Olivier auditorium on 17 July 2012. Once again, Hytner's programming was astute. Having mounted *Henry V* at the time of Britain's invasion of Iraq and the *Henry IV* plays on the eve of an election, he chose to mount *Timon* just as the Libor scandal broke. Paul Mason, writing in the *Guardian*, noted the striking modern parallels, not only with this fraudulent manipulation of interest rates by the banks but with the Leveson enquiry and the scandal surrounding GS4 security for the Olympic Games, events all of which exposed 'a network of corrupted individuals',[164] much like those who feature in Shakespeare and Middleton's play. Beale, remarking on the headlines dominating the papers leading up to the opening night, asserted: 'It was like the God of theatre saying "Go for it".'[165]

As Hytner told his cast and crew on the first day of rehearsals, 'The obvious temptation is to make it a play about now and that is a temptation that we have simply failed to resist.'[166] This was to be a thoroughly modern interpretation, set in London in 2012 and, as the poster and programme made humorously apparent, it was to be a direct commentary on our times. The poster showed Beale, as Timon, sitting at a dinner table, quaffing champagne, with what appeared to be the popstar Madonna on his right, David Beckham on his left, Boris Johnson on his far left and Tony Blair refilling his glass.

The locations featured in the set design alluded firmly to London. Designer Tim Hately remarked that he and Hytner had decided that 'The address ... that Timon lives at is Eaton Square',[167] one of Belgravia's most exclusive addresses, a location that could be glimpsed through the windows of Timon's apartment in 2.2. The opening scene was set in an art gallery, identified by many reviewers as 'The National Gallery', with later set changes providing glimpses of Canary Wharf and Westminster. Even the more abstract setting of the play's second half, after Timon's departure from his life of luxury, was seen by Lloyd Evans as alluding to 'the underpass beneath the National Theatre itself' (*The Spectator*).[168] With its modern-day London setting, the play became 'a lacerating parable for our troubled times' (Fiona Mountford, *Evening Standard*) and 'for the crisis of the modern business elite',[169] referred to by many reviewers as a 'play for today' (Georgina Brown, *Mail on Sunday*; Paul Taylor, *Independent*; Ian Shuttleworth, *FT*).

The production began with the stage littered with small tents with cardboard signs attached to some of them and groups of people sitting among them. The image was redolent of the recent Occupy London campaign, which had seen anti-capitalist protesters camping outside St Paul's Cathedral. These figures were to rise up later in the play as the followers of Alcibiades. As the play began, a wall descended in front of the tents, providing the scene setting for the opening scene – 'The Timon Room', a room in an art gallery, dedicated to its sponsor, in which a glamorous party was taking place.

FIGURE 5 *Deborah Findlay and Simon Russell Beale in* Timon of Athens, *directed by Nicholas Hytner at the National Theatre, 2012.*
© *Johan Persson/ArenaPAL*

The assembled crowd was made up of instantly recognizable contemporary creatives, all greeting each other 'noisily',[170] clasping champagne flutes and posing for photographs. In addition to the Poet, the Painter and the Jeweller, Hytner altered the character of 'The Merchant' to that of 'The Actor', enhancing the sense of a modern A-list party.

For the following scene, in which Timon hosts a banquet for his friends, a huge, richly-tapestried curtain descended and a long banqueting table adorned with candelabras was set up on the stage, as guests entered with flutes of champagne. Throughout the meal, waiters dressed in black inconspicuously cleared plates and served fresh courses. In another perfectly judged contemporary analogy for the world of Shakespeare's play, the masque of Amazons in this scene was replaced by a display of modern ballet (choreographed by the Royal Ballet's Edward Watson), an erotic duet performed by two scantily clad ballerinas.

The ensuing scenes revealed a series of office suites and luxury apartments. The Senator, here renamed Lepidus, was revealed in 2.1, besuited, in a smart office backed by a vista of the City. Lucullus's House in 3.1 was transformed into a room in 'Lucullan Capital', a financial institution in which Lucullus lounged on a leather sofa in front of a glass coffee table littered with copies of the *Financial Times*, drinking wine. The 'public place' of 3.2 became the home of Ventidius, an apartment featuring a large, Damien Hirst-like image of coloured squares on the back wall and 3.3 (Sempronius's house), took place in a room through which the Houses of Parliament could be seen through the back window, establishing Sempronia (Lynette Edwards) as a contemporary politician.

Timon and his entourage appeared in 2.2, clutching London Fashion Week brochures, another indication of his London lifestyle and, in another move, which Susannah Clapp praised as 'not subtly but suitably remade' and absolutely 'right for our times' (Susannah Clapp, *Observer*), the 'anti-banquet' that Timon prepares for his ungrateful acolytes in 3.6 was transformed from Shakespeare's dishes of 'lukewarm water' (3.6) to platters of faeces which Timon upturned onto the head of one of his former friends – a witty and clear means of conveying Timon's utter repugnance for his circle of acquaintances. The skill with which Hytner and Hately updated the settings and the situations led Lloyd Evans to declare 'OK, I was wrong ... I now realize it's perfectly feasible. Antique dramas can make sense in a modern location' (*The Spectator*).

The second half of the play is undoubtedly more difficult to manage than the first due to its static, minimalist nature. As Beale elucidates, the fact that Shakespeare keeps Timon on stage 'for 50 minutes, non-stop' is a 'fearsome' challenge for an actor and 'further proof' for Beale that the play is 'a sketch', an unfinished piece.[171] In spite of the considerable praise for Beale's depiction of Timon's tragic descent, a number of critics found that the production sagged in the fourth act.[172] Hytner himself admits that some of the audience were 'probably less excited at the end than they were at the interval', but finds this inevitable with the 'really weird' second half.[173]

The second half of the play is particularly challenging to directors updating the play to the present day. While the city environment of the play's first three acts lends itself perfectly to a contemporary setting, the woods and cave and, in particular, the earth that delivers forth gold are more difficult to locate. Nunn's production, which set the second half in 'a scrapyard in decayed inner-city London'[174], tried to make sense of Timon's discovery of gold in that location by having an escaping thief bury his loot, later to be found by Timon. Hytner, acknowledging that the second half of the play is 'much stranger, and much less literal' than the first, felt that his task 'was to translate the imagery of the modern city into something that would allow Simon Russell Beale to unfold his own internal landscape'. He and Hately settled on 'an urban wasteland, left behind maybe by a failed building development', which Hytner felt 'echoed Timon's spiritual wasteland'.[175] The urban landscape also developed, as Hately explains, an abstract quality, in keeping with the tone of the second half:

> It came to our minds, both Nick and I, what if we had this environment that was a building site. I think of those steels coming out of the concrete columns, so that was an immediate starting point. And I suddenly thought, this could become quite sculptural and quite interesting. It could also become a forest. It could also become echoes of Greek ruins. So it became more and more abstract. It became more of a metaphor.[176]

In spite of the effectiveness of this desolate landscape, Timon's discovery of gold beneath this derelict building site remained an 'improbability' (Billington, *Guardian*) with Timon lifting off a manhole cover to discover an unsecured vault of gold, a moment that, as Maxie Szalwinska asserted, stretched 'the audience's credulity … to breaking point' (*Sunday Times*).

Hytner states that they did discuss some reason for this in rehearsal – 'I think things have gone so badly that that is possibly where the secret Fort Knox of the city is and he's stumbled on it' – but adds:

I don't know. You get into trouble, don't you? He needs to get rich, or there isn't a second half, and I think we decided 'What the hell', rather than that he finds suitcases full of bank notes – then it really is Ealing Comedy – I preferred to have something crazy and unexplained.[177]

One of the more successful updatings of the second half was that of Alcibiades's attack on Athens, which became 'not a military challenge to Athens in revenge but an uprising of the dispossessed' (Shuttleworth). By cutting Alcibiades's appearance before the senators and banishment in 3.5, Hytner transformed him from a military general to an anti-capitalist, leading a riot of the discontented, who had been seen protesting at the beginning of the play. The rioters took to the streets in protest between Acts 2 and 3 shouting 'Strike Athens!' and 'Shame on You!' and attacked Timon's guests as they left his house after 3.6, an 'inspired take' on the character and his mob (Dominic Cavendish, *Telegraph*), which referenced the Occupy protest movement and the London riots of 2011. In the play's final moments, Alcibiades appeared, having changed from the jeans and khaki parka in which he had led the rioters to a suit and tie, as he took his seat in complicity with the senators at the council table, something which Hytner felt worked particularly well and has proved somewhat prescient: 'Look, there's Alexis Tsipras now, wearing a suit.'[178]

The excision of 3.5 was one of a number of cuts and alterations made by Hytner to the text as it appears in the First Folio (1623). As the programme declared, for 'reasons of sense and structure, approximately 250 lines have been cut or amended' and 'small portions of text included from other Shakespeare plays'.[179] Hytner explained that he had mostly 'cut where it doesn't feel comprehensible, where it doesn't feel that it will be immediately impactful on a contemporary audience'.[180] Cutting and changing the Shakespearean text is something with which Hytner has become increasingly comfortable but, in the case of *Timon*, like others before him, he felt particularly justified due to what he perceived as its unfinished nature: 'the text we have is undoubtedly an uncorrected first draft. There are whole passages that make no sense whatsoever, and others that entirely contradict what's gone before.'[181] However, the volume of changes made was, perhaps, more than could be justified by claiming lack of sense or contradiction. Some were made in order to fit with Hytner's concept: references to 'day' were changed to 'evening' in the first party scene; references to old currency were updated to make them sound contemporary and English; pronouns and terms of address were altered in order to fit the changes in gender of some of the characters; the word 'woods' was changed to 'wilds' in Act 4 and 'root' to 'food' or 'morsel', in keeping with the industrial setting. However, in other cases, words were altered which audiences might have understood, and indeed which one might find in a number of Shakespeare's plays. Within the first scene, 'fix'd' became 'certain' (1.1.9); 'Quick' became 'Sudden' (1.1.93); 'debt' became 'bail' (1.1.98; 1.1.106); 'precedent' became 'former' (1.1.136); 'Vouchsafe', 'Accept' (1.1.155); and 'speaks the common tongue', 'speaks as all men speak' (1.1.176).

The interpolated lines were taken mostly from *Coriolanus* and were used to create more of a sense of what was happening in the streets, among the people. Hytner describes this as 'deliberate and pragmatic and opportunistic':

> It was exactly the time of the Occupy movement ... We caught the moment. The Alcibiades stuff is plainly unusable. It's useless. It's not developed. It's not integrated ... I invented it because what you have on the page simply isn't good enough. So where else would you go other than *Coriolanus*?[182]

As he explained to John Lahr, 'What I'm wanting to do is create from the very beginning the sense that the place is a tinderbox; the street is full of people who are on the point of eruption.'[183] The first scene ended with lines partly lifted from *Coriolanus* and *Hamlet*, establishing that Alcibiades had 'roused the city'; 2.1 finished with lines loosely based on some from *Coriolanus*, suggesting that the rabble was about to 'unroof the city'; and 3.1 included an exchange between Lucilius and Flaminia (a female Flaminius), again with lines drawn from *Coriolanus*, concerning the people and Alcibiades crying for bread and breaking 'ope the locks of the senate'.

A few other additional lines were taken from elsewhere in the Shakespearean canon, including the witty interpolation of the phrase 'Your play needs no excuse' from *A Midsummer Night's Dream* (5.1.350–1), when Timon bid farewell to the actor:

> Well fare you, gentleman: give me your hand;
> Your play needs no excuse. Sir, your work
> Hath suffer'd under praise. (NT Promptbook, Scene 1)

and the final half line of the play, 'Now go we in content to liberty', taken from *As You Like It.* (1.3.134–5)

The process of cutting, altering and interpolating was similar to that carried out for *The Alchemist*, with Hytner employing a dramatist (in this case Ben Power) to work on the play prior to rehearsals beginning. Beale was also firmly involved in the creation of the text from the beginning, as was actor Nick Sampson, who was playing relatively small roles but who had worked with Hytner on *The Madness of George III, The Winter's Tale, Henry V, His Dark Materials, London Assurance, Hamlet* and *Collaborators,* an indication, remarks Beale, of Hytner's 'collaborative' working ethic.[184]

In addition to the textual alterations, the most notable change made to the play was the transformation of a number of the male characters in the play to female ones: Flavius, Timon's steward became Flavia (played by Deborah Findlay),

Flaminius, his servant became Flaminia (Olivia Llewellyn), the senator Sempronius became the MP Sempronia (Lynette Edwards) and both the Jeweller (Jo Dockery) and the Painter (Penny Layden) were portrayed as women. These changes not only provided more roles for women but also created a more accurate portrait of contemporary London: 'As soon as it's in a contemporary world that's what you do.'[185]

In the title role, Beale was praised for his 'compelling' performance, noted, in particular, for its 'psychological acuity' (Billington). Russell Beale managed, in the eyes of most of the reviewers to provide a character with 'little interior life' (Szalwinska) with an emotional and psychological coherence and impact. This was something that Russell Beale was determined to achieve, asserting that: 'There's no point in doing it unless there's some sort of emotional impact.'[186] This impact would stem, he and Hytner decided, from portraying Timon as a man 'who doesn't understand how to experience and respond to love', who 'doesn't like to be touched'[187] and who mistakenly equates 'true friendship' with 'profligate gift-giving'.[188] This fear of physical contact was something on which a number of the reviewers picked up: 'He ... backs neurotically away when anyone tries to kiss or touch him, as if unused to the demands of intimacy' (Billington); 'This is a Timon who shrinks from embraces, who showers his dinner party guests with gifts and presents them with a specially commissioned ballet ... as a way of fending off anything deeper than generalised contact' (Taylor). For Paul Taylor, this 'radical wariness about genuine intimacy', provided an 'emotional link' between the first and second parts of the play, 'between the beaming plutocrat in part one and the furious male bag-lady in part two'.

The production was, like many of Hytner's, praised for its strong all-round cast, which included actors with whom Hytner had worked before – Beale, Nick Sampson and Deborah Findlay, who had played Paulina in *The Winter's Tale*. The reviews were universally positive, one of the most common comments being that the play seemed to be 'freshly-minted' (Mountford; Cavendish), 'as if Shakespeare recently popped into the National for a script meeting' (Mountford). Libby Purves described the text as spoken with 'modern naturalism', such that 'certain lines ... fall so naturally that the occasional "methinks" is almost a surprise' (*The Times*). The Hytner hallmarks of speed (the production running at only 2 hours 30 minutes including an interval), biting humour and accessibility were all in evidence[189] and the production won Hytner the 2012 *Evening Standard* Award for best director.

Othello

Hytner's final Shakespeare production for the NT during his artistic directorship – *Othello* – reunited him with Adrian Lester and Rory Kinnear as Othello and Iago respectively. Hytner had waited some time to get both actors for these roles. As Kinnear explained, '[Hytner] first mooted it with Adrian when they did *Henry V* back in 2003' and had suggested the role of Iago to Kinnear in 2007.[190] Many of the reviews and other commentary surrounding the production focused on these two central performances, the 'long awaited pairing of these two superb actors' (Matt Wolf, *International Herald Tribune*).[191] However, most agreed that it was Hytner's decision to set the play in a contemporary military setting that helped to define the relationships and give the production its clarity and relevance. It was, for Paul Taylor, 'a properly provocative vindication of a decade of modernised Shakespeare at Hytner's National Theatre' (*Independent*).

Like Hytner's productions of *Henry V*, *Hamlet* and *Timon*, the play was given a contemporary setting. As Hytner explained, this was largely because it felt like 'a play that could have been written yesterday'.[192] The early Venetian scenes were moved to a location which resembled London, the first two scenes set in a street of tall nineteenth-century buildings with black-railing balconies and imposing doors, a location in which 'big decisions are taken on behalf of a quasi-imperial power'.[193] Iago and Roderigo emerged with drinks in hand from a hotel, advertising its 'All Day Menu'. In 1.3 the senate meeting took place in an underground war room, a panelled space with a long conference table and black leather chairs. From Act 2 onwards, the setting shifted to a foreign military base with grey portacabins surrounded by a high concrete wall topped with barbed wire, which opened to reveal stark living quarters with plain beige walls. Act 4 scene 1 unfolded in a lavatory, enabling Othello to overhear Iago and Cassio's discussion from one of the cubicles.

Described by Taylor as 'studiedly anti-heroic', these bare, simple settings seemed to enhance the play's brutality, creating what he called 'an un-operatically terrifying take on the play'. This last description is particularly striking given the critical tendency to comment on the 'operatic' nature of Hytner's productions in the 1980s and 1990s, including those of *Measure for Measure, The Tempest* and *King Lear* at the RSC, and indicates a profound journey in Hytner's work, from abstract, archetypal, heightened interpretations of Shakespeare to those grounded in a concrete reality. Even Tim Walker, who initially bemoaned the lack of an 'epic' quality to the production's settings, came to feel that the 'use of utilitarian settings ... start[ed] to pay off as it place[d] the attention firmly on the players' (*Sunday Telegraph*).

In addition to its contemporary setting, the other most commented-upon feature of the production was its determination to make the play about more than simply racial prejudice. As Kinnear reported, the company 'decided' or 'discovered' during rehearsals that 'the racial politics ... [had] been made more of than perhaps there is in the play':[194] 'certainly no one in the army ever brings it up, or doubts that Othello should be the general'.[195] While there is an 'obvious racial dimension'[196] to the play – particularly in the constant references to Othello as 'The Moor' – most of the racist language used against Othello comes in the first three scenes – from Roderigo, Brabantio and Iago in connection with Othello's relationship with Desdemona, not commenting

on him in a professional capacity, and this was made particularly apparent in this production by the broad ethnic mix of
the army. Adrian Lester was determined that Othello and his
relationship with Desdemona should not be defined by his
colour, asserting 'He doesn't kill his wife because he's black,
he isn't jealous because he's black.'[197]

The motivation for the events of the play in this production
stemmed not from any explicit racial prejudice but from
the military environment. This was the tragedy of two men
who had become defined by their military lives, and a young
woman to whom this world was alien. Hytner's conception of
Othello primarily as a play centring around war led him to
appoint a military adviser on the production, Major-General
Jonathan Shaw, 'recently retired after 32 years in the British
Army', having 'commanded the British-led division on Basra
in 2007'.[198] Shaw not only advised on aspects of the depiction
of a military barracks, but also wrote an extensive programme
note, outlining the way in which his experience in the army
had provided him with insight into the relationships and
tensions in *Othello*:

> With the benefit of age, I can appreciate how densely
> Shakespeare has built up the pressures in Othello to put
> him on a psychological hair-trigger for Iago to exploit.
> After my own 32 years in the Army, it is clear that many of
> those pressures result from the military dynamics in both
> his own personality and in the operational circumstances
> into which the characters are thrust ... it is these dynamics
> that Nick Hytner asked me to explore.[199]

As Kinnear explains, although the 'sense of wounded
psyches through exposure to great trauma is not something
Shakespeare unpicks explicitly', it is something that the actors
chose to explore within the contemporary context of this
production.[200] Led by Shaw, Hytner and his company came to
see the military environment as key to the atmosphere and the
simmering violence of the Cyprus scenes, to Iago's motivation,

his relationship with Emilia, Othello's unerring trust in Iago and the problems that unfold in the Othello/Desdemona relationship.

Cyprus was, here, a 'claustrophobic, macho world' where, as Georgina Brown noted, 'even the most decent and level-headed of soldiers can lose their sense of proportion' (*Mail on Sunday*). The soldiers arrive in Cyprus expecting to fight, only to find that the Turkish fleet has been sunk and the conflict is over. As Kinnear elucidates: 'The Turkish fleet, with whom we're all geared up to have a big war, drown. So there's no war and you have all these soldiers hanging around in a military camp, turning in on themselves.'[201]

The sense of barely suppressed violence, resulting from the inaction of a group of soldiers who have prepared to fight, was apparent in the production. Like the fight in 4.8 of Hytner's *Henry V*, the brawl in 2.3 was preceded by the soldiers listening to aggressive rave music as they drank beer and shots, their drinking games becoming increasingly rowdy. Thus, when they re-entered, following Cassio's 'You rogue, you rascal!', they were already pumped up, the fight escalating until most of the soldiers were involved. Lester's Othello also demonstrated a simmering aggression, which surfaced at various points, notably in 3.3, when he leapt over his desk in rage to attack Iago ('Villain, be sure', 3.3.362), angrily kicked a chair and upturned a table in rage ('O that the slave', 3.3.445) and increasingly in his encounters with Desdemona – hitting her and knocking her to the ground in 4.1 ('I am glad to see you mad', 4.1.238) and grabbing her round the neck in 5.2 ('I took you for that cunning whore of Venice', 4.2.91). His final killing of Desdemona was particularly violent, with Othello repeatedly throwing her back onto the bed as she pleaded with him, grabbing her legs and pinning down her arms before holding a pillow over her face.

A violent undercurrent was also evident in the relationship between Iago and Emilia, which Lyndsey Marshall (Emilia) described as 'an abusive relationship',[202] the tensions in which were increased by her position in uniform within the army, by the fact that 'the pressures are more intense because we're together all the time – we're married, we work together, we're in Cyprus together'.[203] On their first appearance together in 2.1, Iago's insulting comments about her 'tongue' (2.1.106) seemed particularly cruel, delivered in front of her colleagues and with the aim of stirring them up to laugh at her. Elsewhere he seemed simply dismissive and aggressive in his attitude towards her, taking the handkerchief off her in 2.3 by hitting her. For Marshall, it was Emilia's desire to stop the abuse and gain Iago's affection that motivated her 'terrible, terrible mistake' of giving him Desdemona's handkerchief: 'I think that she's in a relationship where she just believes that if she gives him this handkerchief, it will be a good night; they'll have a nice time.'[204]

One of the most insightful comments made by Shaw, as far as an understanding of character motivation was concerned, involved the culture of trust within the army. This helped to make sense for Lester of the sometimes seemingly inexplicable way in which Othello places his trust in Iago above that of his new wife. Shaw asserts that the military is 'a culture which is based on trust':

> Othello and Iago have clearly been in many fights together, life-and-death situations in which each has probably entrusted their life to the other and at some time saved the other's life. Iago has proved his 'honesty' on battlefields around the region; Othello has every reason to trust him implicitly. Betrayal is the most heinous of military sins so it is the last to be suspected.[205]

The military context and culture of trust was equally important in understanding Iago's motivations. Shaw asserted: 'So many ex-military will sympathize with how Iago feels, if not how he reacts, after what he sees as Othello's betrayal of trust in promoting Cassio over him.'[206] Kinnear saw this as the primary motivation for Iago's behaviour: 'He's been passed over for promotion in favour of the gilded classes like Cassio.'[207]

Michael Billington felt that the 'precision' of the depiction of the military environment also helped to explicate another often 'obscure' issue in the play: 'why Othello, even before the catastrophe strikes, is effectively demoted, by being replaced as Cypriot governor'. For Billington, in this production it was 'clearly because he has offended military protocol by insisting on taking his wife on a wartime expedition' (*Guardian*). The tragic consequences of Desdemona coming to Cyprus with her husband were made abundantly apparent. This was another area in which Shaw's insights into military life had clearly informed the production:

> Civilian spouses and partners do not go on operations with their partners, based on the long-held view that the two strongest human urges – for sex and violence – should be kept apart.[208]

Within this stark military environment in which even Emilia was depicted as a soldier, Desdemona seemed particularly out of place. Her 'free-spirited, boho behaviour' was, as Andrzej Lukowski noted, 'completely at odds with her husband's', leading him to turn on her 'less from rage than confusion' (*Time Out*). It was equally apparent that Desdemona did not understand her husband's motivations. Shaw offered further insight into this disjunction:

> His instant demotion of Cassio for a brawl on the first night after the removal of the Turkish threat is precisely the kind of exemplary punishment that military commanders use to stamp their authority over a potentially bored and drunken soldiery. Desdemona's entreaties for Cassio, based on the civilian primacy of individual rights, cut right across the demand of military justice for clarity, consistency and speed.[209]

What is apparent from the way in which Hytner and the cast discussed their preparation for the production is Hytner's concentration on creating a specific and detailed context and a strong sense of the world inhabited by the characters. Although many of the insights offered by Shaw fall outside the boundaries of the Shakespearean text, they helped to 'establish the "rules"' of the society depicted on stage, something which Hytner felt was vital to making the contemporary setting work: 'even without specifying the location for the audience, the actors needed to be entirely clear about the way in which the society functioned'. As an example, Hytner cites the scene in which Cassio gets drunk:

> I would say that scene – one of the reasons it worked as well as it did – is that every single one of those actors from Rory Kinnear and Jonny Bailey, right through to the squaddies getting drunk at the back ... were clear about the rules they were living by ... the way the army operates ... it was all there kind of effortlessly because we were so clear and so confident about the rules – social, physical and psychological – that govern the way they behave, and that they therefore break when they are transgressive.[210]

In Mark Shenton's view, the production's success stemmed partly from the fact that the cast had 'been guided to live inside their characters, instead of commenting on them' (*Sunday Express*). The actors were equally assiduous in finding backstories for their characters. Kinnear commented that it seemed vital in terms of the onstage relationship between Iago and Othello 'to create a sense of the kinship and dependency they have had for the past 12 or 13 years'[211] and 'to consider what has happened to Iago just before the play opens'.[212]

Hytner's creation of a clearly defined, realistic, contemporary world seemed, for the most part, to illuminate the text, although Michael Billington felt that the ultra-modern, naturalistic setting worked against Lester's Othello and in favour of Kinnear's Iago, asserting:

although Lester has all the trappings of a great Othello, the production militates against him in the central scenes. To put it bluntly, once you're into a world of laptops and strip lighting, it's hard to believe Othello would be deluded by the absence of a spotted handkerchief.

For 'all the evening's brilliance', it confirmed 'something [Billington had] long suspected: that the more naturalistic the production, the more Iago becomes the play's focal figure'.

Another casualty of the modern setting was a sense of 'grandeur' (Henry Hitchings, *Evening Standard*; Siobhan Murphy, *Metro*). For some this 'muffle[d] the tragedy' (Hitchings) and prevented the ending from gaining its full impact.[213] For others it was precisely this bleak, 'colourless' environment that made the ending so 'heart-wrenching' (Christopher Hart, *Sunday Times*). Desdemona's deathbed was far from the plush four-poster bed of the frontispiece of Nicholas Rowe's 1709 edition of the play: it was, rather, a simple wooden army bed in a strip-lit room with no furnishings. Her nighttime attire was similarly not elaborate – a thin white t-shirt and purple knickers – making her seem – 'all the more vulnerable' (Walker), suffering the indignity of dying with her underwear on display.

The reviews for the production praised 'Hytner's staging ... precisely pitched across the board' (Wolf), describing the production as 'a gripping ... intensely painful psychological thriller' (Charles Spencer, *Telegraph*), 'taut' (Lukowski), 'terrifically exciting, exceptionally coherent' (Susannah Clapp, *The Observer*), 'bracing and completely enthralling' (Shenton). Spencer and Billington commented on recognized Hytner 'hallmarks' in the production – its wit, speed, lucidity and clarity of delivery.[214] The last of these features was remarked upon by many of the critics (Murphy; Hart; Shenton; Julie Carpenter, *Daily Express*; Clapp). As in *Timon* and *Hamlet*, the language was felt by many to be so accessibly delivered, with 'superbly lucid 21st-century naturalism' (Hart), that one at times forgot that the actors were 'speaking in Elizabethan verse' (Murphy).

The clarity and accessibility of the production was, once more, aided by Hytner's judicious cutting and by some minor rewriting of complex lines. Hytner commented in his programme note on one such instance:

> How many precious seconds in a performance of Othello would it take for most of the audience to understand Iago's plan to cause unrest amongst the Cypriots, *whose qualification shall come into no true taste again but by the displanting of Cassio?* More seconds than they have available to work out that he means the Cypriots *will not be pacified again but by the displanting of Cassio,* because everyone in the audience wants to be ready for the next line, and the next. So why can't Iago say what he means?

In this production he did. Complex or wordy passages that were not deemed to advance the plot were frequently excised, all references to tapers, swords (as in *Hamlet*) and sails were cut or altered, being out of keeping with the contemporary setting, as was Othello's reference to 'the castle' (2.1.197), changed to 'our lodgings' to reflect the far more basic accommodation afforded Othello and Desdemona in this production. However, these cuts and changes were minimal, the production still running at three hours without an interval.

The main focus of the reviews was, inevitably, on the central pairing of Iago and Othello. Most critics praised both Lester's Othello and Kinnear's Iago, split as to which became the central performance. For Tim Walker it was Lester's Othello who won the 'monumental battle for supremacy between two great actors at the top of their game'; for Lukowski it was 'Kinnear as Othello's nemesis Iago who [stole] the show'. Lester's poised, authoritative, Othello – reminiscent in some respects of his Henry V – was likened by some to Obama (Hitchings; Georgina Brown, *Mail on*

Sunday), charismatic and eloquent in the early scenes and, in the final act, 'conjuring a verbal symphony of loss, pain, guilt and grief' (Spencer). Kinnear's Iago was similarly praised as 'mesmerising' (Hitchings) and 'compelling' (Lukowski). One of the most regular comments by critics concerned the character's blokey, common-man, quality, comments which resemble those made of his 'ordinary', 'everyman' Hamlet. Like Kinnear's Hamlet, his Iago was also deemed wittily comic. This was a 'creepily amusing' (Hitchings) figure, 'unnerving' (Lukowski) in his casual exploitation of others and 'chilling' in his ordinariness (Murphy).

Other performances were praised for their detail and their freshness, no doubt stemming from Hytner's insistence on a full investment in the world of the play. Jonathan Bailey, as Cassio, a character all too often played as a 'ludicrously trusting dupe' (Ian Shuttleworth, *FT*) began the play with a bounding confidence, bordering on arrogance, only to reveal 'a vulnerable, hopeless side towards the end' (Walker). Lyndsey Marshall's Emilia was more fully integrated into this production by her status as a soldier in the army, her performance described as 'strong' (Walker), particularly in the final scene which, in Ian Shuttleworth's view, she 'magnificently storm[ed]... from beginning to end' (Shuttleworth), while Olivia Vinall's Desdemona seemed particularly young – 'She's married Othello, who is more than twice her age in our production'.[215] Initially she was wide-eyed and playful, brimming with a naïve confidence and increasingly vulnerable: 'a little girl lost in a world where innocence cannot survive' (Spencer).

What almost all of the critics were agreed upon was that this production further confirmed that Hytner, who had just announced his resignation as Artistic Director of the NT, would be sorely missed[216] and 'a very tough act to follow' (Shenton). It was, wrote Lukowski, 'sobering to think this might be the last time the NT boss ... directs one of the Bard's works here'. It was, indeed, the last Shakespeare that Hytner was to direct under his own regime. Whether he will be invited back to guest direct a Shakespeare remains unknown, although given his plans for a theatrical empire of his own, this seems increasingly unlikely in the near future.

5

Conclusion

By the time Hytner retired as Artistic Director of the NT in 2015, it was widely agreed that his had been the most successful reign at its helm. Summaries in the press at various stages of his tenure all hail his success. After only one year in post, an article appeared on the front of the *Guardian*'s G2 section entitled, 'Bravo! How Nicholas Hytner transformed British theatre',[1] detailing ways in which Hytner had already 'electrified the building'. Hytner had, in the view of Maddy Costa, succeeded particularly in 'addressing the concerns of the nation', a feat epitomized in his *Henry V*.[2] Director Jude Kelly agreed. Praising Hytner for 'forcing the National to consider how ideology relates to contemporary theatre-making', she cited *Henry V*, in particular, as indicative of the fact that 'the National wants to have a voice, wants to go into battle with its country and with its artform'.[3] Six years later Hytner remained, according to *The Times*, 'the punchiest power in theatreland',[4] while in 2012, John Lahr, writing in the *New Yorker* asserted that the National 'under the canny stewardship of Nicholas Hytner' was 'on a roll unmatched in its nearly fifty-year history'.[5] When, in 2013, Hytner finally announced his retirement, the accolades flowed. Dominic Cavendish wrote that 'in 10 years of risk-taking' Hytner had 'transformed the National Theatre',[6] Michael Billington stated that he had 'restored to the theatre a strong sense of purpose'[7] and Charlotte Higgins described him as having presided over 'what has been, by near universal acclaim, a golden decade in the history of the National Theatre'.[8]

Particularly striking, given what some of Hytner's predecessors had felt about the job, was Hytner's own enduring enjoyment of the role. Benedict Nightingale writing in 2009, nearly six years into Hytner's regime, explicitly contrasted the responses of Hytner and his direct predecessor Trevor Nunn to the question, 'How are you enjoying the job as the National Theatre director?'. While Nunn had answered 'Not at all', Hytner responded 'Enormously, enormously ... I have been enjoying every moment of it'.[9] On the announcement of his resignation, Hytner stated that it had been 'a joy and a privilege' to lead the theatre, adding: 'I have had the most exciting and most fulfilling job in the English-speaking theatre.'[10] While Hytner asserted a degree of caution in the early days of the job, citing the 'law of theatrical gravity: what goes up will come down' and stating 'The great thing is never to feel too pleased with yourself',[11] it seems that such a law never really came into play.

Hytner's achievements as Artistic Director move well beyond his own successful productions, into the areas of programming, outreach, education, equality and development, a number of which areas have had an impact on the perception and accessibility of the work of Shakespeare at the NT, in particular the Travelex seasons, NT Live, Sunday opening, investment in digital expansion, encouragement of younger, more diverse audiences, greater gender and racial equality in casting and the appointment of more female directors.

The creation of a National Theatre on the South Bank (opening in 1976) was intimately connected to the work of Shakespeare. The long and complex route to the building of the current theatre was initiated by a desire to found 'a house for Shakespeare', where his work would be constantly performed,[12] and the Memorandum and Articles of Association, incorporated in 1963 and still in operation, state that 'the Company is established to promote and assist in the advancement of education ... to procure and increase the appreciation and understanding of the dramatic art in all its forms as a memorial to William Shakespeare'.[13] In the fifty-two years between its founding in 1963 and Hytner's retirement in 2015, the NT has staged sixty-four Shakespeare plays (including tours and Education productions in the NT auditoria) – thirteen during Hytner's twelve-year regime. In addition to Hytner's own productions, detailed in the previous chapter, there have been five productions of Shakespeare plays in the main repertoire – *Measure for Measure* (a co-production with Complicite, dir. Simon McBurney, Olivier, 2004), *All's Well That Ends Well* (dir. Marianne Elliott, Olivier, 2009), *Comedy of Errors* (Olivier, 2011), *Twelfth Night* (Cottesloe, 2011) and *King Lear* (dir. Sam Mendes, Olivier, 2014) – as well as two Education Department productions in the main auditoria, *Twelfth Night* (Cottesloe, 2010) and *Romeo and Juliet* (Shed, 2013).

On the announcement of his appointment as Artistic Director, one of Hytner's expressed aims had been to welcome new actors, directors and audiences into the building, and to reflect in terms of 'casting and repertoire' the meaning of the word 'national' in the twenty-first century. He also expressed a desire to encourage more diverse forms of theatre and to embrace the work of European practitioners.[14] These Shakespeare productions embraced some of Hytner's aims – *Measure for Measure* being a co-production with Complicite, a company profoundly influenced by the work of French physical theatre practitioner Jacques Lecoq, and *Twelfth Night* and *Romeo and Juliet* both being aimed at primary school audiences. Both *All's Well That Ends Well* and *Comedy of Errors* also illustrate the NT's commitment to greater diversity and equality under Hytner, the latter featuring black actors in the four leading roles of the Antipholi and Dromios – Lenny Henry, Chris Jarman, Lucian Msamati and Daniel Poyser – and the former being only the second Shakespeare play to have been directed by a woman in the Olivier auditorium and only the sixth Shakespeare production to have been directed by a woman in the NT's history. In 2009,

Benedict Nightingale suggested that one of 'Hytner's feats' of his regime at that point had been 'to give women directors opportunities that they never had in the National's early days', citing Elliott's directing of *All's Well* as an example of this.[15]

The Travelex scheme, introduced in 2003, was one of Hytner's first major policies as Artistic Director. Acknowledging that 'ticket price is a barrier to young people going to the theatre',[16] Hytner and the National Theatre's Executive director Nick Starr, introduced £10 tickets for two-thirds of the auditorium for performances in the Olivier, securing sponsorship from Lloyd Dorfman, founder and chief executive of Travelex, to support the initiative. Beginning with *Henry V* – initially as part of a three-year deal – the scheme continued to run throughout Hytner's reign, with ticket prices increasing to £12 in 2011. The scheme was described by Michael Billington as 'simply the most radical idea anyone has come up with in years to broaden the theatregoing audience'.[17] In 2004, Costa cited it as 'Hytner's greatest achievement'.[18] Statistics quoted in 2003 suggested that in the first year '31% of the £10 seats [were] bought by people coming for the first time',[19] and in 2013, Libby Purves asserted that 20 per cent of all tickets at the NT were being bought 'by newcomers, many of them to any kind of theatre'.[20] For actor and director Simon Callow, the strength of this scheme was not only its ability to bring more young people and first time theatre-goers into the building, but also the fact that it had 'created an image of the National Theatre as a very accessible place'.[21] The scheme has by no means focused exclusively on Shakespeare, but with nine Shakespeare productions in the Olivier benefiting, it has evidently succeeded in bringing Shakespeare to new, younger audiences.

Another project that has also widened audiences for Shakespeare productions at the National is NT Live. This was first introduced in 2009, with *Phèdre*, starring Helen Mirren, broadcast live to 150 cinemas. The initiative, like Travelex, was spurred on by Hytner's desire to make the theatre more 'National', to ensure that it was representing the country both in terms of age and location demographics. *All's Well That Ends Well, Hamlet, The Comedy of Errors, Timon of Athens, Othello* and *King Lear* were all broadcast as part of NT Live, reaching audiences of 'more than a million and a half people in twenty-two countries ... in venues as far-flung as Bulgaria and Tasmania'.[22] In addition, as part of the scheme, some key Shakespeare productions from other theatres have been broadcast: The Donmar Warehouse's *King Lear* (dir. Robin Lough, 2011), with Derek Jacobi in the title role, and *Coriolanus* (dir. Josie Rourke, 2014) starring Tom Hiddleston; The Manchester International Festival's *Macbeth* (dir. Rob Ashford and Kenneth Branagh) with Branagh as Macbeth; and the Barbican's *Hamlet* (dir. Lyndsey Turner, 2015) starring Benedict Cumberbatch. In 2015, the NT introduced a schools streaming service, offering teachers the opportunity to stream NT productions into their classrooms for free. Unlike the RSC Live Schools' Broadcasts, which are broadcast on specific dates and at set times, the NT productions are on demand in schools, meaning that the productions can be accessed at any time, watched in their entirety or scene by scene and even re-watched for revision purposes. This scheme was launched with broadcasts of the 2010 *Hamlet* and 2013 *Othello,* alongside *Frankenstein* (2011). In November 2015, the first set of statistics relating to the broadcasts, were released. NT on demand was in 1130 schools (a quarter of all secondary schools in the UK); 70 per cent of the schools were outside London and the South East, spread across ninety-four counties in England, Scotland, Wales and Northern Ireland, indicating the wide reach of the project. As Alice King-Farlow, Director of Learning at the NT asserts, it is not only the digital innovation that has helped to give these productions such a wide audience, but also the fact that Hytner's *Hamlet* and *Othello* are such 'accessible', 'exciting' productions which secondary school students find thrilling.[23]

That young people should be able to see Shakespeare in performance is, in Hytner's view, of vital importance. In 2002 he warned of 'arts apartheid', stating that 'a generation of poor and middle-class children are being forced to study Shakespeare and the classics without ever seeing a play'.[24] Seeing Shakespeare in performance and performing in his plays as a child was one of the factors that influenced Hytner profoundly in his future career. He was worried that there were 'children leaving our schools now who have not seen a play, let alone performed in one'.[25] According to Vanessa Thorpe, 'Statistics held by the National Theatre' in 2002 indicated the number of schools paying a membership fee that 'entitled them to discounted tickets' had 'almost halved'. In addition to making it possible for more young people to see Shakespeare as a result of discounted tickets and live cinema broadcasts, Hytner's regime has also seen a flourishing of the Education Department, NT Learning, with a range of Shakespeare productions for primary school pupils, study days for pupils and teachers, sixth-form conferences connected to the Shakespeare productions in the Olivier and the commissioning of two productions, dubbed 'side-dishes' by Hytner, intended to play alongside main house Shakespeare productions in the Olivier and help young audiences to find a 'way in'.[26]

The NT Education department was founded in 1983, but it was not until 2007 under Hytner's regime, that it gained its 'first permanent education space, the John Lyon Education Studio',[27] with the completion of the redevelopment of the NT Studio. The space has subsequently been used for many of NT Learning's activities, which range from workshops for primary school pupils to adult-learning events. Finally, in 2014, the major £70,000,000 redevelopment plan of the theatre, which Hytner oversaw, included the creation of a purpose-built Clore Learning Centre, next to the new Dorfman Theatre, which enables the Education department to run a more extensive programme of events, working with '30% more people' than was previously possible.[28]

Although Shakespeare Education productions had happened at the NT in the years before Hytner became Artistic Director, it was in 2006 that a dedicated programme, mounting an annual abridged production of a Shakespeare play for primary school audiences was established, under the title 'Primary Classics'. These abridged versions of *Pericles* (2006), *Romeo and Juliet* (2007), *A Midsummer Night's Dream* (2008), *Macbeth* (2009) and *Twelfth Night* (2010), toured to a range of London schools with small-scale performances at the NT (in 2009 and 2010 in the Cottesloe Theatre) and were supported by a range of workshops and teacher training days.[29] The play texts, adapted by Carl Heap, were subsequently published with introductory notes aimed at helping teachers or other theatre practitioners to mount their own productions. King-Farlow describes these productions as fitting precisely with Hytner's attitude towards Shakespeare: 'to take a fresh look and ask what it says to an audience today'.[30] This is even more the case, in her view, with 'Primary Theatre for Key Stage 2', a programme that replaced 'Primary Classics' in 2010, and which, in 2013 and 2014, mounted a cut-down adaptation of *Romeo and Juliet* by Ben Power. The production originally toured to schools, culminating in a two-week residency in the NT's 'Temporary theatre' (formerly called The Shed) in October/November 2013. The production was accompanied by workshops for schools, teachers and families and received Hytner's full support.

For secondary pupils, NT Learning has produced a range of resources to accompany the Shakespeare productions in the main repertoire, with extensive Education packs, study days for teachers and workshops. The theatre has also seen the introduction of Shakespeare Student Conferences – the first being on *Othello* in 2013 and the second on *King Lear* in 2014. These conference-style events are aimed at Key Stage 4 and 5 students and include a range of lectures, masterclasses and Q-and-A events with academics and members of the cast and production teams. Hytner himself took part in the 2013 *Othello* conference, in conversation with Dan Rebellato, taking questions from the student audience, something at which King-Farlow describes Hytner as being particularly adept: 'he is very inspiring and very clear'.[31] In addition to being happy to talk about his productions, Hytner has also been 'very open to demonstrating his rehearsal process',[32] something which he did for an event connected to *Hamlet*, unpacking the process of rehearsal from design to performance, working on the text with understudies and taking the mixed-age audience through the process undertaken in his rehearsal room.

In 2008, when Hytner was directing George Bernard Shaw's *Major Barbara*, he met with Anthony Banks, associate director in NT Learning, expressing some concern at the potential inaccessibility of the play to younger audiences, and suggesting that some of the more complex classical plays in the NT repertoire might benefit from what he referred to as 'side dishes', helping these audiences to find a 'way in'.[33] The first of these 'side dishes' was commissioned in 2009, to accompany Marianne Elliott's production of *All's Well* in the Olivier. Writer Lucinda Coxon produced a contemporary sequel to Shakespeare's problem play, entitled *The Eternal Not*, exploring the dysfunctional marriage between Bertram and Helena, which was staged in the Olivier foyer prior to some performances of *All's Well*. A second 'side dish', *Prince of Denmark*, was commissioned in 2010 from Michael Lesslie, this time a prequel to *Hamlet*, which was playing in the Olivier, set around ten years before Shakespeare's play. The play was written to be performed by members of the National Youth Theatre and focused exclusively on the younger characters in *Hamlet*. The production, which was staged in the Cottesloe auditorium, was predominantly targeted at Key Stage 3 students but had a wider appeal, particularly to students studying *Hamlet* for GCSE and A-level.

Adult-learning events have also expanded under Hytner's regime, partly 'in anticipation' of the move to the Clore Learning Centre, with 'In Context' and 'In Depth' events accompanying many of the productions in the repertoire, allowing the theatre's wider audience to explore the plays in detail, often with the participation of the associate director and members of the cast. Hytner has also taken part in workshops aimed at teachers, including an event tied to the Shakespeare Schools Festival, in which he directed Act 2, scene 4 from *Twelfth Night* on the stage of the Lyttleton Theatre, focusing on some of the major concerns seen in his productions of Shakespeare at the National Theatre: the desire to root a play in a concrete environment, the need to keep a production flowing from one scene to the next and a willingness to change Shakespeare's words, 'if the word means the opposite of what it is supposed to mean'.[34]

Asked to sum up the impact of Hytner's regime on the Education Department of the National Theatre and its Shakespeare provision, King-Farlow cites two major 'shifts': a shift to 'focussing back on the National', to an Education department which has a much 'closer relationship to the work on the National Theatre stages', 'opening up, exploring and illuminating that work'; and 'a second shift, away from doing work solely about performing, to including work on writing, backstage and technical crafts – thinking about theatre-making as a whole, and all the skills within the building'. But, for King-Farlow the main drive of Hytner's artistic directorship, which has had a profound impact on the theatre's Education work has been accessibility: 'opening things up – expanding digitally – and 'widening the groups of people who are coming to the National'.[35]

In his capacity as Head of the National Theatre, Hytner has also seen it as his responsibility to get involved in politics, becoming a political spokesman on the Arts not only for the NT but also on behalf of smaller regional theatres, tackling topics including cultural philanthropy, censorship, arts funding and education. Charlotte Higgins, writing in 2012, described Hytner as 'an unofficial spokesman for his colleagues in less well-funded positions'.[36] Hytner has regularly given speeches on these topics, taken part in debates and written articles in the national newspapers, some of which (for example on the topic of multiracial casting in response to criticism of his casting of Clive Rowe in *Carousel*) have already been cited.

In 2012, Hytner used the opportunity of the *Evening Standard* Theatre Awards, where he was being given two awards, to speak out against cuts to arts funding, which had become an issue of major concern to theatres following the Conservatives' victory at the 2010 general election and the appointment of Maria Miller as Culture Secretary in 2012. Hytner asserted that, in order for the sort of philanthropy that the NT partly relies on to thrive, 'every theatre' needed to be funded to a sufficient level to attract such donors.[37] Days later he responded to criticisms by Maria Miller that his claims that she had done little to support cultural philanthropy were 'outrageous', by adding that 'the policies of the Department for Culture, Media and Sport were "vague and woolly and aspirational"'.[38] In 2013, he once again engaged directly with Miller in the public press, by responding to her assertion that 'arts organisations must make the case for their economic worth' with a co-authored article with Nick Starr in the *Guardian*, arguing for the 'economic potential' of the arts and culture, asserting that 'they are fundamental to our success as a nation' and accusing the government of having an arts policy 'that adds up to little more than a reduction in investment'.[39] Prior to the general election of 2015, Hytner joined others in lobbying for the arts both in terms of funding and their position within education. As part of an advisory board, producing an independent report entitled 'Leading the Field', Hytner and his fellow campaigners urged a future government to 'strongly champion the intrinsic value of the arts', campaigning, in particular, on behalf of regional theatres.[40] The issue of arts funding is particularly pertinent to Shakespeare productions, both at the National Theatre and in regional theatres, since full-scale Shakespeare productions, with their large casts (usually a minimum of fifteen actors) require significant funding.

By 2015, when Hytner left the NT, he had received a number of awards for his productions, including the *Evening Standard* Lebedev Special award for his directorship of the NT in 2012 and a Special Award at the Olivier awards, jointly with

Nick Starr, in 2014. In 2012 Hytner was knighted, an honour about which he is characteristically modest, encouraging staff at the NT to continue to refer to him as 'Nick'. Hytner's lack of pomposity and commitment to equality within the theatre building and the rehearsal room has been a notable feature of his time at the theatre. Stephen Fay, writing about Hytner in rehearsal for *The Recruiting Officer* in 1992, remarked that his authority resides partly in his own 'appropriate humility' (Stephan Fay, 'Hunting the Hit-Man, *The Independent on Sunday,* 1 March 1992), while Rupert Christiansen notes that he is 'famous for taking suggestions from anybody, be they star actor or assistant stage manager'.[41]

For a man who is known for being affable in the rehearsal room and for choosing to work on elaborate productions with large casts, one of Hytner's chief personal qualities on which his colleagues and friends frequently comment is his shyness. In spite of his ability to control a rehearsal room and to lead stimulating discussion among his actors, Hytner is notoriously bad at small talk. Alan Bennett describes him as 'opaque, no good one-to-one, much better in a group',[42] Richard Eyre speaks of his 'conversational tic' of 'not returning the ball'[43] and Nigel Hawthorne, before his death, recalled a lunch with Hytner: 'It was a ghastly occasion – there were awkward silences throughout, couldn't get anything out of him. Then he gave me a lift back to London in his car and suddenly he was talking non-stop: I'm sure it was because he didn't have to look me in the eye.'[44] And yet, Hytner is extremely adept at interviews, able to speak eloquently and with passion about all aspects of his theatrical work, not afraid to acknowledge mistakes that he has made in the past, commenting on previous productions, 'I can't necessarily always remember how we got there, but I can remember why they no longer feel very good to me',[45] and modest about his successes, which he often attributes to his actors.

To sum up the features of his directing career – particularly in the area of Shakespeare – is to note a change, from early, full-blown productions with elaborate, often abstract sets and eclectic costuming, mixing references to Shakespeare and the present day to crystal clear, firmly contemporary and meticulously specific productions in the latter half of his time at the NT, combined with a greater confidence about altering and cutting the Shakespearean text (some might say an irreverence) in order to make it readily intelligible. What remains central to his work is a balance between 'the desire to elevate and the desire to entertain'[46] – to create productions that speak firmly to the political and social concerns of the present, while seeking opportunities for humour and spectacle; to combine 'trust in [the] text with imagistic boldness'.[47] And yet, Hytner's own abiding memory of his time at the NT, as described to John Lahr in 2012, is not a moment of elaborate spectacle, or great drama, but one of quiet simplicity – the finale of *Much Ado About Nothing* in 2007:

> I pulled Beatrice and Benedick out of the dance. As the show is ending, everybody else is partying, and they've found a quiet corner. Once they find each other, they've got so much to talk about. That's all they're going to do for the rest of their lives: talk *to* each other, not *at* each other. The world is there for them. They can leave it and join in at will. Contentment is in being in quiet retreat … "It's what I want".[48]

This seems, perhaps, ironic given Hytner's apparent lack of confidence in one-on-one situations and yet it reveals a more sensitive side to the showman, which has inevitably been an important contributor to the success of his Shakespeare productions: an ability to find the quiet, human, tender moments amid those on a more epic scale.

Hytner has transformed the National Theatre physically, financially and in terms of its repertoire and audiences. When his previous incumbents left the role of Artistic Director they seemed determined never to run a theatre building again, all resuming successful freelance careers. However, Hytner has clearly discovered his metier in the role of Artistic Director, a role that he is reluctant to surrender. Even before his departure from the National Theatre, rumours were rife that he and Nick Starr were to establish a theatrical building of their own, taking on similar roles to those they had undertaken at the NT. Finally, in August 2015, only a few months after the end of his tenure at the NT, the pair announced the first stage of their new venture: the establishment of a new theatre company, to be called London Theatre Company and the acquisition of a 900-seat theatre in a location on the river at Tower Bridge, due to open in 2017. Here they plan a repertoire of new work, combined with 'a re-invention of a great work from the past'[49] – similar fare to that delivered so successfully at the NT over twelve years. Hytner himself will direct at least two shows per year in the theatre. And it seems unlikely that things will stop there, Hytner expressing his hope that this theatre will be 'the first of several' theatres that he and Starr will acquire.[50] It seems likely that the next decade will see more successful Hytner productions, predominantly new writing, some musicals (though not 'another big Broadway revival')[51] – and, perhaps, some Shakespeare.

APPENDIX

Productions by Nicholas Hytner

A Selected Chronology

1985	English National Opera	*Xerxes*	Handel
	Chichester Festival Theatre	*The Scarlet Pimpernel*	Beverley Cross
1986	Manchester Royal Exchange	*As You Like It*	Shakespeare
		Edward II	Marlowe
		The Country Wife	Wycherley
1988	Royal Shakespeare Company	*The Tempest*	Shakespeare
		Measure for Measure	Shakespeare
1989	National Theatre	*Ghetto*	Joshua Sobol
	Drury Lane	*Miss Saigon*	Claude-Michel Schönberg and Alain Boublil
1990	Almeida Theatre	*Volpone*	Jonson
	National Theatre	*Wind in the Willows*	Alan Bennett
1991	RSC	*King Lear*	Shakespeare
	NT	*The Madness of George III*	Alan Bennett (Film 1994)

1992		*The Recruiting Officer*	Farquhar
1993	Aldwych Theatre	*The Importance of Being Earnest*	Wilde
1997	NT	*The Cripple of Inishmaan*	Martin McDonagh
1998	Lincoln Centre, New York	*Twelfth Night*	Shakespeare
2001	NT	*The Winter's Tale*	Shakespeare
2001		*Mother Clap's Molly House*	Mark Ravenhill
2003		*Henry V*	Shakespeare
2004		*Stuff Happens*	David Hare
		The History Boys	Alan Bennett (Film 2006)
2005		*Henry IV Parts 1 and 2*	Shakespeare
2006		*The Alchemist*	Jonson
2007		*The Man of Mode*	Etherege
		Much Ado About Nothing	Shakespeare
2010		*Hamlet*	Shakespeare
2011		*One Man, Two Guvnors*	Richard Bean (from Goldoni)
2012		*Timon of Athens*	Shakespeare
2013		*Othello*	Shakespeare
2014		*Great Britain*	Richard Bean

NOTES

Introduction

1   BBC, 'Hytner takes National's top job', *BBC News*,
25 September 2001, http://news.bbc.co.uk/1/hi/
entertainment/1562108.stm (last accessed 20 November
2015).

2   Wills Morgan, *South Bucks, Burnham & Iver Observer*, 4
April 2003, quoted in Daniel Rosenthal, *The National Theatre
Story* (London: Oberon, 2013), 706.

3   Rosenthal, 707.

4   Ibid.

5   Ibid.

6   Vanessa Thorpe, 'F*** you, says BBC as 50,000 rage at
Spr*ng*r', *Observer*, 9 January 2005.

7   Rosenthal, 788.

8   Esther Addley, 'Storm grows over National Theatre play
dubbed racist and offensive by critics', *Guardian*, 14 February
2009.

9   Mark Lawson, 'Phone-hacking: hold the main stage!',
Guardian, 1 July 2014.

10   The Memorandum and Articles of Association of the National
Theatre Board (first incorporated on 8 February 1963 and
subsequently updated), states that one of the main purposes
of the theatre is to act as 'a memorial to William Shakespeare'
(p. 1). 'Memorandum and Articles of Association of the
National Theatre Board', held in the archive of the Royal
National Theatre.

Chapter 1

1   Nicholas Hytner, Interview with author, National Theatre, 30 April 2014.

2   Robert Miola, *The Comedy of Errors: Critical Essays* (London: Routledge, 2000), 32.

3   Robert Speaight, quoted in Miola, 32.

4   Nicholas Hytner, 'Faking It', *Areté*, Issue 41, Autumn 2013, 6.

5   Ibid.

6   Ibid.

7   Ibid.

8   Nicholas Hytner, Interview with author, London, 19 August 2015.

9   Hytner, 'Faking It', 6.

10   Ibid.

11   Hytner, Interview, 30 April 2014.

12   Ibid.

13   Ibid.

14   Andrew Dickson, 'A Life in the Theatre: Nicholas Hytner', *Guardian*, 16 October 2010.

15   Hytner, Interview, 30 April 2014.

16   Ibid.

17   Ibid.

18   Ibid.

19   Benedict Nightingale, 'Student Drama: Talent and Temerity' in *The University of Cambridge: An 800th Anniversary Portrait*, ed. Peter Pagnamenta (London: Third Millennium Publishing, 2009), 299.

20   Hytner, Interview, 19 August 2015.

21   Nicholas Hytner quoted in Rupert Christiansen, 'Hytner's Latest Challenge', *Weekend Telegraph*, 1 April 1989.

22   Nigel Chapman, 'Ariel, stasis', *Stop Press with Varsity*, 25 January 1975, 2.

23   Paul Harris, 'A Knight at the Theater: But just call him Nick',
      Jewish Telegraph, 2010, http://www.jewishtelegraph.com/
      prof_51.html (last accessed 10 September 2015).

24   Eve Wersocki Morris and Molly Hytner, 'Sir Nicholas Hytner:
      "It's Time to Go"', *Impact Magazine*, 27 January 2014, http://
      www.impactnottingham.com/2014/01/sir-nicholas-hytner-its-
      time-to-go/ (last accessed 10 September 2015).

25   Derek Harvey, Review of *All's Well*, *Cambridge Evening
      News*, 3 March 1976.

26   Nightingale, 300.

27   glbtq, 'Hytner, Sir Nicholas', *An Encyclopedia of Gay,
      Lesbian, Bisexual, Transgender and Queer Culture*, http://
      www.glbtq.com/arts/hytner_nicholas.html (last accessed 10
      September 2015).

28   Natalie Anglesey, 'Director credits his childhood in
      Manchester as where his love of theatre began', *Manchester
      Evening News*, 3 January 2014.

29   Christiansen, 'Hytner's Latest Challenge'.

30   Nicholas Hytner, 'A Hotline to Shakespeare', in *The Hidden
      Hall*, ed. Peter Pagnamenta (London: Third Millenium
      Publishing, 2004), 146.

31   Hytner, Interview, 30 April 2014.

32   Hytner, 'A Hotline', 146.

33   Ibid.

34   Ibid.

35   Nigel Chapman, 'Shaw sallied into Newnham', *Varsity*, 3 May
      1975, 6.

36   Paul Hartle and Peter Molloy, Review of *The Threepenny
      Opera*, *Varsity*, 29 November 1975, 8.

37   Steve Berry, Review of *A Chaste Maid in Cheapside*, *Varsity*,
      6 November 1976, 8.

38   Programme for *A Kick in the Stalls*, Summer 1976, Footlights
      Archive, 2/2/82, University of Cambridge Library.

39   Programme for *Tag*, Summer 1977, Footlights Archive, 2/2/84,
      University of Cambridge Library.

40 Hartle and Molloy, 'Review of *The Threepenny Opera*'.

41 Hytner, Interview, 30 April 2014.

42 Julian Evans and Nigel Chapman, 'Review of *The Rise and Fall of the City of Mahagonny*', *Varsity*, 5 March 1977, 9.

43 Elizabeth Forbes, 'University and Student Performances', *Opera*, May 1977, 504–5.

44 Max Loppert, 'People: 174 Nicholas Hytner', *Opera*, July 1991, 757.

45 Nightingale, 300.

46 According to the minutes of the Footlights meeting on 11 March 1977, Hytner asked the Footlights to say that they would provide a guarantee of £100 in order to 'bamboozle' Eastern Arts into supplying a further guarantee of £200 (Footlights minute book, 11 March 1977, contained in the Footlights Archive, 1/2/7, University of Cambridge Library).

47 Hytner, Interview, 30 April 2014.

48 Nightingale, 300.

49 Hytner, Interview, 30 April 2014.

50 Ibid.

51 Loppert, 'People: 174 Nicholas Hytner', 758.

52 Norman Platt, 'Justifying the Dunghill', *Opera*, June 1989, 682.

53 Loppert, 'People: 174 Nicholas Hytner', 757–8.

54 Ibid.

55 Max Loppert, 'Handel in London', *Opera,* April 1985, 374.

56 Loppert, 'People', 754.

57 Hytner quoted by Loppert, 'People', 760.

58 Loppert, 'People', 758.

59 Hytner, Interview, 30 April 2014.

60 Loppert, 'People', 755.

61 Hytner, Interview, 30 April 2014.

62 Hytner quoted by Loppert, 'People', 756.

63 Hytner, Interview, 30 April 2014.

64 Ibid.

65 Nicholas Hytner, 'Stand and Unfold Yourself', unpublished lecture, delivered at The University of Notre Dame, London, 5 March 2013, 2.

66 Nicholas Hytner, 'The purpose of playing', *Opera*, April 1988, 420.

67 Ibid., 419.

68 Loppert, 'People', 756.

69 Hytner, Interview, 19 August 2015.

70 The programme note states that Hytner invited his former fellow Footlights to write *Aladdin* (Programme for *Aladdin*, Exeter Northcott Theatre, 18 December 1981–23 January 1982, Exeter Library Special Collections, Show file 3/38).

71 Wadham appeared in *The Ruling Class, Much Ado About Nothing, The Winter's Tale* and *The Madness of George III*.

72 Mitchell appeared in *The Scarlet Pimpernel, Mother Clap's Molly House* and *Great Britain*.

73 Desmond Barrit appeared in *The Scarlet Pimpernel, Wind in the Willows, The Tempest, The History Boys, Stuff Happens, The Habit of Art* and *The Recruiting Officer*.

74 Alex Jennings appeared in *The Scarlet Pimpernel, The Country Wife, Measure for Measure, The Importance of Being Earnest, Ghetto, The Alchemist, The Winter's Tale, The Recruiting Officer, Stuff Happens, The Habit of Art, Collaborators* and *The Lady in the Van* film.

75 Mark Thompson designed *The Ruling Class, Jumpers, Chips with Everything, The Scarlet Pimpernel, Mumbo Jumbo, The Country Wife, Measure for Measure, Volpone, Wind in the Willows, The Madness of George III, Henry IV parts 1 and 2, The Alchemist, England People Very Nice, One Man Two Guvnors* and *The Lady in the Van*.

76 David Fielding designed *Murderer, Aladdin, Xerxes, The Tempest* and *King Lear*.

77 Di Seymour designed *Absurd Person Singular, Barefoot in the Park, Tom Jones, Alice* and *As You Like It*.

78 Mark Henderson designed the lighting for *The Scarlet*

Pimpernel, Jumpers, Mumbo Jumbo, Edward II, The Tempest and *Measure for Measure.*

79   Sams was musical director for *The Scarlet Pimpernel, Jumpers, Magic Flute, As You Like It, Edward II, Country Wife, Don Carlos, The Tempest, Measure for Measure, Ghetto* and *Wind in the Willows.*

80   Christiansen, 'Hytner's Latest Challenge'.

81   Hytner, Interview, 19 August 2015.

82   Reviews of *The Scarlet Pimpernel* taken from *London Theatre Record*, Volume 5, Issue 25/6, December 1985, 1230–2.

83   'stunning' (S.A.S., Review of *Murderer, Exeter Express and Echo,* 25 June 1981); 'glossy' (Anon., Review of *Murderer, Herald Express,* Torquay, 29 June 1981); 'glittering' and 'eye-catching' (Chris Court, Review of *Aladdin, Western Morning News,* 23 December 1981); 'done with style, and a high polish' (Peter Roberts, Review of *The Recruiting Officer, Herald Express,* 11 May 1981). Reviews of *The Scarlet Pimpernel* described it as 'spectacular' (Francis King, *Sunday Telegraph* and Jim Hiley, *The Listener,*) and 'lavish' (Jack Tinker, *Daily Mail*).

84   'fast-moving' (A.P.S., Review of *Aladdin, The Mid-Devon Advertiser*, 31 December 1981 and Court, Review of *Murderer*); 'directed with pace and panache' (Derek Lean, Review of *Barefoot in the Park*, *The Western Morning News*, 14 May 1983); 'vigorous' (Michael Coveney, Review of *Jumpers, FT,* 5 March, 1984).

85   Coveney praised the 'exemplary clarity' of *Jumpers* (Coveney, Review of *Jumpers*).

86   Coveney described *Jumpers* as an 'intelligent production' (Coveney, Review of *Jumpers*); Alan Hulme wrote of it as 'intelligently directed' (Alan Hulme, Review of *Jumpers, Manchester Evening News*, 2 March, 1984).

87   Alastair McKenzie, Production Manager, Notice contained in show file for *The Country Wife*, 16 March 1982, Exeter Northcott Theatre Archive, Show file 3/35.

88   Nicholas Cottis, Review of *The Recruiting Officer, Guardian*, 11 May 1982.

89 John Barber, Review of *Jumpers, Telegraph*, 2 March 1984.

90 Michael Billington, Review of *Jumpers, Guardian*, 2 March 1984.

91 Robert Cushman, 'A Measure of Success', *London Daily News*, 28 May 1987.

92 Robin Thornber, Review of *Edward II, Guardian*, 25 October 1986.

93 David Self, Review of *The Country Wife, Kaleidoscope*, broadcast on Radio 4 on 22 December 1986, 9.45–10.15 p.m.

94 Michael Billington, 'Kingdoms of Experience', *Country Life*, 24 September 1987.

95 Nicholas Hytner, Interview, Supplement to touring programme for *As You Like It*, 7 April–17 May 1986, ed. Judy Meewezen, Manchester Royal Exchange Archive.

96 Joan Seddon, 'The gospel according to Hytner', *Manchester Evening News*, 27 August 1987.

97 'visually, sensually ... one of the most exciting and exhilarating I've seen on the arena stage of the Royal Exchange Theatre in Manchester' (Thornber, Review of *Edward II*); 'strongly symbolic staging' (Grevel Lindop, Review of *Edward II, TLS*, 7 November, 1986); 'high, flamboyant theatricality' (John Peter, Review of *Don Carlos, Sunday Times*, 20 September 1987); a 'dazzling high camp production' (Michael Ratcliffe, Review of *The Country Wife, Observer*, 21 December 1986).

98 Christopher Stocks described *Edward II* as 'very operatic' (Christopher Stocks, 'Directing Marlowe', *Gay Life*, November 1986) while Patrick O'Neill commented on its 'operatic quality' (Patrick O'Neill, Review of *Edward II, Daily Mail*, 24 October, 1986). Billington, writing about *Don Carlos*, asserted that Hytner made use of 'the emblematic, pictorial style he has employed in opera productions' (Billington, 'Kingdoms of Experience').

99 'modern and outrageous' (Michael Coveney, Review of *Edward II, FT*, 27 October 1986); 'grotesque' (Grevel Lindop, Review of *The Country Wife, TLS*, 2 January 1987); 'decadent' (Robin Thornber, Review of *The Country*

Wife, Guardian, 20 December 1986). Writing about *The Country Wife*, Hulme described Hytner as 'the enfant terrible of the Royal Exchange' (Alan Hulme, Review of *The Country Wife, Manchester Evening News*, 19 December, 1986).

100 'a terrific, driving production' (Mary Harron, Review of *Mumbo Jumbo, Observer*, 17 May 1987); 'vigorous' (Martin Cropper, Review of *Edward II, The Times*, October 27 1986); 'energetic' (John Peter, Review of *The Country Wife, Sunday Times*, 28 December 1986); 'brisk' (Michael Schmidt, Review of *Don Carlos, Independent*, 14 September 1987).

101 Michael Schmidt, Review of *As You Like It, Kaleidoscope*, broadcast on Radio 4 on 10 January 1986, 9.45–10.15 p.m.

102 Lindop, Review of *Edward II*.

103 Nicholas Hytner, quoted in Cushman, 'A Measure of Success'.

104 Cushman, 'A Measure of Success'.

105 Harvey Crane, 'Macabre Theatre', *The Stage*, 9 July 1981.

106 Stocks, 'Directing Marlowe'.

107 Michael Ratcliffe, Review of *Don Carlos, Observer*, 13 September 1987.

108 Coveney, Review of *Edward II*.

109 Peter, Review of *The Country Wife*.

110 Thornber, Review of *The Country Wife*.

111 Lindop, Review of *The Country Wife*.

112 Seddon, 'The gospel according to Hytner'.

113 Hytner, Interview, 19 August 2015.

114 Stocks, 'Directing Marlowe'.

115 Peter, Review of *The Country Wife*.

116 Seddon, 'The gospel according to Hytner'.

117 Hytner, Interview, 19 August 2015.

118 Hytner, Supplement to touring programme.

119 Hytner, 'Stand and Unfold yourself', 1.

120 Nicholas Shrimpton, 'Shakespeare Performances in London,

Manchester and Stratford Upon Avon, 1985–6', *Shakespeare Survey* 40, 1987, 174.

121 Hytner, 'Stand and Unfold yourself', 1.

122 Hytner, Interview, 19 August 2015.

123 Ibid.

124 Ibid.

125 Jeremy Sams, Interview, Supplement to touring programme for *As You Like It*, ed. Judy Meewezen.

126 Di Seymour, Interview, Supplement to touring programme for *As You Like It*, ed. Judy Meewezen.

127 Sams, Supplement to touring programme.

128 Seymour, Supplement to touring programme.

129 Sams, Supplement to touring programme.

130 Seymour, Supplement to touring programme.

131 Hytner, Supplement to touring programme.

132 Ibid.

133 Ibid.

134 Duncan Bell, Interview, Supplement to touring programme for *As You Like It*, ed. Judy Meewezen.

135 Anon, Review of *As You Like It, The Yorkshire Post*, 10 January 1986.

136 Hytner, Supplement to touring programme.

137 Bell, Supplement to touring programme.

138 Hytner, 'Stand and Unfold yourself', 2.

139 Hytner, Supplement to touring programme.

140 Ibid.

141 Hytner, 'Stand and Unfold yourself', 12.

142 John Peter, 'Outside the Rules', *Sunday Times*, 12 January 1986.

143 Schmidt, Review of *As You Like It*.

144 Michael Ratcliffe 'Return to Arden', *Observer*, 12 January 1986.

145 Robin Thornber, Review of *As You Like It, Guardian*, 11 January 1986.

146 John Barber, Review of *As You Like It, Telegraph*, 13 January 1986.

147 Ratcliffe, 'Return to Arden'.

148 Michael Coveney, Review of *As You Like It, The FT*, 13 January 1986.

149 Seymour, Supplement to touring programme.

150 K. Thomas, *Man and the Natural World: Changing Attitudes in England 1500–1800* (Harmondsworth: Penguin, 1984), 194.

151 Schmidt, reviewing the production on Kaleidoscope, described the court as being 'made to seem like a Fascist camp' ('Review of *As You Like It*'), while Ratcliffe saw it as 'a place of fascistic repression and conspiracy' (Ratcliffe, 'Return to Arden').

152 Ratcliffe, 'Return to Arden'.

153 Agnes Latham (ed.), *As You Like It* (London: Methuen, 1975), xci.

154 'Review of *As You Like It*', *FT*, 13 June 1973, quoted in Cynthia Marsh (ed.), *As You Like It: Shakespeare in Production* (Cambridge: Cambridge University Press, 2004).

155 Mike Hubbard, Interview, Supplement to touring programme for *As You Like It*, ed. Judy Meewezen.

156 Seymour, Supplement to touring programme.

157 The props list lists a 'Gun rack with 2 guns' and '4 Dead animals on gun rack' (prompt copy for *As You Like It*, Manchester Royal Exchange archive).

158 Alan Hulme, Review of *As You Like It, Manchester Evening News*, 10 January 1986.

159 Ratcliffe 'Return to Arden'.

160 Coveney, Review of *As You Like It*.

161 Seymour, Interview, Supplement to touring programme.

162 Ibid.

163 Ibid.

164 Schmidt, Review of *As You Like It*; Hulme, Review of *As You Like It*.

165 Hytner, Interview, 19 August 2015.

166 Peter, 'Outside the Rules'.

167 Ratcliffe, 'Return to Arden'.

168 Hytner, Interview, 19 August 2015.

169 Seymour, Supplement to touring programme.

170 Speaking to Schmidt on Kaleidoscope, Billington noted that McTeer 'flings herself on little hillocks, repeatedly', Schmidt responding – 'Yes, there were mannerisms in her acting which I was troubled by. That was one of them. There was perhaps too much flailing about' (Schmidt, Review of *As You Like It*).

171 Seymour, Supplement to touring programme.

172 Ibid.

173 Ibid.

174 Ibid.

175 Ibid.

176 Coveney, Review of *As You Like It*.

177 Ibid.

178 Schmidt, Review of *As You Like It*.

179 Thornber, Review of *As You Like It*.

180 Patrick O'Neil, Review of *As You Like It, Daily Mail,* 10 January 1986.

181 Barber, Review of *As You Like It*.

182 Hulme, Review of *As You Like It*.

183 Peter, 'Outside the Rules'.

184 Anon, Review of *As You Like It, Yorkshire Post*.

185 Hytner, quoted in Cushman, 'A Measure of Success'.

Chapter 2

1 Richard Eyre, *National Service* (London: Bloomsbury, 2003), 15–16.

2 Rosenthal, *National*, 448.

3   Hytner, Interview, 19 August 2015.

4   Ibid.

5   Ibid.

6   Ibid.

7   Reviews of *Measure for Measure* taken from *London, Theatre Record*, Volume 7, Issue 23, November 1987, 1495–9 and Volume 8, Issue 21, October 1988, 1414–18 (unless otherwise stated.)

8   Roger Allam, 'The Duke in Measure for Measure' in *Players of Shakespeare 3*, eds Russell Jackson and Robert Smallwood, (Cambridge: Cambridge University Press, 1994), 22.

9   Ibid., 27.

10   Michael Billington, Review of *Measure for Measure*, *Country Life*, 12 November 1987.

11   Hytner, Interview, 19 August 2015.

12   Stanley Wells, 'Shakespeare Performances in England', *Shakespeare Survey 42* (Cambridge: Cambridge University Press, 1990), 134.

13   Robert Smallwood, 'Introduction' in *Players of Shakespeare 3*, eds Russell Jackson and Robert Smallwood, (Cambridge: Cambridge University Press, 1994), 7.

14   Wells, 'Shakespeare Performances', 134.

15   Brian Gibbons (ed.) *Measure for Measure* (Cambridge: Cambridge University Press, 2006), 71.

16   Janet Watts, 'A New Duke of Dark Corners', *Observer*, 8 November 1987.

17   Terry Grimley, 'Stratford's New Man Measures Up', *The Birmingham Post*, 7 November 1987.

18   Ibid.

19   Watts, 'A New Duke of Dark Corners'.

20   Allam, 'The Duke', 23.

21   Hytner, Interview, 19 August 2015.

22   Ibid.

23   'It is characteristic of Mr Hytner to have established this

nether penitential world so intelligently and effectively'
(Coveney, 1987).

24 'Mr Hytner's great gift is that he thinks theatrically'
(Billington, Review of *Measure, Country Life*).

25 'Hytner's directorial pace sweeps even these rather
substanceless performances briskly along' (Kemp, 1988).

26 Grimley, 'Stratford's New Man'.

27 Watts, 'A New Duke of Dark Corners'.

28 'It feels to me like it's the Duke's play' (Hytner, Interview, 19
August 2015).

29 Wells, 'Shakespeare Performances', 134–5.

30 Allam, 'The Duke', 22.

31 Ibid., 25.

32 Hytner, Interview, 19 August 2015.

33 Allam, 'The Duke', 23.

34 Smallwood, *Players*, 7.

35 Hytner, Interview, 19 August, 2015.

36 Michael D. Friedman, '"Oh Let Him Marry Her!":
Matrimony and Recompense in *Measure for Measure*',
Shakespeare Quarterly 46:4 (1995): 454.

37 Hytner, Interview, 19 August 2015.

38 Reviews of *The Tempest* taken from *Theatre Record*, Volume
8, Issue 15, July 1988, 1005–9 and Volume 9, Issue 11, May
1989, 689–94.

39 Virginia Mason Vaughan, *The Tempest: Shakespeare in
Performance* (Manchester: Manchester University Press,
2011), 91, 94.

40 Ibid., 91.

41 Vaughan, *The Tempest*, 98.

42 Hytner, Interview, 19 August 2015.

43 Alden T. Vaughan and Virginia Mason Vaughan, *Shakespeare's
Caliban* (Cambridge: Cambridge University Press, 1993),
196–7.

44 'The comic capers of Caliban, Trinculo and a stroppy Scots

Stephano have rarely been funnier' (Jane Edwardes, *Time Out*, 1989); 'Few Trinculos have been as genuinely comic' (Jack Tinker, *Daily Mail*, 1989).

45 Vaughan, *The Tempest*, 92.

46 Ibid., 93.

47 Christine Dymkowski, *The Tempest: Shakespeare in Production* (Cambridge: Cambridge University Press, 2000), 11.

48 *The Tempest*, dir. Nicholas Hytner, RSC, Royal Shakespeare Theatre, Promptbook, 1988, Shakespeare Birthplace Trust Archive, RSC/SM/1/1988/TEM1.

49 Hytner, Interview, 19 August 2015.

50 Stanley Wells, 'Shakespeare Performances', 144–5.

51 Hytner, Interview, 19 August 2015.

52 Elizabeth Story Donno (ed.), *Twelfth Night* (Cambridge: Cambridge University Press, 2004), 35.

53 Hytner, Interview, 19 August 2015.

54 'The music, by Jeremy Sams, is aptly and pleasantly weird' (Jones, 1989); 'Jeremy Sams's music supplies appropriately reflective tunes mysterious as the sound of the sea in a hollow shell' (Kellaway, 1988); 'Much assisted by Jeremy Sams's atmospheric music, the transformation scenes, masques and tableaux materialize and dissolve wonderfully' (Kemp, 1989).

55 David Lindley (ed.), *The Tempest* (Cambridge: Cambridge University Press, 2013), 17.

56 Peter Holland, programme note for *The Tempest*, Royal Shakespeare Theatre, Stratford-upon-Avon, 1988.

57 'John Wood makes a remarkable Prospero, stressing his lines to offer unexpected meanings' (Jones, 1989); 'His line readings are full of strange pauses and emphases, or lack of them' (Koenig, 1989); 'Unusually placed pauses, strange stresses and syncopations result in a kind of elocutionary extravaganza' (Kemp, 1989).

58 'to hear Mr Wood speak those immortal lines in a voice which seems to range over unlimited octaves is to be dazzled by the actor's art' (Tinker, 1989).

59 Hytner, Interview, 19 August 2015.

60 Ibid.

61 Holland, programme note.

62 Hytner, Interview, 19 August 2015.

63 Sheridan Morley, Review of *Measure for Measure, Punch*, 21 October 1988.

64 Hytner, Interview, 19 August 2015.

65 Rosenthal, 449.

66 Rosenthal, 448.

67 Ibid., 447.

68 Reviews of *Ghetto* taken from *Theatre Record*, Volume 9, April 1989, 549–56.

69 David Nathan, Interview with Maria Friedman, *Applause Magazine*, March 1997.

70 Rosenthal, 447.

71 Eyre, *National Service*, 72.

72 Hytner, Interview, 19 August 2015.

73 Eyre, *National Service*, 84.

74 Reviews of *Miss Saigon* taken from *Theatre Record*, Volume 9, Issue 19, September 1989, 1229–39.

75 Rosenthal, 455.

76 Tim Teeman, 'Leading man', *The Times*, 12 May 2001.

77 Reviews of *Volpone* taken from *Theatre Record*, Volume 10, Issue 7, April 1990, 463–8.

78 Rebecca Yearling, 'Volpone on the Stage', in *Volpone: A Critical Edition*, ed. Matthew Steggle (London: Bloomsbury Arden, 2011), 43–4.

79 Ibid., 45.

80 Hytner, Interview, 19 August 2015.

81 Ibid.

82 Hytner, 'Stand and Unfold Yourself', 11.

83 Reviews of *Wind in the Willows* taken from *Theatre Record*, Volume 10, Issue 25/6, December 1990, 1666–71.

84 The production was subsequently revived for Christmas in

November 1991 (running until March 1992). It then returned between December 1993 and June 1994 and again for Christmas 1994–5 (Rosenthal, 'National Theatre Productions 1963–2013', appendix).

85 Michael Romain, 'A Tragedy of Need, or a Kind of Everest', *RSC Magazine*, Spring, 1991, 10.

86 Ibid.

87 Ibid.

88 Nicholas Hytner, quoted in Romain, 'A Tragedy'.

89 Ibid.

90 Reviews of *King Lear* taken from *Theatre Record*, Volume 10, Issue 14, July 1990, 916–20 and Volume 11, Issue 9, May 1991, 531–3 (unless otherwise stated).

91 Carol Rutter, 'Eel Pie and Ugly Sisters in *King Lear*' in *Lear from Study to Stage: Essays in Criticism*, eds James Ogden and Arthur Hawley Scouten (Cranbury: Associated University Presses, 1997), 172.

92 Peter Holland, 'Shakespeare Performances in England', *Shakespeare Survey* 44 (1991): 181.

93 Hytner, Interview, 19 August 2015.

94 Holland, 'Shakespeare Performances', 181.

95 Ibid. Of course, Sam Mendes's production at the NT in 2013–14 took the image even further, surrounding the whole stage in the second half of the play with a huge corn field.

96 Ibid., 179.

97 Stanley Wells, 'General Introduction' in *William Shakespeare: The Complete Works*, eds Stanley Wells, Gary Taylor, John Jowett, William Montgomery (Oxford: Oxford University Press, 2nd edn, 2005), xxxix.

98 R. A. Foakes (ed.), *King Lear* (London: Arden, 1997), 113.

99 Stanley Wells, 'The Once and Future King Lear' in *The Division of the Kingdoms: Shakespeare's Two Versions of King Lear*, eds Gary Taylor and Michael Warren (Oxford: Oxford University Press, 1987), 18.

100 Nicholas Hytner, 'A stage for second thoughts', *The Times*, 30 June 1990.

101 Foakes, *Lear*, 178.

102 Lesley Kordecki and Karla Koskinen, *Re-visioning Lear's Daughters: Testing Feminist Criticism and Theory* (London: Palgrave Macmillan, 2010), 42.

103 Holland, 'Shakespeare Performances', 179.

104 Robert Clare, 'Quarto and Folio: A Case for Conflation', in *Lear from Study to Stage: Essays in Criticism*, eds James Ogden and Arthur Hawley Scouten (Cranbury: Associated University Presses, 1997), 90.

105 Holland, 'Shakespeare Performances', 179.

106 Ibid.

107 Ibid., 179–81.

108 Romain, 'A Tragedy', 11.

109 Ibid.

110 Deborah Warner, at the National Theatre in 1990 staged the scene as Lear's birthday party – a family affair with little suggestion that 'the division of the kingdom was a matter of state (Holland, 'Shakespeare Performances', 183). Sam Mendes, directing the production at the National Theatre in 2013–14 experimented with a similar concept, before settling on a formal press conference, with long tables set with microphones and around thirty of Lear's retinue surrounding the stage.

111 Hytner, Interview, 19 August 2015.

112 Romain, 'A Tragedy', 11.

113 Wood, quoted in Romain, 12.

114 Holland, 'Shakespeare Performances', 181–2.

115 Ibid.

116 Ibid.

117 Eyre, 161.

118 Romain, 'A Tragedy', 12.

119 Holland, 'Shakespeare Performances', 182.

120 Hytner, Interview, 19 August 2015.

121 Benedict Nightingale, 'Some Recent Productions', in *Lear*

from Study to Stage: Essays in Criticism, eds James Ogden and Arthur Hawley Scouten (Cranbury: Associated University Presses, 1997), 235.

122 Holland, 'Shakespeare Performances', 182.

123 Kordecki and Koskinen, *Re-visioning*, 2.

124 Samuel Taylor Coleridge, *Notes and Lectures Upon Shakespeare and Some of the Old Poets and Dramatists* (London: William Pickering, 1849), 313.

125 Maynard Mack, *King Lear in Our Time* (Los Angeles: University of California Press, 1972), 32.

126 Maurice Charney, *Shakespeare's Villains* (Maryland: Farleigh Dickinson University Press, 2012), 95.

127 Romain, 'A Tragedy', 11.

128 Kordecki and Koskinen, *Re-visioning*, 11.

129 Hytner, Interview, 19 August 2015.

130 Holland, 'Shakespeare Performances', 182.

131 Hytner, Interview, 19 August 2015.

132 Christine Eccles, 'Switching the breeches parts', *Independent*, 29 June 1990.

133 Alois Brandl, *Shakespeare* (Berlin: E. Hofmann, 1894), 179.

134 Foakes, *Lear*, 52.

135 Ibid.

136 Hytner, Interview, 19 August 2015.

137 'Hytner's work, as operatically opulent and inventive as ever, succeeded because the invention, fresh and revisionist, cohered, local effects growing into dramatic architecture' (Holland, 'Shakespeare Performances', 179).

138 'Hytner's *Lear* depended on theatricality, often of baroque extremes, for a dramatic argument' (Holland, 'Shakespeare Performances', 179).

139 'Nothing ... is taken for granted: every character's precise function is re-examined' (Billington, 1991).

140 'Hytner takes command of the play's intellectual battlefield if not the emotional one' (Miller, 1991); 'there is still

13 – 73

no questioning ... the intelligence of Nicholas Hytner's production' (Nightingale, 1991).

141 Hytner, Interview, 19 August 2015.

Chapter 3

1   Stephen Fay, 'Hunting the Hit-Man', *Independent on Sunday*, 1 March 1992.

2   Rosenthal, *National Theatre*, 480.

3   Fay, 'Hunting'.

4   Rosenthal, 'NT Productions 1963–2013' in *National Theatre*.

5   Kenneth Hurran, quoted in Rosenthal, *National Theatre*, 496.

6   Clive Hirschhorn, quoted in Rosenthal, *National Theatre*, 496.

7   Rosenthal, *National Theatre*, 496–7.

8   Nicholas Hytner, 'What you see is what you get', *Independent*, 8 September 1993.

9   Hytner, 'What you see'.

10   Watts, 'A New Duke'.

11   Hytner, 'What you see'.

12   Dickson, 'A Life in the Theatre'.

13   Hytner, Interview, 19 August 2015.

14   Patricia Lennox, Interview with Philip Bosco, in *North American Players of Shakespeare*, ed. Michael W. Shurgot (Newark, DE: University of Delaware Press, 2007), 55.

15   Ibid.

16   Mel Gussow, 'Creating Onstage Magic with Water', *New York Times*, 28 July 1998.

17   Clifford A. Ridley, 'Helen Hunt as Viola in *Twelfth Night*', *philly.com*, 25 July 1998, http://articles.philly. com/1998-07-25/entertainment/25737408_1_twelfth-night-viola-duke-orsino (last accessed 18 September 2015).

18   Lennox, *North American Players*, 55.

19 Gussow, 'Creating Onstage Magic'.

20 Charles Isherwood, Review of *Twelfth Night, Variety*, 17 July 1998.

21 Hytner, Interview, 19 August 2015.

22 Joanna Coles, Review of *Twelfth Night, Guardian*, 18 July 1998.

23 Donno (ed.) *Twelfth Night*, 35.

24 Hytner, Interview, 19 August 2015.

25 Bob Crowley, Interview, *New York Times*, 28 July 1998.

26 Ted Merwin, Review of *Twelfth Night, Theatre Journal* 51.2 (1999): 191–2.

27 Isherwood, Review of *Twelfth Night*.

28 Merwin, Review of *Twelfth Night*, 191–2.

29 Gussow, 'Creating Onstage Magic'.

30 Nicholas Hytner, 'Entering Shakespeare's Dreams', *New York Times*, 7 December 1998.

31 Nicholas Hytner, 'Stand and Unfold Yourself', 3–4.

32 Ibid.

33 Merwin, Review of *Twelfth Night*, 191–2.

34 Nicholas Hytner, quoted in Gussow, 'Creating Onstage Magic'.

35 Gussow, 'Creating Onstage Magic'.

36 Bob Crowley, quoted in Gussow, 'Creating Onstage Magic'.

37 Merwin, Review of *Twelfth Night*, 191–2.

38 Isherwood, Review of *Twelfth Night*.

39 Gussow, 'Creating Onstage Magic'.

40 Don Shewey, 'Gender Bending of Yore', *The Advocate*, 1 September 1998, 51.

41 Janet Adelman, 'Male Bonding in Shakespeare's Comedies' in *Rough Magic: Renaissance Essays in Honor of C. L. Barber*, eds Peter Erickson and Coppelia Kahn (Newark, DE: University of Delaware Press, 1985), 88–9.

42 Stephen Orgel, 'Nobody's Perfect: Or Why Did the English

Stage Take Boys for Women?', *South Atlantic Quarterly* 88 (1989): 27.

43 Shewey, 'Gender Bending', 52.

44 Coles, *Twelfth Night*.

45 Hytner, Interview, 19 August 2015.

46 Shewey, 'Gender Bending', 52.

47 Merwin, Review of *Twelfth Night*, 191–2.

48 Ben Brantley, 'Festival Review', *New York Times*, 17 July 1998.

49 Anthony Tommasini, 'For "Twelfth Night", A Daxophone, Tibetan Bowls and an Indian …', *New York Times*, 21 August 1998.

50 Ibid.

51 Ibid.

52 Ibid.

53 Hytner, 'Stand and Unfold Yourself', 11.

54 Alan C. Dessen, *Re-scripting Shakespeare* (Cambridge: Cambridge University Press, 2002), 7–8.

55 Alan C. Dessen, 'Teaching What's Not There' in *Shakespeare in Performance: A Collection of Essays*, ed. Frank Occhiogrosso (Newark, DE: University of Delaware Press, 2003), 104–5.

56 Hytner, 'Stand and Unfold Yourself', 12.

57 Vincent Canby, Review of *Twelfth Night, New York Times*, July 26, 1998.

58 Ridley, Review of *Twelfth Night*.

59 Isherwood, Review of *Twelfth Night*.

60 Ibid.

61 Lennox, *North American Players*, 60–1.

62 Ibid., 62.

63 Ibid., 63.

64 Hytner, Interview, 19 August 2015.

65 Ridley, Review of *Twelfth Night*.

66   Brantley, 'Festival Review'.

67   Isherwood, Review of *Twelfth Night*.

68   Brantley, 'Festival Review'.

69   Ridley, Review of *Twelfth Night*.

70   Lennox, *North American Players*, 55–7.

71   Ibid., 59–60.

72   Brantley, 'Festival Review'.

73   Coles, Review of *Twelfth Night*.

74   Dickson, 'A Life in Theatre'.

75   Richard A. Blake, 'The Crucible', *America*, 15 February 1997, 24–7, http://digital.lib.lehigh.edu/trial/reel_new/films/list/0_7_7 (last accessed 15 September, 2015).

76   Matt Wolf, 'No Thorns in Hytner's Hollywood', *The Times*, 21 January 1997.

77   Jonathan Coe, '*The Crucible*', *New Statesman*, 28 February 1997, 43.

78   Wolf, 'No Thorns'.

79   John Lahr, 'Curtain Raiser: Nicholas Hytner's theatrical golden age', *The New Yorker*, 23 April 2012.

80   John Sloan, *Authors in Context: Oscar Wilde* (Oxford: Oxford World Classics, 2009), 175.

81   Reviews of *The Importance of Being Earnest* taken from *Theatre Record*, Volume 13, Issue 5, 26 February–11 March 1993, 259–64.

82   Reviews of *The Winter's Tale* taken from *Theatre Record*, Volume 21, 21 May–1 June 2001, 671–7 (unless otherwise stated).

83   Ashley Martin-Davis, Interview, NT Education Workpack: *The Winter's Tale*, *National Theatre*, 7, http://www. nationaltheatre.org.uk/sites/all/libraries/files/documents/ winters_tale.pdf (last accessed 15 September 2015).

84   Michael Dobson, 'Shakespeare Performance in England 2001', *Shakespeare Survey* 55 (2002): 320.

85   A. D. Nuttall, *William Shakespeare: The Winter's Tale* (London: Edward Arnold, 1966), 40.

86 Philip M. Weinstein, 'An Interpretation of Pastoral in *The Winter's Tale*', *Shakespeare Quarterly*, Vol. 22:2 (1971): 97–8.

87 Patricia Tatspaugh, *Shakespeare at Stratford: The Winter's Tale* (London: Arden, 2002), 138.

88 Ibid., 145.

89 J. H. P. Pafford (ed.) *The Winter's Tale* (London: Methuen, 1963), lxxvi.

90 'Nicholas Hytner's gripping new production' (Foss); 'a magnificent production' (Coveney); 'it works beautifully' (Brown).

91 'Nicholas Hytner's production … falls woefully short of what it should be' (Gross); 'his production disappoints' (de Jongh).

92 'In the last act, when the dead come to life and old sorrows are laid aside, the production does become briefly moving' (Spencer); 'A moving resolution' (Foss).

93 'the superlative magic of the finale' (de Jongh).

94 Claire Skinner, Interview, NT Education Workpack: *The Winter's Tale*, *National Theatre*, 7, http://www.nationaltheatre.org.uk/sites/all/libraries/files/documents/winters_tale.pdf (last accessed 15 September 2015).

95 'Jennings is a really fine actor, often on the verge of greatness, especially when working with Hytner' (Coveney); 'Jennings conquers it with much more assurance than he showed in such other classic roles for other directors at the RSC. It's the best thing he's done since he last worked with Hytner' (Alastair Macaulay, *FT*).

96 Daniel Rosenthal, 'The man who needn't be king', *The Times*, 21 May 2001.

97 Heather O'Neill, 'Jealousy Will Get You Nowhere', an interview with Alex Jennings, *Independent*, 16 May 2001.

Chapter 4

1 David Lister, 'National Theatre's incoming director promises cheap seats and new productions to explore edge of drama', *Independent*, 24 January, 2003.

2   Adrian Lester, 'Adrian Lester on Henry V', *Shakespeare on Stage*, ed. Julian Curry (London: Nick Hern, 2010), 121.

3   Michael Billington, 'Welcome to the Cheap Seats', *Guardian*, 29 April 2003.

4   Nicholas Hytner, '*Henry V*: Directing: Contemporary Context', *Stagework*, http://www.stagework. org.uk/webdav/harmonise@Page%252F@ id=6012&Document%252F@id=2546.html (last accessed, 15 November 2015).

5   Abigail Rokison, 'Laurence Olivier' in *Gielgud, Olivier, Ashcroft, Dench: Great Shakespeareans, Vol. XVI*, ed. Russell Jackson (London: Bloomsbury Arden, 2013), 93.

6   Billington, 'Welcome to the Cheap Seats'.

7   Rosenthal, *National Theatre*, 690.

8   Nicholas Hytner, 'Nicholas Hytner on Henry V', Platforms, *National Theatre*, http://www.nationaltheatre.org.uk/ discover-more/platforms/platform-papers/nicholas-hytner-on-henry-v (last accessed 15 November 2015).

9   Peter Reynolds and Lee White, '*Henry V*: Rehearsal Diaries: Eleven: Space and Spectacle', *Stagework*, http:// www.stagework.org.uk/webdav/harmonise@Page%252F@ id=5,583&Section%252F@id=-404html (last accessed 15 November 2015).

10   Reviews of *Henry V* taken from *Theatre Record*, Volume 23, 7–20 May 2003, 625–31 (unless otherwise stated).

11   Rosenthal, *National*, 695.

12   Michael Dobson, 'Shakespeare Performances in England, 2003', *Shakespeare Survey 57* (Cambridge: Cambridge University Press, 2004), 281–2.

13   Ibid., 281.

14   Michael White and Paul Webster, 'Sante, Tony: Chirac's peace offering', *Guardian*, 7 May 2003.

15   Lister, 'National Theatre's incoming director'.

16   David Lister, 'Adrian the First steps into battle as Henry V in theatrical landmark', *Independent*, 16 August, 2002.

17 Jasper Rees, 'A King for our Times', *Telegraph*, 29 April, 2003.

18 Billington, 'Welcome to the Cheap Seats'.

19 Penny Downie, '*Henry V*: The Chorus: Penny Downie: Steeped in History', *Stagework*, http://www.stagework.org.uk/webdav/ harmonise@Page%252F@id=6012&Document%252F@ id=2705.html (last accessed 15 November 2015).

20 Rosenthal, *National*, 695.

21 Downie, 'Steeped in History'.

22 Hytner, Interview, 19 August 2015.

23 Gwilym Jones, 'Piece Out His – or Her – Imperfections', *Around the Globe* 51 (Summer 2012): 12.

24 Andrew Gurr (ed.), 'Introduction' in *Henry V* (Cambridge: Cambridge University Press, 2005), 7.

25 Macready (1819–39) and Phelps (1852) both split the Act 2 Chorus, as did Terry Hands in his 1975 RSC production (Gurr (ed.) *Henry V*, 50).

26 Rupert Wickham, 'Henry V: Nationality and Race: French a Credible Opposition', *Stagework*, http://www. stagework.org.uk/webdav/harmonise@Page%252F@ id=6012&Document%252F@id=2507.html (last accessed, 15 November 2015).

27 Reynolds and White, 'Diaries, Twenty-Eight: Previews Continued'.

28 Ibid.

29 Reynolds and White, 'Diaries, Twenty-Eight: Previews Continued'.

30 Ibid., 'Seventeen: Shock and Awe'.

31 Hytner, Interview, 19 August 2015.

32 Ibid.

33 Robert Blythe, '*Henry V*: Nationality and Race: Captain Llewelleyn', *Stagework*, http://www.stagework.org.uk/webdav/ harmonise@Page%252F@id=6012&Document%252F@ id=2511.html (last accessed 15 November 2015).

34 Hytner, 'Nicholas Hytner on Henry V'.

35 Dobson, 'Shakespeare Performances in England, 2003', 281.

36 Lester, 'Adrian Lester on Henry V', 122.

37 Hytner, Interview, 19 August 2015.

38 Hytner, 'Nicholas Hytner on Henry V'.

39 Ibid.

40 Lester, 'Adrian Lester on Henry V', 121.

41 Ibid., 122.

42 Reynolds and White, 'Diaries: Five: 21st Century Actors, 17th Century Text'.

43 Ibid. 'Four: the Readthrough'.

44 Ibid. 'Six: the First Week'.

45 Ibid. 'Eight: The Cabinet Room'.

46 Ibid. 'Twenty-three: The Technical Rehearsal'.

47 Hytner, Interview, 19 August 2015.

48 Dobson, 'Shakespeare Performances in England, 2003', 284.

49 Michael Dobson, 'Shakespeare Performances in England, 2005', *Shakespeare Survey* 59 (2006): 323–8.

50 Reviews of *1 and 2 Henry IV* taken from *Theatre Record,* Volume 25, Issue 9, 23 April–6 May 2005, 568–75 (unless otherwise stated).

51 Dobson, 'Shakespeare Performances in England, 2005', 328.

52 Ibid.

53 Nicholas Hytner, quoted in Bella Merlin, *With the Rogue's Company* (London: Oberon, 2005), 5.

54 Peter Reynolds and Samantha Potter, '*Henry IV Parts 1 and 2* Preparatory Workpack', *NT: Learning: Teaching Resources*, 20, http://d1wf8hd6ovssje.cloudfront.net/documents/henry_iv.pdf (last accessed 15 November, 2015).

55 Ibid.

56 Hytner quoted in Merlin, *Rogue's*, 6.

57 Merlin, *Rogue's*, 57.

58 Ibid., 56.

59 Ibid.

60 Hytner, 'Stand and Unfold Yourself', 2.

61 Merlin, *Rogue's*, 72.

62 Ben Ringham, quoted in Merlin, *Rogue's,* 72.

63 Max Ringham, quoted in Merlin, *Rogue's,* 72.

64 Reynolds and Potter, 'Henry IV Parts 1 and 2 Preparatory Workpack', 20.

65 Hytner, quoted in Merlin, *Rogue's*, 21.

66 Ibid., 2.

67 Hytner, Interview, August 2015.

68 Ibid., 46.

69 Merlin, *Rogue's*, 22.

70 Hytner, quoted in Merlin, *Rogue's*, 18.

71 Dobson, 'Shakespeare Performances', 326.

72 Ibid., 326.

73 Mark Thompson, Design Notes, cited in Merlin, *Rogue's*, 19.

74 Dobson, 'Shakespeare Performances', 327.

75 Reynolds and Potter, 'Henry IV Parts 1 and 2 Preparatory Workpack', 21.

76 Ibid.

77 Merlin, *Rogue's*, 23–4.

78 Alan C. Dessen, 'The Director as Shakespeare Editor', *Shakespeare Survey* 59 (2006), 186.

79 Ibid., 187.

80 Nicholas Hytner, 'Nicholas Hytner talks to Heather Neill', *Theatre Voice*, http://www.theatrevoice.com/audio/interview-nicholas-hytner-talks-to-heather-neill/ (last accessed 10 September 2015).

81 Ibid.

82 Nicholas Hytner, quoted in Robert Butler, *The Alchemist Exposed* (London: Oberon, 2006), 11.

83 Derek Bond, '*The Alchemist*: Worksheet', *National Theatre Education*, 11, http://www.nationaltheatre.org.uk/sites/all/libraries/files/documents/Alchemist_wkstAu2eEp.pdf (last accessed 15 November 2015).

84 Hytner, quoted in Butler, *Exposed*, 11.

85 Bond, 'The Alchemist: Worksheet', 10.

86 Hytner, 'Nicholas Hytner talks to Heather Neill'.

87 Ibid.

88 Derek Bond, 'The Alchemist: Worksheet', 10.

89 Hytner, Interview, 19 August 2015.

90 Hytner, 'Nicholas Hytner talks to Heather Neill'.

91 Reviews of *The Alchemist* taken from *Theatre Record*, Volume 26, Issue 19, 10–23 September 2006, 1010–15 (unless otherwise stated).

92 Reviews of *Much Ado About Nothing* taken from *Theatre Record*, Volume 27, Issue 25–6, 3–31 December 2007, 1497–501 (unless otherwise stated).

93 Nicholas Hytner, 'Nicholas Hytner talks lots about *Much Ado About Nothing*', *Theatre Voice*, 5 October 2007, http://www.theatrevoice.com/audio/nicholas-hytner-talks-about-much-ado/ (last accessed 10 September, 2015).

94 Hytner, 'Stand and Unfold Yourself', 4.

95 Nicholas Hytner quoted in Annette Vieusseux, '*Much Ado About Nothing:* Rehearsal Diaries', *Stagework*, http://www.stagework.org.uk/stageworks/muchado/rehearsaldiaries.html (last accessed 15 November 2015).

96 Ibid.

97 Hytner, 'Nicholas Hytner talks lots'.

98 Ibid.

99 Ibid.

100 Hytner, in Vieusseux, 'Rehearsal Diaries'.

101 Vieusseux, 'Rehearsal Diaries'.

102 Nicholas Hytner, quoted in eds Jonathan Bate and Eric Rasmussen, *Much Ado About Nothing*, RSC edition (London: Palgrave Macmillan, 2009), 149.

103 Ibid., 154.

104 Zoe Wanamaker quoted in Jasper Rees, '*Much Ado About Nothing*: "We didn't sleep together, did we?"', *Telegraph*, 12 December, 2007.

105 Hytner, 'Nicholas Hytner talks lots'.

106 Rees, 'We didn't sleep together'.

107 Ibid.

108 'The age of the actors actually adds to the pleasure and point of the piece' (Charles Spencer, *Telegraph*); 'they make their maturity the governing idea of the play' (Susannah Clapp, *Observer*); 'Wanamaker and Beale's maturity delivers an unexpected depth and charge to Beatrice and Benedick's guarded romantic feelings' (Mark Shenton, *Sunday Express*).

109 Hytner, quoted in Bate and Rasmussen, *Much Ado*, 146.

110 Ibid.

111 Vieusseux, Rehearsal Diary.

112 Simon Russell Beale, '*Much Ado About Nothing*: Beatrice and Benedick; Simon Russell Beale talks us through the wedding scene', *Stagework*, http://www.stagework.org.uk/stageworks/ muchado/beatriceandbenedick45.html (last accessed 15 November 2015).

113 Carol Chillington Rutter, 'Shakespeare Performances in England (and Wales), 2008', *Shakespeare Survey* 62 (2009): 362–3.

114 Hytner, quoted in Bate and Rasmussen, *Much Ado*, 149.

115 Nicholas Hytner, '*Much Ado About Nothing*: Nick Hytner on Claudio's visit to Hero's Grave', *Stagework*, http://www. stagework.org.uk/stageworks/muchado/grave.html (last accessed 10 September 2015).

116 Ibid.

117 'Hytner works miracles with scenes that I normally dread' (Jane Edwardes, *Time Out*).

118 'An especially fine and moving performance from Oliver Ford-Davies as Hero's initially urbane and later agonised father' (Spencer).

119 Bate and Rasmussen (eds) *Much Ado*, 142.

120 Hytner, 'Nicholas Hytner talks lots'.

121 Nicholas Hytner, '*Much Ado About Nothing*: The different roles of the director', *Stagework*, http://www.stagework.org.

uk/stageworks/muchado/directing32.html (last accessed 10 September 2015).

122 Rutter, 'Shakespeare Performances in England (and Wales), 2008', 363.

123 Hytner, 'Nicholas Hytner talks lots about Much Ado'.

124 Hytner, quoted in Bate and Rasmussen, *Much Ado*, 152.

125 Ibid.

126 'Don John gains riveting psychological complexity' (Bassett).

127 'Andrew Woodall even manages to give the usually one-dimensional villain Don John a clinically depressive motivation for his destructive nihilism' (Taylor).

128 Vieusseux, 'Rehearsal Diaries'.

129 Ibid.

130 Nicholas Hytner, '*Much Ado About Nothing:* Nick Hytner on his Rehearsal Process', *Stagework*, http://www.stagework. org.uk/stageworks/muchado/directing33.html (last accessed 10 September 2015).

131 Vieusseux, 'Rehearsal Diaries'.

132 Vieusseux, 'Rehearsal Diaries'.

133 Rees, 'We didn't sleep together, did we?'.

134 Nicholas Hytner, 'With Shakespeare the play is just the starting point', *Guardian*, 12 April 2003.

135 Hytner, 'Stand and Unfold Yourself', 4.

136 Ibid.

137 Ibid., 5.

138 Ibid., 4.

139 Ibid.

140 Bridget Escolme, 'Madness and Infantilism in Some Versions of Hamlet', in *Performance, Madness and Psychiatry*, eds Anna Harpin and Juliet Foster (London: Palgrave Macmillan, 2014), 179–80.

141 Reviews of *Hamlet* taken from *Theatre Record*, Volume 30, Issue 20, 24 September–7 October 2010, 1128–34 (unless otherwise stated).

142 Carol Chillington Rutter, 'Shakespeare Performances in
     England, 2010', *Shakespeare Survey* 64 (2011): 376.

143 Hytner, 'Stand and Unfold Yourself', 10.

144 Ibid.

145 Daniel Starza Smith, 'Review of Shakespeare's *Hamlet*
     (directed by Sir Nicholas Hytner) at the Olivier Theatre,
     National Theatre, London, 20 November 2010', *Shakespeare*,
     7:4 (2011): 473.

146 Ibid., 472.

147 Nicholas Hytner, 'The solution is the actor', Programme note
     for *Othello*, Olivier Auditorium, National Theatre, 2013.

148 'The cadence of every line seems to have been reappraised';
     'He refreshes the key speeches' (Hitchings); 'Rory Kinnear's
     performance ... superb in its ... quarrying of the all-too-
     familiar lines' (Purves); 'The natural rhythms and apparent
     spontaneity of his speech were remarkable; simultaneously,
     not a syllable of poetry escaped him untested.' (Starza Smith,
     'Review', 471.)

149 'I have rarely seen a Hamlet more real, more natural, less
     "acted"' (Neil Norman, Review of *Hamlet, Daily Express*, 8
     October, 2010); 'Kinnear's Hamlet is sympathetic, unstagey ...
     and so natural' (McGinn).

150 'Kinnear's performance has two defining features: unflaggingly
     crisp diction and an intelligent, incisive command of the
     nuances of Shakespeare's writing' (Hitchings); 'caustic,
     exact, gimlet-sharp prince' (Clapp); 'Kinnear speaks with
     ear-popping clarity' (Allfree).

151 Starza Smith, 'Review', 471; Charles Spencer, *Telegraph*.

152 Charles Spencer, Review of *The Revenger's Tragedy*,
     Telegraph, 6 June, 2008.

153 Alastair Macaulay, Review of *The Man of Mode*, *FT*,
     7 February 2007.

154 'How one feels the grief at the death of his father' (Tim
     Walker, *Sunday Telegraph*); 'His voice cracks with grief when
     he remembers his father' (Hart).

155 Kinnear, 'Rory Kinnear Talks about Playing Hamlet'.

156 Hytner, 'Stand and Unfold Yourself', 9.

157 Ibid., 10.

158 Hytner, 'Stand and Unfold Yourself', 12.

159 John Jowett (ed.), *Timon of Athens* (Oxford: Oxford University Press, 2004), 1.

160 Jowett, *Timon,* 1.

161 Jowett, *Timon,* 2.

162 Michael Billington, 'Best Shakespeare productions: What's your favourite Timon of Athens?', *Guardian*, 3 May 2014.

163 Hytner, 'Stand and Unfold Yourself', 8.

164 Paul Mason, 'Timon of Athens: the Power of Money', *Guardian*, 20 July, 2012.

165 Simon Russell Beale, 'Simon Russell Beale on Timon of Athens', Platform, recorded at the NT in August 2012, *Soundcloud*, 2012, https://soundcloud.com/nationaltheatre/simon-russell-beale-platform (last accessed 15 November 2015).

166 Nicholas Hytner, Interview, 'The Making of Timon: Staging the Play', *National Theatre*, http://www.nationaltheatre.org.uk/video/the-making-of-timon-staging-the-play (last accessed 15 November 2015).

167 Tim Hately, Interview, 'The Making of Timon: Staging the Play'.

168 Reviews of *Timon* taken from *Theatre Record*, Volume 32, Issue 15, 15–28 July 2012, 804–9 (unless otherwise stated).

169 Mason, 'Timon of Athens: the Power of Money'.

170 *Timon of Athens*, dir. Nicholas Hytner, National Theatre, Promptbook, 2012, National Theatre Archive, RNT/SM/1/594b.

171 Simon Russell Beale, 'Simon Russell Beale talks about his star performance as Timon', *Theatre Voice*, 31 August 2012, http://www.theatrevoice.com/audio/simon-russell-beale-talks-about-his-star-performance-as-timon/ (last accessed 15 November 2015).

172 'Sir Nicholas Hytner's production sags after the interval' (Letts, *Daily Mail*); 'The energy dips in the second half'

(Brown, *Mail on Sunday*); 'The inescapable problems of the play emerge in the peculiar second half' (Andrzej Lukowski, *Time Out*).

173 Hytner, Interview, 19 August 2015.

174 Anthony B. Dawson and Gretchen E. Minton (eds), *Timon of Athens* (London: Arden, 2008), 130.

175 Hytner, 'Stand and Unfold Yourself', 8.

176 Hately, 'The Making of Timon'.

177 Hytner, Interview, 19 August 2015.

178 Hytner, Interview, 19 August 2015.

179 Programme for *Timon of Athens*, Olivier Auditorium, National Theatre, 2012.

180 Hytner, 'The Making of Timon'.

181 Hytner, 'Stand and Unfold Yourself', 12.

182 Hytner, Interview, 19 August 2015.

183 John Lahr, *Joy Ride: A Theatre Primer* (London: Bloomsbury, 2015), 412.

184 Simon Russell Beale, Interview with Author, London, 6 June 2015.

185 Hytner, Interview, 19 August 2015.

186 Russell Beale, 'Simon Russell Beale on Timon of Athens'.

187 Ibid.

188 Simon Russell Beale quoted in Paul Taylor, 'The Making of a Modern Timon', *Independent*, 14 July 2012.

189 'The first half is fast, venomously satirical, as exciting an hour of theatre as you will see' (Letts, *Daily Mail*).

190 Rory Kinnear, quoted in Holly Williams, 'Rory Kinnear, national treasure', *Independent*, 13 April 2013.

191 Reviews of *Othello* taken from *Theatre Record*, Volume 33, Issue 9, 23 April–6 May 2013, 388–92 (unless otherwise stated).

192 Hytner, NT Live recording of *Othello*.

193 Ibid.

194 Kinnear, quoted in Williams, 'Rory Kinnear, national treasure'.

195 Rory Kinnear, quoted in Stephen Moss, 'Othello and Iago are
     a bit cracked', *Guardian*, 10 April 2013.

196 Peter Erickson, 'Images of White Identity in *Othello*' in
     Othello: New Critical Essays, ed. Philip C. Kolin (London:
     Routledge, 2013), 133.

197 Adrian Lester, quoted in Stephen Moss, 'Othello and Iago are
     a bit cracked'.

198 Jonathan Shaw, Programme note: 'Othello, from a military
     perspective', Programme for *Othello*, Olivier Auditorium,
     National Theatre, 2013.

199 Ibid.

200 Rory Kinnear quoted in Sarah Hemming, 'Villain of the piece',
     FT, 12 April 2013.

201 Kinnear, quoted in Sarah Hemming, 'Villain of the piece'.

202 Lyndsey Marshall, Interview, 'Emilia and Desdemona:
     Women in "Othello"', *National Theatre Live*, http://ntlive.
     nationaltheatre.org.uk/productions/40168-othello (last
     accessed 10 September 2015).

203 Lyndsey Marshall, Interview, National Theatre Platform:
     'Rory Kinnear and Lyndsey Marshall in Conversation',
     National Theatre, August 2013, http://www.nationaltheatre.
     org.uk/video/rory-kinnear-and-lyndsey-marshal-in-
     conversation (last accessed 10 September 2015).

204 Marshall, 'Emilia and Desdemona'.

205 Shaw, 'Othello, from a military perspective'.

206 Ibid.

207 Kinnear, quoted in Moss, 'Othello and Iago are a bit cracked'.

208 Shaw, 'Othello, from a military perspective'.

209 Ibid.

210 Hytner, Interview, 30 April, 2014.

211 Kinnear, quoted in Moss, 'Othello and Iago are a bit cracked'.

212 Hemming, 'Villain of the piece'.

213 'I'd say it scores a successful victory on points without
     delivering the final, knockout blow' (Billington).

214 'This Othello has all the hallmarks of Hytner at his best – it's

witty, agile, lucid and deeply felt' (Spencer); 'With Nicholas Hytner directing, we also expect a production that will be witty, well-spoken and illuminating' (Billington).

215 Olivia Vinall, Interview, 'Emilia and Desdemona: The Women in Othello', *National Theatre Live*, http://ntlive. nationaltheatre.org.uk/productions/40168-othello (last accessed 10 September 2015).

216 'My word, we will miss Hytner when he leaves the NT in 2015' (Spencer, *Telegraph*).

Chapter 5

1 Maddy Costa, 'Bravo! How Nicholas Hytner transformed British theatre', *Guardian*, 22 March 2004.

2 Ibid.

3 Jude Kelly, 'The national wants to go into battle', *Guardian*, 22 March 2004.

4 John Bungey, 'The luvvie power list 2010: theatre's 50 most influential people', *The Times*, 15 December 2010.

5 Lahr, 'Curtain Raiser'.

6 Dominic Cavendish, 'Culture Updates', *Telegraph*, 11 April 2013.

7 Michael Billington, 'Appreciation', *Guardian*, 11 April 2013.

8 Charlotte Higgins, 'I'm a History Boy, Hytner tells National', *Guardian*, 11 April 2013.

9 Benedict Nightingale, 'The NT – stage of soapbox', *The Times*, 9 February 2009.

10 Jack Malvern, 'Cue successor as Hytner bows out after a glorious run at National', *The Times*, 11 April 2013.

11 Maev Kennedy, 'NT director scores a hit, a very palpable hit', *Guardian*, 27 July 2003.

12 Tim Goodwin, *Britain's Royal National Theatre: The First 25 years*, London: Royal National Theatre/Nick Hern Books, 1988, 5.

13 The National Theatre consitution, First provisional draft,
Olivier archive, BL.Add.30331; Memorandum and articles
of Association, incorporated the 8th day of February, 1963.
Olivier archive, BL.Add.80331.

14 Billington, 'Welcome to the Cheap Seats'.

15 Nightingale, 'The NT – stage of soapbox'.

16 David Lister, 'How to get children switched on to the drama
of theatre', *Independent*, 9 November 2002.

17 Billington, 'Welcome to the Cheap Seats'.

18 Costa, 'Bravo!'.

19 Kennedy, 'NT director scores a hit'.

20 Libby Purves, 'The BBC has to detach itself from the rating
mentality', *The Times*, 7 March 2013.

21 Simon Callow, quoted in Costa, 'Bravo!'.

22 Lahr, 'Curtain Raiser'.

23 Alice King-Farlow, Interview with author, National Theatre,
London, 3 December 2015.

24 Fiachra Gibbons, 'Theatre chief warns of arts apartheid',
Guardian, 4 November 2002.

25 Vanessa Thorpe, 'Bard is a mystery to our lost generation,
warns arts boss', *Observer*, 3 November 2002.

26 Anthony Banks, Interview with author, National Theatre,
London, 28 February 2011.

27 Rosenthal, 827.

28 Rosenthal, 836.

29 See Abigail Rokison, *Shakespeare for Young People*, London:
Arden Bloomsbury, 2013, Ch. 5.

30 King-Farlow, Interview.

31 Ibid.

32 Ibid.

33 Banks, Interview.

34 Nicholas Hytner, 'Nicholas Hytner Directs Act 2 scene 4 from
Twelfth Night, You Tube, May 2011, https://www.youtube.com/
watch?v=EAG733T1fpw (last accessed 18 December 2015).

35 King-Farlow, Interview.

36 Charlotte Higgins, 'The Arts are on a Knife edge', *Guardian*, 1 December 2012.

37 Amira Hashish, 'Nicholas Hytner makes impassioned plea against arts cuts', *Evening Standard*, 25 November 2012.

38 Charlotte Higgins, 'National Theatre boss rebukes culture secretary over arts funding stance', *Guardian*, 30 November 2012.

39 Nicholas Hytner and Nick Starr, 'Sir Nicholas Hytner: Arts are Economic Gold for Britain', *Guardian*, 24 April 2013.

40 Matthew Hemley, 'Equity and UK Theatre lead pre-election arts lobby', *The Stage*, 2 April 2015.

41 Rupert Christiansen, 'How Hytner became a contender', *Daily Telegraph*, 24 February 1997.

42 Ibid.

43 Eyre quoted in Lahr, 'Curtain Raiser'.

44 Christiansen, 'How Hytner became a contender'.

45 Nicholas Hytner, Interview with author, National Theatre, 30 April 2014.

46 Nicholas Hytner, 'The Diary', *FT*, 25 June, 2001.

47 Michael Billington, 'Very much his own man', *Guardian*, 26 September 2001.

48 Lahr, 'Curtain Raiser'.

49 Chris Bennion, 'Nicholas Hytner announces plan for 900-seat theatre', *Telegraph*, 20 August 2015.

50 Nicholas Hytner, Interview with author, London, 15 August 2015.

51 Ibid.

BIBLIOGRAPHY

A.P.S. Review of *Aladdin*. *Mid-Devon Advertiser*, 31 December 1981.

Addley, Esther. 'Storm grows over National Theatre play dubbed racist and offensive by critics'. *Guardian*, 14 February 2009.

Adelman, Janet. 'Male Bonding in Shakespeare's Comedies'. In *Rough Magic: Renaissance Essays in Honor of C. L. Barber*, Peter Erickson and Coppelia Kahn (eds), 73–103. Newark, DE: University of Delaware Press, 1985.

Allam, Roger. 'The Duke in Measure for Measure'. In *Players of Shakespeare 3*, Russell Jackson and Robert Smallwood (eds), 21–41. Cambridge: Cambridge University Press, 1994.

Anglesey, Natalie. 'Director credits his childhood in Manchester as where his love of theatre began'. *Manchester Evening News*, 3 January 2014.

Anon. Review of *Murderer. Herald Express,* Torquay, 29 June 1981.

Barber, John. Review of *Jumpers. Telegraph*, 2 March 1984.

Barber, John. Review of *As You Like It. Telegraph*, 13 January 1986.

Bate, Jonathan and Rasmussen, Eric, eds. *Much Ado About Nothing*, RSC edition. London: Palgrave Macmillan, 2009.

BBC. 'Hytner takes National's top job'. *BBC News*, 25 September 2001. Available online: http://news.bbc.co.uk/1/hi/entertainment/1562108.stm (last accessed 20 November 2015).

Beale, Simon Russell. '*Much Ado About Nothing:* Beatrice and Benedick: Simon Russell Beale talks us through the wedding scene'. *Stagework*. Available online: http://www.stagework.org.uk/stageworks/muchado/beatriceandbenedick45.html (last accessed 15 November 2015).

Beale, Simon Russell. 'Simon Russell Beale on Timon of Athens', Platform, recorded at the NT in August 2012.

Soundcloud. 2012. Available online: https://soundcloud.com/
nationaltheatre/simon-russell-beale-platform (last accessed 15
November 2015).

Beale, Simon Russell. 'Simon Russell Beale talks about his star
performance as Timon'. *Theatre Voice*, 31 August 2012.
Available online: http://www.theatrevoice.com/audio/simon-
russell-beale-talks-about-his-star-performance-as-timon/ (last
accessed 15 November 2015).

Bennion, Chris. 'Nicholas Hytner announces plan for 900-seat
theatre'. *Telegraph*, 20 August 2015.

Berry, Steve. Review of *A Chaste Maid in Cheapside*. *Varsity*. 6
November 1976.

Billington, Michael. Review of *Jumpers*. *Guardian*, 2 March 1984.

Billington, Michael. 'Kingdoms of Experience'. *Country Life*, 24
September 1987.

Billington, Michael. Review of *Measure for Measure*, *Country Life*,
12 November 1987.

Billington, Michael. 'Very much his own man'. *Guardian*, 26
September 2001.

Billington, Michael. 'Welcome to the Cheap Seats'. *Guardian*, 29
April 2003.

Billington, Michael. 'Appreciation'. *Guardian*, 11 April 2013.

Billington, Michael. 'Best Shakespeare productions: What's your
favourite Timon of Athens?'. *Guardian*, 3 May 2014.

Blake, Richard A. 'The Crucible'. *America*, 15 February 1997,
24–7. Available online: http://digital.lib.lehigh.edu/trial/reel_new/
films/list/0_7_7 (last accessed 15 September 2015).

Blythe, Robert. '*Henry V*: Nationality and Race: Captain
Llewelleyn'. *Stagework*. Available online: http://www.
stagework.org.uk/webdav/harmonise@Page%252F@
id=6012&Document%252F@id=2511.html (last accessed 15
November 2015).

Bond, Derek. '*The Alchemist*: Worksheet'. *National Theatre
Education*. Available online: http://www.nationaltheatre.org.uk/
sites/all/libraries/files/documents/Alchemist_wkstAu2eEp.pdf (last
accessed 15 November 2015).

Brandl, Alois. *Shakespeare*. Berlin: E. Hofmann, 1894.

Brantley, Ben. 'Festival Review'. *New York Times*, 17 July 1998.

Bungey, John. 'The luvvie power list 2010: Theatre's 50 most
influential people'. *The Times*, 15 December 2010.

Butler, Robert. *The Alchemist Exposed*. London: Oberon, 2006.

Canby, Vincent. Review of *Twelfth Night*. *New York Times*, 26 July 1998.

Cavendish, Dominic. 'Culture Updates'. *Telegraph*, 11 April 2013.

Chapman, Nigel. 'Ariel, stasis'. *Stop Press with Varsity*, 25 January 1975, 2.

Chapman, Nigel. 'Shaw sallied into Newnham'. *Varsity*, 3 May 1975, 6.

Charney, Maurice. *Shakespeare's Villains*. Maryland: Farleigh Dickinson University Press, 2012.

Christiansen, Rupert. 'Hytner's Latest Challenge'. *Weekend Telegraph*, 1 April 1989.

Christiansen, Rupert. 'How Hytner became a contender'. *Telegraph*, 24 February 1997.

Clarke, Robert. 'Quarto and Folio: A Case for Conflation'. In *Lear from Study to Stage: Essays in Criticism*, James Ogden and Arthur Hawley Scouten (eds), 79–108. Cranbury: Associated University Presses, 1997.

Coe, Jonathan. '*The Crucible*'. *New Statesman*, 28 February 1997.

Coleridge, Samuel Taylor. *Notes and Lectures upon Shakespeare and Some of the Old Poets and Dramatists*. London: William Pickering, 1849.

Coles, Joanna. Review of *Twelfth Night*. *Guardian*, 18 July 1998.

Costa, Maddy. 'Bravo! How Nicholas Hytner transformed British theatre'. *Guardian*, 22 March 2004.

Cottis, Nicholas. Review of *The Recruiting Officer*. *Guardian*, 11 May 1982.

Court, Chris. Review of *Aladdin*. *Western Morning News*, 23 December 1981.

Coveney, Michael. Review of *Jumpers*. *FT*, 5 March, 1984.

Coveney, Michael. Review of *As You Like It*. *FT*, 13 January 1986.

Coveney, Michael. Review of *Edward II*. *FT*, 27 October 1986.

Crane, Harvey. 'Macabre Theatre'. *The Stage*, 9 July 1981.

Cropper, Martin. Review of *Edward II*. *The Times*, 27 October 1986.

Crowley, Bob. Interview. *New York Times*, 28 July 1998.

Cushman, Robert. 'A Measure of Success'. *London Daily News*, 28 May 1987.

Dawson, Antony B. *Hamlet: Shakespeare in Performance.*
    Manchester: Manchester University Press, 1997.
Dawson, Anthony B. and Minton, Gretchen E. (eds). *Timon of
    Athens.* London: Arden, 2008.
Dessen, Alan C. *Re-scripting Shakespeare.* Cambridge: Cambridge
    University Press, 2002.
Dessen, Alan C. 'Teaching What's Not There'. In *Shakespeare in
    Performance: A Collection of Essays*, Frank Occhiogrosso (ed.),
    104–12. Newark, DE: University of Delaware Press, 2003.
Dessen, Alan C. 'The Director as Shakespeare Editor', *Shakespeare
    Survey 59* (2006), 182–92.
Dickson, Andrew. 'A Life in the Theatre: Nicholas Hytner'.
    Guardian, 16 October 2010.
Dobson, Michael. 'Shakespeare Performance in England 2001',
    Shakespeare Survey 55 (2002): 285–321.
Dobson, Michael. 'Shakespeare Performances in England, 2003',
    Shakespeare Survey 57 (2004): 258–89.
Dobson, Michael. 'Shakespeare Performances in England, 2005',
    Shakespeare Survey 59 (2006): 298–337.
Donno, Elizabeth Story (ed.). *Twelfth Night.* Cambridge:
    Cambridge University Press, 2004.
Downie, Penny. '*Henry V*: The Chorus: Penny Downie:
    Steeped in History'. *Stagework.* Available online: http://
    www.stagework.org.uk/webdav/harmonise@Page%252F@
    id=6012&Document%252F@id=2705.html (last accessed 15
    November 2015).
Dymkowski, Chris. *The Tempest: Shakespeare in Production.*
    Cambridge: Cambridge University Press, 2000.
Eccles, Christine. 'Switching the breeches parts'. *Independent*, 29
    June 1990.
Erickson, Peter. 'Images of White Identity in *Othello*'. In *Othello:
    New Critical Essays*, Philip C. Kolin (ed.), 133–45. London:
    Routledge, 2013.
Escolme, Bridget. 'Madness and Infantilism in Some Versions of
    Hamlet'. In *Performance, Madness and Psychiatry*, Anna Harpin
    and Juliet Foster (eds), 165–86. London: Palgrave Macmillan,
    2014.
Evans, Julian and Chapman, Nigel. 'Review of *The Rise and Fall of
    the City of Mahagonny*'. *Varsity*, 5 March 1977.
Eyre, Richard. *National Service.* London: Bloomsbury, 2003.

Fay, Stephen. 'Hunting the Hit-Man', *Independent on Sunday*,
1 March 1992.

Foakes, R. A. (ed.). *King Lear*. London: Arden, 1997.

Forbes, Elizabeth. 'University and Student Performances', *Opera*
(May 1977): 504–5.

Friedman, Michael D. '"Oh Let Him Marry Her!": Matrimony and
Recompense in *Measure for Measure*', *Shakespeare Quarterly* 46
(4) (1995): 454–64.

Gibbons, Brian (ed.) *Measure for Measure*. Cambridge: Cambridge
University Press, 2006.

Gibbons, Fiachra. 'Theatre chief warns of arts apartheid'.
Guardian, 4 November 2002.

glbtq. 'Hytner, Sir Nicholas'. *An Encyclopedia of Gay, Lesbian,*
Bisexual, Transgender and Queer Culture. Available online:
http://www.glbtq.com/arts/hytner_nicholas.html (last accessed 10
September 2015).

Goodwin, Tim. *Britain's Royal National Theatre: The First*
25 Years. London: Royal National Theatre/Nick Hern Books,
1988.

Grimley, Terry. 'Stratford's New Man Measures Up'. *Birmingham*
Post, 7 November 1987.

Gurr, Andrew (ed.). *Henry V*. Cambridge: Cambridge University
Press, 2005.

Gussow, Mel. 'Creating Onstage Magic with Water'. *New York*
Times, 28 July 1998.

Harris, Paul. 'A Knight at the Theater: But just call him Nick'.
Jewish Telegraph. 2010. Available online: http://www.
jewishtelegraph.com/prof_51.html (last accessed 10 September
2015).

Harron, Mary. Review of *Mumbo Jumbo. Observer*, 17 May 1987.

Hartle, Paul and Molloy, Peter. Review of *The Threepenny Opera*.
Varsity, 29 November 1975.

Harvey, Derek. Review of *All's Well. Cambridge Evening News*,
3 March 1976.

Hashish, Amira. 'Nicholas Hytner makes impassioned plea against
arts cuts'. *Evening Standard*, 25 November 2012.

Hately, Tim. Interview. 'The Making of Timon: Staging the Play'.
National Theatre. Available online: http://www.nationaltheatre.
org.uk/video/the-making-of-timon-staging-the-play (last accessed
15 November 2015).

Hemley, Matthew. 'Equity and UK Theatre lead pre-election arts lobby'. *The Stage,* 2 April 2015.

Hemming, Sarah. 'Villain of the piece'. *FT*, 12 (April 2013).

Higgins, Charlotte. 'National Theatre boss rebukes culture secretary over arts funding stance'. *Guardian*, 30 November 2012.

Higgins, Charlotte. 'The Arts are on a Knife edge'. *Guardian*, 1 December 2012.

Higgins, Charlotte. 'I'm a History Boy, Hytner tells National'. *Guardian*, 11 April 2013.

Holland, Peter. 'Shakespeare Performances in England', *Shakespeare Survey* 44 (1991): 157–90.

Hulme, Alan. Review of *Jumpers*. *Manchester Evening News,* 2 March 1984.

Hulme, Alan. Review of *As You Like It*. *Manchester Evening News*, 10 January 1986.

Hulme, Alan. Review of *The Country Wife*. *Manchester Evening News*, 19 December 1986.

Hytner, Nicholas. 'The purpose of playing', *Opera* (April 1988), 419–23.

Hytner, Nicholas. 'A stage for second thoughts'. *The Times*, 30 June 1990.

Hytner, Nicholas. 'What you see is what you get'. *Independent*, 8 September 1993.

Hytner, Nicholas. 'Entering Shakespeare's Dreams'. *New York Times*, 7 December 1998.

Hytner, Nicholas. 'The Diary', *FT*, 25 June, 2001.

Hytner, Nicholas. 'With Shakespeare the play is just the starting point'. *Guardian*, 12 April 2003.

Hytner, Nicholas. 'A Hotline to Shakespeare'. In *The Hidden Hall*, Peter Pagnamenta (ed.), 146–7. London: Third Millennium Publishing, 2004.

Hytner, Nicholas. 'Stand and Unfold Yourself'. Unpublished lecture, delivered at The University of Notre Dame, London, 5 March 2013.

Hytner, Nicholas. 'Faking It'. *Areté* 41 (Autumn 2013): 6.

Hytner, Nicholas. '*Henry V*: Directing: Contemporary Context'. *Stagework*. Available online: http://www.stagework.org.uk/webdav/harmonise@Page%252F@id=6012&Document%252F@id=2546.html (last accessed 15 November 2015).

Hytner, Nicholas. Interview. 'The Making of Timon: Staging

the Play'. *National Theatre*. Available online: http://www.
nationaltheatre.org.uk/video/the-making-of-timon-staging-
the-play (last accessed 10 September 2015).

Hytner, Nicholas. '*Much Ado About Nothing*: Nick Hytner on
Claudio's visit to Hero's Grave'. *Stagework*. Available online:
http://www.stagework.org.uk/stageworks/muchado/grave.html
(last accessed 10 September 2015).

Hytner, Nicholas. '*Much Ado About Nothing:* Nick Hytner on his
Rehearsal Process'. *Stagework*. Available online: http://www.
stagework.org.uk/stageworks/muchado/directing33.html (last
accessed 10 September 2015).

Hytner, Nicholas. '*Much Ado About Nothing:* The different roles
of the director'. *Stagework*. Available online: http://www.
stagework.org.uk/stageworks/muchado/directing32.html (last
accessed 10 September 2015).

Hytner, Nicholas. 'Nicholas Hytner on Henry V', Platforms,
National Theatre. Available online: http://www.nationaltheatre.
org.uk/discover-more/platforms/platform-papers/nicholas-hytner-
on-henry-v (last accessed 15 November 2015).

Hytner, Nicholas. 'Nicholas Hytner talks lots about *Much Ado
About Nothing*'. *Theatre Voice*. 5 Oct 2007. Available online:
http://www.theatrevoice.com/audio/nicholas-hytner-talks-about-
much-ado/ (last accessed 10 September 2015).

Hytner, Nicholas. 'Nicholas Hytner talks to Heather Neill'. *Theatre
Voice*. Available online: http://www.theatrevoice.com/audio/
interview-nicholas-hytner-talks-to-heather-neill/ (last accessed 10
September 2015).

Hytner, Nicholas and Starr, Nick. 'Sir Nicholas Hytner: Arts are
economic gold for Britain'. *Guardian*, 24 April 2013.

Isherwood, Charles. Review of *Twelfth Night. Variety*, 17 July 1998.

Jones, Gwilym. 'Piece Out His – or Her – Imperfections', *Around
the Globe* 51 (Summer 2012): 12.

Jowett, John (ed.). *Timon of Athens*. Oxford: Oxford University
Press, 2004.

Kelly, Jude. 'The national wants to go into battle'. *Guardian*, 22
March 2004.

Kennedy, Maev. 'NT director scores a hit, a very palpable hit'.
Guardian, 27 July 2003.

Kinnear, Rory. 'Rory Kinnear talks about playing Hamlet'.
National Theatre, January 2011. Available online: http://www.

nationaltheatre.org.uk/video/rory-kinnear-talks-about-playing-hamlet (last accessed 10 September 2015).

Kordecki, Lesley and Koskinen, Karla. *Re-visioning Lear's Daughters: Testing Feminist Criticism and Theory*. London: Palgrave Macmillan, 2010.

Lahr, John. 'Curtain Raiser: Nicholas Hytner's theatrical golden age'. *New Yorker,* 23 April 2012.

Lahr, John. *Joy Ride: A Theatre Primer*. London: Bloomsbury, 2015.

Latham, Agnes, (ed.). *As You Like It*. London: Methuen, 1975.

Lawson, Mark. 'Phone-hacking: hold the main stage!'. *Guardian*, 1 July 2014.

Lean, Derek. Review of *Barefoot in the Park*. *The Western Morning News*, 14 May 1983.

Lennox, Patricia. Interview with Philip Bosco. In *North American Players of Shakespeare,* Michael W. Shurgot (ed.), 54–67. Newark, DE: University of Delaware Press, 2007.

Lester, Adrian. 'Adrian Lester on Henry V'. *Shakespeare on Stage*, Julian Curry (ed.), 117–42. London: Nick Hern, 2010.

Lindley, David, (ed.) *The Tempest*. Cambridge: Cambridge University Press, 2013.

Lindop, Grevel. Review of *Edward II*. *TLS*, 7 November, 1986.

Lindop, Grevel. Review of *The Country Wife*. *TLS*, 2 January 1987.

Lister, David. 'Adrian the First steps into battle as Henry V in theatrical landmark'. *Independent*, 16 August, 2002.

Loppert, Max. 'Handel in London', *Opera* (April 1985): 368–76.

Loppert, Max. 'People: 174 Nicholas Hytner', *Opera* (July 1991): 754–61.

Macaulay, Alastair. Review of *The Man of Mode*. *FT*, 7 February 2007.

Mack, Maynard. *King Lear in Our Time*. Los Angeles: University of California Press, 1972.

Malvern, Jack. 'Cue successor as Hytner bows out after a glorious run at National'. *The Times*, 11 April 2013.

Marsh, Cynthia (ed.). *As You Like It: Shakespeare in Production*. Cambridge: Cambridge University Press, 2004.

Marshall, Lyndsey. Interview, 'Emilia and Desdemona: Women in "Othello"'. *National Theatre Live*. Available online: http://ntlive.nationaltheatre.org.uk/productions/40168-othello (last accessed 10 September 2015).

Marshall, Lyndsey. Interview. National Theatre Platform: 'Rory Kinnear and Lyndsey Marshall in Conversation'. *National Theatre*. August 2013. Available online: http://www.nationaltheatre.org.uk/video/rory-kinnear-and-lyndsey-marshal-in-conversation (last accessed 10 September 2015).

Martin-Davis, Ashley. Interview. NT Education Workpack: *The Winter's Tale*. *National Theatre*. Available online: http://www.nationaltheatre.org.uk/sites/all/libraries/files/documents/winters_tale.pdf (last accessed 15 September 2015).

Mason, Paul. 'Timon of Athens: the Power of Money'. *Guardian*, 20 July 2012.

Merlin, Bella. *With the Rogue's Company*. London: Oberon, 2005.

Merwin, Ted. 'Review of *Twelfth Night*', *Theatre Journal* 51 (2) (1999): 191–2.

Miola, Robert. *The Comedy of Errors: Critical Essays*. London: Routledge, 2000.

Moss, Stephen. 'Othello and Iago are a bit cracked'. *Guardian*, 10 April 2013.

Nathan, David. Interview with Maria Friedman. *Applause Magazine*, March 1997.

Nightingale, Benedict. 'Some Recent Productions'. In *Lear from Study to Stage: Essays in Criticism*, James Ogden and Arthur Hawley Scouten (eds), 226–46. Cranbury: Associated University Presses, 1997.

Nightingale, Benedict. 'Student Drama: Talent and Temerity'. In *The University of Cambridge: An 800th Anniversary Portrait*, Peter Pagnamenta (ed.), 298–301. London: Third Millennium Publishing, 2009.

Nightingale, Benedict. 'The NT – stage of soapbox'. *The Times*, 9 February 2009.

Nuttall, A. D. *William Shakespeare: The Winter's Tale*. London: Edward Arnold, 1966.

O'Neill, Heather. 'Jealousy Will Get You Nowhere'. Interview with Alex Jennings. *Independent*, 16 May 2001.

O'Neill, Patrick. Review of *As You Like It*. *Daily Mail*, 10 January 1986.

O'Neill, Patrick. Review of *Edward II*. *Daily Mail*, 24 October, 1986.

Orgel, Stephen. 'Nobody's Perfect: Or Why Did the English Stage Take Boys for Women?', *South Atlantic Quarterly* 88 (1989): 7–29.

Pafford, J. H. P. (ed.). *The Winter's Tale*. London: Methuen, 1963.

Peter, John. 'Outside the Rules'. *Sunday Times*, 12 January 1986.

Peter, John. Review of *The Country Wife*. *Sunday Times*, 28 December 1986.

Peter, John. Review of *Don Carlos*. *Sunday Times*, 20 September 1987.

Platt, Norman. 'Justifying the Dunghill'. *Opera* (June 1989): 678–84.

Purves, Libby. 'The BBC has to detach itself from the rating mentality'. *The Times*, 7 March 2013.

Ratcliffe, Michael. 'Return to Arden'. *Observer*, 12 January 1986.

Ratcliffe, Michael. Review of *The Country Wife*. *Observer*, 21 December 1986.

Ratcliffe, Michael. Review of *Don Carlos*. *Observer*, 13 September 1987.

Rees, Jasper. 'A King for our Times'. *Telegraph*, 29 April, 2003.

Rees, Jasper. '*Much Ado About Nothing*: "We didn't sleep together, did we?"'. *Telegraph*, 12 December 2007.

Reynolds, Peter and Potter, Samantha. '*Henry IV Parts 1 and 2* Preparatory Workpack'. *NT: Learning: Teaching Resources*. Available online: http://d1wf8hd6ovssje.cloudfront.net/documents/henry_iv.pdf (last accessed 15 November 2015).

Reynolds, Peter and White, Lee '*Henry V*: Rehearsal Diaries'. *Stagework*. Available online: http://www.stagework.org.uk/webdav/harmonise@Page%252F@id=6016&Section%252F@id=29.html (last accessed 15 November 2015).

Ridley, Clifford A. 'Helen Hunt as Viola in *Twelfth Night*'. *philly.com*, 25 July 1998. Available online: http://articles.philly.com/1998-07-25/entertainment/25737408_1_twelfth-night-viola-duke-orsino (last accessed 18 September 2015).

Roberts, Peter. Review of *The Recruiting Officer*. *Herald Express*, 11 May 1981.

Rokison, Abigail. 'Laurence Olivier'. In *Gielgud, Olivier, Ashcroft, Dench: Great Shakespeareans Vol. XVI*, Russell Jackson (ed.), 61–109. London: Arden Bloomsbury, 2013.

Rokison, Abigail. *Shakespeare for Young People*, London: Arden Bloomsbury, 2013.

Romain, Michael. 'A Tragedy of Need, or a Kind of Everest'. *RSC Magazine* (Spring 1991): 10–12.

Rosenthal, Daniel. 'The man who needn't be king'. *The Times*, 21 May 2001.

Rosenthal, Daniel. *The National Theatre Story*. London: Oberon, 2013.

Rutter, Carol. 'Eel Pie and Ugly Sisters in *King Lear*'. In *Lear from Study to Stage: Essays in Criticism*, James Ogden and Arthur Hawley Scouten (eds), 172–225. Cranbury: Associated University Presses, 1997.

Rutter, Carol Chillington. 'Shakespeare Performances in England (and Wales), 2008', *Shakespeare Survey* 62 (2009): 349–85.

Rutter, Carol Chillington. 'Shakespeare Performances in England, 2010'. *Shakespeare Survey* 64 (2011): 340–77.

S.A.S. Review of *Murderer*. *Exeter Express and Echo*, 25 June 1981.

Schmidt, Michael. Review of *As You Like It*. *Kaleidoscope*. Broadcast on Radio 4, 10 January 1986, 9.45–10.15 p.m.

Schmidt, Michael. Review of *Don Carlos*. *Independent*, 14 September 1987.

Seddon, Joan. 'The gospel according to Hytner'. *Manchester Evening News*, 27 August 1987.

Self, David. Review of *The Country Wife*. *Kaleidoscope*. Broadcast on Radio 4, 22 December 1986, 9.45–10.15 p.m.

Shewey, Don. 'Gender Bending of Yore'. *The Advocate*, 1 September 1998, 51.

Shrimpton, Nicholas. 'Shakespeare Performances in London, Manchester and Stratford Upon Avon, 1985–6', *Shakespeare Survey* 40 (1987): 169–84.

Skinner, Claire. Interview. NT Education Workpack: *The Winter's Tale*. *National Theatre*. Available online: http://www.nationaltheatre.org.uk/sites/all/libraries/files/documents/winters_tale.pdf (last accessed 15 September 2015).

Sloan, John. *Authors in Context: Oscar Wilde*. Oxford: Oxford World Classics, 2009.

Smallwood, Robert. 'Introduction'. In *Players of Shakespeare 3*, edited by Russell Jackson and Robert Smallwood, 1–20. Cambridge: Cambridge University Press, 1994.

Spencer, Charles. Review of *The Revenger's Tragedy*. *Telegraph*, 6 June 2008.

Starza Smith, Daniel. 'Review of Shakespeare's *Hamlet* (directed by Sir Nicholas Hytner) at the Olivier Theatre, National Theatre, London, 20 November 2010', *Shakespeare* 7 (4) (2011): 471–3.

Stocks, Christopher. 'Directing Marlowe'. *Gay Life,* November 1986.

Tatspaugh, Patricia. *Shakespeare at Stratford: The Winter's Tale.* London: Arden, 2002.

Taylor, Paul. 'The Making of a Modern Timon'. *Independent*, 14 July 2012.

Teeman, Tim. 'Leading man', *The Times*, 12 May 2001.

The Independent, 'How to get children switched on to the drama of theatre'. *Independent*, 9 November 2002.

The Independent, 'National Theatre's incoming director promises cheap seats and new productions to explore edge of drama'. *Independent*, 24 January 2003.

Thomas, K. *Man and the Natural World: Changing Attitudes in England 1500–1800*. Harmondsworth: Penguin, 1984.

Thornber, Robin. Review of *As You Like It*. *Guardian*, 11 January 1986.

Thornber, Robin. Review of *Edward II*. *Guardian*, 25 October 1986.

Thornber, Robin. Review of *The Country Wife, Guardian*, 20 December 1986.

Thorpe, Vanessa. 'Bard is a mystery to our lost generation, warns arts boss'. *Observer*, 3 November 2002.

Thorpe, Vanessa. 'F*** you, says BBC as 50,000 rage at Spr*ng*r'. *The Observer*, 9 January 2005.

Tommasini, Anthony. 'For "Twelfth Night", A Daxophone, Tibetan Bowls and an Indian …'. *The New York Times*, 21 August 1998.

Vaughan, Alden T. and Vaughan, Virginia Mason. *Shakespeare's Caliban*. Cambridge: Cambridge University Press, 1993.

Vaughan, Virginia Mason. *The Tempest: Shakespeare in Performance*. Manchester: Manchester University Press, 2011.

Vieusseux, Annette. '*Much Ado About Nothing:* Rehearsal Diaries'. *Stagework*. Available online: http://www.stagework.org.uk/ stageworks/muchado/rehearsaldiaries.html (last accessed 15 November 2015).

Vinall, Olivia. Interview, 'Emilia and Desdemona: The Women in *Othello*'. *National Theatre Live*. Available online: http://ntlive. nationaltheatre.org.uk/productions/40168-othello (last accessed 10 September 2015).

Watts, Janet. 'A New Duke of Dark Corners'. *Observer*, 8 November 1987.

Weinstein, Philip M. 'An Interpretation of Pastoral in *The Winter's Tale*', *Shakespeare Quarterly* 22 (2) (1971): 97–109.

Wells, Stanley. 'The Once and Future King Lear'. In *The Division of the Kingdoms: Shakespeare's Two Versions of King Lear*, Gary Taylor and Michael Warren (eds), 1–22. Oxford: Oxford University Press, 1987.

Wells, Stanley. 'Shakespeare Performances in England', *Shakespeare Survey* 42 (1990): 129–48.

Wells, Stanley. 'General Introduction'. In *William Shakespeare: The Complete Works*, Stanley Wells, Gary Taylor, John Jowett and William Montgomery (eds), xv–xlii. Oxford: Oxford University Press, 2nd edn. 2005.

Wersocki Morris, Eve and Hytner, Molly. 'Sir Nicholas Hytner: "It's Time to Go"'. *Impact Magazine*, 27 January 2014. Available online: http://www.impactnottingham.com/2014/01/sir-nicholas-hytner-its-time-to-go/ (last accessed 10 September 2015).

White, Michael and Webster, Paul. 'Sante, Tony: Chirac's peace offering'. *Guardian*, 7 May 2003.

Wickham, Rupert. 'Henry V: Nationality and Race: French a Credible Opposition'. *Stagework*. Available online: http://www.stagework.org.uk/webdav/harmonise@Page%252F@id=6012&Document%252F@id=2507.html (last accessed 15 November 2015).

Williams, Holly. 'Rory Kinnear, national treasure'. *Independent*, 13 April 2013.

Wolf, Matt. 'No Thorns in Hytner's Hollywood'. *The Times*, 21 January 1997.

Yearling, Rebecca. 'Volpone on the Stage'. In *Volpone: A Critical Edition*, Matthew Steggle (ed.), 31–54. London: Bloomsbury Arden, 2011.

INDEX

69 Theatre Company 6, 7

Adams, Douglas 10
Adamson, Samuel 129
  Southwark Fair 1, 107
Addy, Mark: Dogberry (*Much Ado*) 137
Adelman, Janet 90
Akuwudike, Jude: Pistol (*Henry V*) 111
Alfano, Franco: *Leggenda di Sakuntala* 15
Allam, Roger: Duke (*Measure for Measure*) 39, 42–4, 47
Allen, Joan
  Elizabeth Proctor (*The Crucible*) 96
Allfree, Claire 131, 135, 143
Almeida Theatre 62–3
Anderson, Paul 60
Arden Shakespeare 70, 101
Arditti, Michael 10
arts funding 177–8
Ashcroft, Peggy: Beatrice (*Much Ado*) 134
Ashford, Rob (dir. *Macbeth*) 173
Ayckbourn, Alan: *Absurd Person Singular* 18
Ayliff, H. K. (dir. *Hamlet*) 140

BAFTA (British Academy Film and Television Award) 95
Bailey, Jonathan, Cassio (*Othello*) 163, 166
Baker, Sean, Angelo (*Measure for Measure*) 46
Banks, Anthony 176
Barber, John 19, 29, 35
Barbican Theatre 38, 56–7, 81, 173
Barnes, Peter: *The Ruling Class* 18

Barrit, Desmond 19, 49, 56–7
Barton, John (dir. *Measure for Measure*) 7, 46
Bassett, Kate 100, 109–10, 119, 123, 131, 137, 143
Beale, Simon Russell 6, 128, 130–1, 155
  Benedick (*Much Ado*) 131, 133–4, 136–8
  Subtle (*The Alchemist*) 6, 130
  Timon (*Timon of Athens*) 148–52, 156
Bean, Richard
  England People Very Nice 1–3, 107
  Great Britain 2–3, 107
  One Man Two Guvnors 3, 8, 107
Bell, Duncan
  Ariel (*The Tempest*) 57
  Orlando (*As You Like It*) 27–8, 32, 35
Bennett, Alan 3, 8, 64, 83, 97, 179
  Habit of Art, The 107
  History Boys, The 96, 107
  Hymn and *Cocktail Sticks* 107
  Lady in the Van, The 96–7
  Madness of George III, The 59, 83–4, 95, 155
  Madness of King George, The (film) 95–7
  People 107
  Wind in the Willows, The 8, 58, 64–5, 83–4, 95, 98
Betti, Ugo: *Queen and the Rebels* 11
Billington, Michael 19, 32, 39, 43, 45, 47–8, 51–2, 58, 61, 63–6, 74–5, 79–81, 98, 101, 105, 108, 120, 123–6, 130–3, 135,

137, 142, 148, 152,
156, 162–4, 169, 172
Birmingham Rep. 140
Blair, Tony 110, 144, 149
Blythe, Robert: Fluellen (*Henry V*)
115–17
Bouffes du Nord 148
Bosco, Philip: Malvolio (*Twelfth
Night*) 86, 93–5
Boublil, Alain and Schönberg,
Claude-Michel: *Miss
Saigon* 17, 52, 60–2,
65, 84–5, 119
Boucicault, Dion: *London
Assurance* 155
Bradbrook, Muriel 9
Bradley, David, Henry IV 125
Branagh, Kenneth
(dir. *Henry V* [film]) 114–15
Macbeth 173
Brandl, Alois 80
Brantley, Ben 94–5
British Broadcasting Corporation
(BBC) 2, 10
Britten, Benjamin
Peter Grimes 15
Turn of the Screw, The 15
Broadway 61, 65, 85, 92, 95, 181
Broadway Theatre, New York 61
Brook, Peter
dir. *King Lear* 71, 81
dir. *A Midsummer Night's
Dream* 22
dir. *Timon of Athens* 148
Brown, Georgina 99, 101–2, 128,
131, 143–5, 149, 160,
165
Burden, Suzanne: Celia (*As You
Like It*) 24
Burnside, Mike 62
Burton, William (dir. *The Tempest*)
50

Calder, David: Polonius (*Hamlet*)
144
Callow, Simon 172
Cambridge Corn Exchange 13–14
Cambridge Music Theatre 14
Cambridge University 5, 9–15, 19,
49, 61, 64, 83

Amateur Dramatic Club, The
(ADC) 10–13
Cambridge Footlights, The 10,
13–14, 18, 64
Cambridge University Opera
Society 14
European Theatre Group, The
10
Preston Society, The 11
Trinity Hall 5, 9, 11
Camden Festival 15
Campbell, Alastair 110
Canby, Vincent 93
Carpenter, Julie 136, 164
Cavendish, Dominic 153, 156, 169
Center Stage 96–7
Century Theatre 6–7
Romeo and Juliet 7
Chapman, Nigel 10
Charney, Maurice: *Shakespeare's
Villains* 77
Chichester Festival Theatre 19, 86
Chirac, Jacques 110
Christiansen, Rupert 179
Christopher, James 76, 81
Clapp, Susannah 99, 101–2, 105,
123–6, 130, 135, 143,
151, 164
Clare, Robert 70
Coe, Jonathan 96
Coleridge, Samuel Taylor 77
Coles, Joanna 87, 95
colour-blind/racial-blind casting
45–6, 85, 111
commedia dell'arte 5
Complicite: *Measure for Measure*
171
conspiracy 122
Conway, Lydia 59
Copley, John: *Aida* 15
Costa, Maddy 169, 172
Cottis, Nicholas 20
Courtenay, Tom 7, 20
Coveney, Michael 22, 29, 34–5,
40, 47, 53–5, 60, 63,
81, 99, 101, 103, 105
Coxon, Lucinda: *The Eternal Not*
176
Crane, Harvey 22
Cross, Beverley: *The Scarlet*

Pimpernel 19, 27, 32, 59, 61, 130
Crowley, Bob 59–60, 86–9
Cumberbatch, Benedict: Hamlet 173
Curry, Julian 114, 118

Daldry, Stephen 95, 105
  dir. *Billy Elliot* 105
Daniels, Phil 103
  Autolycus (*Winter's Tale*) 104
  Pompey (*Measure for Measure*) 45
Dench, Judi: Hermione and Perdita (*The Winter's Tale*) 7
Department for Culture, Media and Sport 178
Dessen, Alan C. 127
  Re-scripting Shakespeare 92
  'Teaching What's Not There' 93
Dexter, Sally: Regan (*King Lear*) 78
Dickson, Andrew 96
Disney 6
Dobson, Michael 99, 110, 119–20, 126
Dockery, Jo: Jeweller (*Timon of Athens*) 156
Donaldson, Ann 53
Donmar Warehouse 98, 140, 173
Donno, Elizabeth Story 87
Doran, Gregory
  dir. *Hamlet* 140
  dir. *Timon of Athens* 148
Dorfman, Lloyd 172
Downie, Penny: Chorus (*Henry* V) 111–12
Dunn, Tony 44, 63, 65
Dymkowski, Christine 50

Eastern Arts 14
Edwardes, Jane 101, 116, 120, 123, 126, 137–8
Edwards, Christopher 50, 57
Edwards, Lynette: Sempronia (*Timon of Athens*) 151, 156
Elliott, Marianne (dir. *All's Well*) 171–2, 176
Elliott, Michael 7
English National Opera (ENO) 15–16, 52, 59, 84, 97

Escolme, Bridget 142
Etherege, George: *The Man of Mode* 145
Evans, Lloyd 149, 151
Evening Standard British Film Awards 95
Evening Standard Theatre Awards 16, 61, 157, 178
Eyre, Richard 37, 60–1, 64, 75, 179
  Artistic Director of the NT 5, 37, 60

Farquhar, George: *The Recruiting Officer* 18, 20, 83–4, 179
Fay, Stephen 83–4
Festival Theatre, Stratford Ontario 86
Fielding, David 19, 66
Fielding, Susannah: Hero (*Much Ado*) 136
Fiennes, Ralph: Edmund (*King Lear*) 79
film 18, 86, 90, 95–8, 105, 108–10, 114 *see also* individual titles
Findlay, Deborah 156
  Paulina (*The Winter's Tale*) 104, 156
  Flavia (*Timon of Athens*) 150, 155
First Folio (Shakespeare) 48, 53, 69–71, 117, 145, 153
  see also individual plays
Foakes, R. A. 70, 80
Forbes, Elizabeth 14
Ford-Davies, Oliver, Leonato (*Much Ado*) 137
Foss, Roger 99, 101, 119, 125
Frankcom, Sarah (dir. *Hamlet*) 140
Friedman, Maria: Hayyah (*Ghetto*) 59

Gambon, Michael 98
  Falstaff (*Henry IV Parts 1 and 2*) 123–5
Gardner, Lyn 19
Garrick, David: *The Tempest* (adpt.) 50

Gibbons, Brian 41
Gielgud, John 55
    Benedick (*Much Ado*) 134
    Sir Politic Would-be (*Volpone*)
        63
Glendinning, Robert: *Mumbo
        Jumbo* 21–2, 40
Glyndebourne 61
Goldoni, Carlo: *The Servant of
        Two Masters* 8
Goodbody, Buzz (dir. *As You Like
        It*) 30
Gore-Langton, Robert 105
Gorky, Maxim: *Philistines* 145
Graham, Martha 54
Grahame, Kenneth 64
    Wind in the Willows, The 8, 64
Grand Théâtre de Genève 61
Grandage, Michael (dir. *Hamlet*)
        140
Gray, Dominic 48, 52–3
Gross, John 61, 65, 100–1, 104,
        119

Hall, Peter
    Artistic Director of the NT 5
    dir. *Hamlet* 7
    dir. *Volpone* 63
Hamer, Cate: Celia (*Volpone*) 62–3
Handel 16
    Giulio Cesare 16
    Xerxes 15–16, 84
Hands, Terry
    Artistic Director of the RSC
        38, 58
    dir. *Henry V* 7
    dir. *The Merry Wives of Windsor*
        5–6
Hare, David: *Stuff Happens* 1, 107
Hart, Christopher 133, 143–5, 164
Hately, Tim 149, 151–2
Hawksford, Daniel: Claudio (*Much
        Ado*) 136
Hawthorne, Nigel 179
Heap, Carl 175
Hemming, Sarah 131, 133
Henderson, Mark 19, 40, 52–3
Henry, Lenny 171
Her Majesty's Theatre, London 19

Hiddleston, Tom: Coriolanus 173
Higgins, Charlotte 169, 177
Higgins, Claire: Gertrude (*Hamlet*)
        142–3
Hiley, Jim 42, 45, 60
Hirschhorn, Clive 49, 54–5, 57,
        62, 81
Hitchings, Henry 144, 164–6
Hodge, John: *Collaborators* 107
Hogg, Christopher 1
Holland, Peter 9, 54, 57, 67–70,
        74, 76–7, 79
Horton, Priscilla: Cordelia (*King
        Lear*) 80
Howard, Alan, (*Henry V*) 7
Hoyle, Martin 42, 45, 52–5
Hubbard, Mike 31
Hulme, Alan 32, 35
Hunt, Helen: Viola (*Twelfth Night*)
        86, 93
Hurren, Kenneth 60, 65, 97
Hytner, Nicholas
    Artistic Director of the NT 1,
        3, 5, 60, 82, 104–5,
        107–8, 119, 157, 166,
        169–72,174, 177
    associate director, Lincoln Center
        85
    associate director, Manchester
        Royal Exchange 20–1,
        25
    associate director, NT 37
    awards 16, 61, 85, 95, 157,
        178–9
    films
        Center Stage, The 96–7
        Crucible 96–7
        History Boys, The 96
        Lady in the Van, The 96–7
        Madness of King George, The
            95–7
        Object of My Affection, The
            86, 90, 96–8
    knighthood 179
    musicals
        Alice 19
        Carousel 59, 83–6, 95, 177
        Ghetto 17, 37, 58–61, 64–5,
            79, 83

Miss Saigon 17, 52, 60–2, 65,
       84–5, 119
Threepenny Opera, The 13
operas
   Aida 15
   Coronation of Poppaea, The 14
   Cunning Little Vixen, The 97
   Don Giovanni 97
   Force of Destiny, The 97
   Giulio Cesare 16
   *King Goes Forth to France,
       The* 16
   King Priam 15
   Knot Garden, The 16
   La Clemenza di Tito 61
   Leggenda di Sakuntala 15
   Magic Flute The 16, 52, 59
   Maria Tudor 15
   *Marriage of Figaro, The (Le
       Nozze di Figaro)* 15, 61
   Peter Grimes 15
   Queen of Spades, The 15
   Rienzi 15–16
   *Rise and Fall of the City of
       Mahagonny, The* 10, 13
   Turn of the Screw, The 15
   Xerxes 15–16, 84
pantomimes
   Aladdin 18
plays
   Absurd Person Singular 18
   As You Like It 3, 21–36, 40,
       92, 129
      casting 25, 28
      costume 30, 34
      Court, The 25, 29–31, 34–5
      Forest of Arden, The 26,
          29–32, 34
      cuts 23–4, 26
      lighting
      music 26–7, 35, 40, 92
      rehearsals 24–5, 27–8
      set design 21, 25–7, 29–35
      textual changes 23–4, 92
   Alchemist, The 6, 63, 128–30,
       155
   Barefoot in the Park 18
   Chaste Maid in Cheapside, A
       12–13

Chips with Everything 19
Collaborators 107
Cressida 98
Cripple of Inishmaan, The 83
Country Wife, The 21–3, 40,
       59, 62, 130
Don Carlos 21–2, 35, 40,
       60, 62
Edward II 20–3, 40, 62, 129
England People Very Nice
       1–3, 107
Great Britain 2–3, 107
Habit of Art, The 107
Hamlet 25, 88, 107, 129,
       139–47
   casting 145
   rehearsals 144
   set design 147
   textual changes 146–7
Hard Problem, The 107
Henry IV Parts 1 and 2 56,
       107, 119–29, 131, 138,
       148
   casting 56, 126
   cuts 127
   ending 124
   lighting 122
   music 122
   rehearsals 122, 125, 127
   set design 120–2
   textual changes 127–8
Henry V 25, 88, 107–21, 123,
       129, 131, 138, 141,
       148, 155, 157, 160,
       169, 172
   casting 84–5, 108, 110–11
   cuts 117
   ending 113
   Harfleur 112, 113, 116
   music 115
   rehearsals 108, 116, 118–19
   set design 108–9, 121
   use of *Henry IV* 114
   textual changes 116–17
His Dark Materials 107
History Boys, The 96, 107
Hymn and *Cocktail Sticks* 107
*Importance of Being Earnest,
       The* 97–8

Jumpers 19–22, 27, 40
King Lear 9, 39, 56, 58, 65,
        66–82
    casting 56, 79–80, 84
    costumes 66
    cuts 70–1
    mock trial 69–71
    rehearsals 70–1
    set design 66–9, 71–2
    storm 67–8
    use of Folio text 69–71
Lady in the Van, The 96–7
London Assurance 155
Love's Labour's Lost 11–12, 63
    cuts 12, 63
    design 11
Madness of George III, The 59,
        83–4, 95, 155
Major Barbara 17, 176
Man of Mode, The 145
Measure for Measure 9, 17,
        38–47, 57–9, 61–2, 66,
        84–5, 87, 92, 94, 102,
        113, 120, 129–30, 158
    casting 44–6, 84–5
    costumes 17, 39
    ending 46–7, 57, 102, 113
    lighting 40
    music 40
    set design 17, 39–40, 42–4
Mother Clapp's Molly House
        97, 105
Mrs Warren's Profession 12
Much Ado About Nothing 107,
        128–9, 131–9, 180
    casting 133–4, 137
    cuts 139
    ending 138, 180
    music 132–3, 139
    rehearsals 132, 136, 138–9
    set design 131–2
Mumbo Jumbo 21–2, 40
Murderer 18
One Man Two Guvnors 3, 8, 107
Orpheus Descending 98
Othello 3, 25, 88, 107, 129,
        139, 147, 157–67
    casting 157
    cuts 165

Cyprus 159–60, 161, 162
    ending 164
    music 160
    rehearsals 158
    set design 157–8, 163–4
    textual changes 165
    Venice 157
People 107
Phèdre 172
Rafta, Rafta 1, 107
Recruiting Officer, The 18, 20,
        83–4, 179
Ruling Class, The 18
Scarlet Pimpernel, The 19, 27,
        32, 59, 61, 130
Southwark Fair 1, 107
Stuff Happens 1, 107
Tempest, The 38–9, 45, 47–59,
        61, 66–7, 75, 87, 94,
        102, 113, 120, 129,
        158
    banquet 53
    casting 48
    ending 56–7, 102, 113
    lighting 50, 52–3
    masque 53–4
    music 50, 52–4
    set design 51–2
    storm 50–1
Timon of Athens 25, 63, 88,
        107, 129, 139, 147–57
    casting 156
    cuts 63, 153–5
    rehearsals 148, 153, 155
    set design 149, 151–2
    textual changes 153–5
Tom Jones 18
Travelling Light 107
Twelfth Night 45, 52, 57, 85–95,
        98, 113, 129, 132, 135,
        171, 175, 177
    casting 93
    costumes 89, 92
    cuts 92–3
    ending 91, 113
    lighting 93
    music 92–3
    set design 86–9, 92–3
    textual changes 92–3

Volpone 62, 64, 128–9, 132
Wind in the Willows, The 8, 58,
    64–5, 83–4, 95, 98
Winter's Tale, The 57, 98–105
    Bohemia 99, 100–1
    casting 103
    ending 101–3, 113
    set design 99, 101
    sexuality 98
    'Stand and Unfold Yourself'
        122

International Shakespeare
    Conference 47
Isherwood, Charles 89

Jackson, Barry (dir. *Hamlet*) 140
Jacobi, Derek: King Lear 173
Janáček: *The Cunning Little Vixen*
    97
Jarman, Chris 171
Jennings, Alex 19, 59, 97, 103, 130
    Alan Bennett (*Lady in the Van*) 97
    Ernest (*The Importance of Being
        Earnest*) 97
    Face (*The Alchemist*) 6, 130
    Kittel (*Ghetto*) 59
    Leontes (*Winter's Tale*) 99,
        103–4
    Lucio (*Measure for Measure*) 44
Jones, Dan 49–51, 55, 57
Jones, Griff Rhys 10, 64
Jones, James Earl: Benedick (*Much
    Ado*) 134
Jongh, Nicholas de 42, 44, 99,
    113, 124, 134
Jonson, Ben 64, 128–30
    First Folio 128
    Alchemist, The 6, 63, 128–30,
        155
        Face 6
        Sir Epicure Mammon 6
        Subtle 6
    Volpone 62, 64, 128–9, 132
    sub-plot 63–4
        Bonario 62
        Celia 62–3
        Corbaccio 62
        Corvino 62

Mosca 62
    Sir Politic Would-Be 63–4
    Volpone 62
    Voltore 62
Joseph, Patterson
    Oswald (*King Lear*) 84
    Worthy (*The Recruiting Officer*)
        84
Jowett, John 147
Jung, Carl 48, 51–2, 72, 87

Kae-Kazim, Hakeem: Claudio
    (*Measure for Measure*)
    46, 84
Kaleidoscope 22
Kane, John, Caliban (*The Tempest*)
    48–9
Keightley, Chris 10
Kellaway, Kate 49–50, 53
Kelly, Jude 169
Kemp, Peter 39, 44, 52, 57
Kennedy, Douglas 61
Kent Opera 15
Kerr Scott, Linda
    Djigan (*Ghetto*) 59, 79
    Fool (*King Lear*) 79–81
Khan-Din, Ayub: *Rafta, Rafta* 1,
    107
King-Farlow, Alice 173, 175, 177
Kingsley, Louise 79, 81
Kingston, Alex: Cordelia (*King
    Lear*) 75, 78
Kinnear, Rory 157–60
    Hamlet 141, 145–6, 166
    Iago (*Othello*) 157, 161, 163,
        165–6
    Pytor (*Philistines*) 145
    Sir Fopling Flutter (*The Man of
        Mode*) 145
    Vincentio (*The Revenger's
        Tragedy*) 145
Koenig, Rhoda 49, 52, 98
Kohler, Estelle
    Goneril (*King Lear*) 76
    Isabella (*Measure for Measure*)
        46
Kordecki, Lesley 70
Kwei-Armah, Kwame: *Elmina's
    Kitchen* 1

Lahr, John 155, 169, 180
Lan, David 59
Laurenson, James
    Ghost (*Hamlet*) 144
    Player King (*Hamlet*) 141
Lawson, Dennis, Mosca (*Volpone*)
        62
Layden, Penny: Painter (*Timon of
        Athens*) 156
Leeds Playhouse 18, 24
Le Prevost, Nicholas: Benedick
        (*Much Ado*) 134
Lecoq, Jacques 171
Lennox, Patricia 86, 95
Lesslie, Michael: *Prince of
        Denmark* 176
Lester, Adrian
    Henry V 84–5, 108, 110–14,
        116, 118
    Othello 157, 159, 160–1, 163–5
Letts, Quentin 134, 145
Lincoln Center, New York 85–6,
        95
    Vivian Beaumont Theatre 86–7
Lindley, David 53
Lindop, Grevel 22
Lister, David 111, 143–5
Llewellyn, Olivia: Flaminia (*Timon
        of Athens*) 156
London Critics' Circle Theatre
        Awards 61
London Theatre Company 181
Loppert, Max 16–17
Lough, Robin (dir. *King Lear*) 173
Lyric Hammersmith 21

Macaulay, Alastair 65, 101, 103,
        128
Macfadyen, Matthew: Hal (*Henry
        IV Parts 1 and 2*)
        123–5
Mack, Maynard 77
Macready, Charles (dir. *King Lear*)
        80
Malahide, Patrick 143
Manchester Grammar School 7–9
Manchester High School 7
Manchester International Festival
        173

Manchester Opera House 5, 6
Manchester Palace Theatre 5, 6
Manchester Royal Exchange 3, 17,
        19–38, 40, 92, 140
Manchester University Theatre 6
Marlowe, Christopher 23, 64
    Edward II 20–3, 40, 62, 129
Marmion, Patrick 45
Marshall, Lyndsey: Emilia
        (*Othello*) 160–1, 166
Martin-Davies, Ashley 99
Mason, Brewster: Falstaff (*The
        Merry Wives of
        Windsor*) 6
Mason, Paul 148
masque 47, 53–4, 132, 150
Maxwell, James 21
    Prospero (*The Tempest*) 7, 21
    The Grand Inquisitor (*Don
        Carlos*) 21
McAfee, Annalena 63
McBurney, Simon (dir. *Measure for
        Measure*) 171
McDiarmid, Ian 62
    Volpone 62
McDonagh, Martin: *The Cripple of
        Inishmaan* 83
McGinn, Caroline 143, 145
McGrath, Rory, Mulville, Jimmy
        and Fincham, Peter:
        Aladdin 18
McKenzie, Alastair 20
McTeer, Janet: Rosalind (*As You
        Like It*) 24–5, 28–9, 35
Mendes, Sam 95, 104–5
    dir. *American Beauty* 105
    dir. *King Lear* 171
Merlin, Bella 122, 127
Middleton, Thomas
    Chaste Maid in Cheapside, A
        12–13
    Revenger's Tragedy, The 145
    Timon of Athens 147, 148
Miller, Arthur: *The Crucible* 96–7
Miller, Carl 67, 73
Miller, Jonathan (dir. *The Tempest*)
        48
Miller, Maria 178
Miller, Paul (dir. *Hamlet*) 140

Milne, A. A.: *Toad of Toad Hall* 8, 64
Mirren, Helen 98, 172
Mitchell, Iain 19
Monge, Julio: Antonio (*Twelfth Night*) 90
Monteverdi: *The Coronation of Poppaea* 14
Morley, Sheridan 47, 55, 58–60, 64, 98–9, 101, 120
Morrison, Campbell: Stephano (*The Tempest*) 49
Morrison, John: *Tom Jones* 18
Mortimer, Vicki 132
Mountford, Fiona 149, 156–7
Mozart 23
    Don Giovanni 97
    La Clemenza di Tito 61
    Magic Flute, The 16, 52, 59
    Marriage of Figaro, The (*Le Nozze di Figaro*) 15, 61
Msamati, Lucian 171
Mulville, Jimmy 10, 18
Murphy, Siobhan 164–6
Murray, Braham 6, 7
Murray, Brian: Sir Toby Belch (*Twelfth Night*) 91, 94
musicals 2, 13, 19, 23, 38, 58, 60–1, 83–5, 181 *see also* individual titles

Napier, John 61
Nathan, John 59, 110, 138
National Portrait Gallery 110
National Theatre (NT) 1–3, 5, 8, 37–8, 56, 58–61, 63–4, 82–4, 95, 98–105, 107–67, 169–81
    Clore Learning Centre 174, 176
    Cottesloe Theatre 171, 175–6
    Dorfman Theatre 174
    John Lyon Education Studio 174
    Lyttleton Theatre 2, 83, 105, 177
    Memorandum and Articles of Association 3, 170
    National Theatre Studio 14, 174
    NT Education/ Learning 171, 173–7
    NT Live 105, 170, 172–3

Olivier Theatre 3, 38, 58, 65, 83, 98, 104, 109, 121, 131, 148, 171–2, 174, 176
    'Primary Classics' 175
    'Primary Theatre for Key Stage 2' 175
    schools' streaming 173
    Shed, The (Temporary Theatre) 171, 175
    Sunday opening 170
National Youth Theatre 176
Negga, Ruth, Ophelia (*Hamlet*) 144
News of the World, The 2
New Sussex Opera 15
Nightingale, Benedict 11, 65, 67, 74–7, 81, 99, 116–17, 123, 128, 130–1, 138, 170, 172
Noble, Adrian
    dir. *As You Like It* 32
    dir. *The Winter's Tale* 100
Noble, Cecilia: Hostess and Queen of France (*Henry V*) 111
Norman, Neil 143
Normington, John: Antipholus of Syracuse (*The Comedy of Errors*) 5
Northcott Theatre, Exeter 18, 24, 62
Nunn, Trevor
    Artistic Director of the NT 5, 60, 104–5, 170
    dir. *Timon of Athens* 148, 152
    dir. *The Winter's Tale* 7, 100
Nuttall, A. D. 100

Object of My Affection, The 86, 90, 96–8
Old Vic Theatre 30, 134
Olivier, Laurence 108–10, 126
    dir. *Henry V* (film) 108–10, 114–15, 117
    Justice Shallow and Hotspur (*Henry IV Parts 1 and 2*) 126
Olivier awards 2, 16, 61, 85, 178
O'Neil, Patrick 35

opera 2–3, 13–23, 26, 35, 42–3,
        52, 54, 58, 61, 83, 97,
        158 *see also* individual
        titles
Opera Magazine 14, 16–17
Orgel, Stephen 90
Osborne, Charles 42, 46
*Oxford Complete Works of
        Shakespeare* 69

Pacini, Giovanni: *Maria Tudor* 15
Pafford, J. H. P. 101
Paris Opera 16
Paton, Maureen 52–3, 60
Peacock, Trevor: Verges (*Much
        Ado*) 137
Pennington, Michael: *Timon of
        Athens* 148
Pentonville prison 44
Peter, John 22, 29, 35, 43–4,
        103–4, 113–16
Platt, Norman 15
Players of Shakespeare 44
Portman, Rachel 132
Potter, Samantha 122, 127
Pountney, David 15
    Madam Butterfly 15
Power, Ben 155, 175
Poyser, Daniel 171
Public Broadcasting Service (PBS)
        95
Puccini: *Madam Butterfly* 15, 60
Pullan, David, Froth (*Measure for
        Measure*) 45
Pullen, Melanie Clark, Perdita
        (*Winter's Tale*) 101
Pullman, Philip 107
Purves, Libby 146, 157, 172

Quinn, Michael 67, 75, 78–9

Racine: *Phèdre* 172
Raistrick, George: Elbow (*Measure
        for Measure*) 45
Ratcliffe, Michael 29–30, 48, 51,
        55, 57, 61
Ravenhill, Mark: *Mother Clapp's
        Molly House* 97, 105
Rebellato, Dan 175

Redgrave, Vanessa: Beatrice (*Much
        Ado*) 134
Renaissance Theatre Company 80
Reynolds, Peter 113, 118–19
Richard Rodgers Estate 84
Richards, I. A. 12
Richardson, Ian 5–6
    Angelo (*Measure for Measure*) 7
    Antipholus of Ephesus (*The
        Comedy of Errors*) 5
    Ford (*The Merry Wives of
        Windsor*) 5–6
    Sir Epicure Mammon (*The
        Alchemist*) 6
Ridley, Clifford A. 94
Rissik, Andrew 44
Roache, Linus: Edgar (*King Lear*)
        79
Rodgers, Richard and
        Hammerstein II, Oscar:
        Carousel 59, 83–6, 95,
        177
Rodway, Norman: Gloucester
        (*King Lear*) 79
Rosenthal, Daniel 59, 61, 84, 117
Rourke, Josie (dir. *Coriolanus*) 173
Rowe, Clive: Mr Snow (*Carousel*)
        84–5, 177
Rowe, Nicholas 164
Royal Ballet 150
Royal Opera House 16
Royal Shakespeare Company (RSC)
        5, 7, 9, 11, 17, 32,
        37–59, 65–82, 87, 120,
        134, 140, 158
    RSC Live Schools' Broadcasts 173
Royal Shakespeare Theatre (RST)
        5, 7, 38, 66
Rudd, Paul: Orsino (*Twelfth Night*)
        86, 89, 93–4
Rutherford, Malcolm 72–3, 78
Rutter, Carol Chillington 67,
        136–7, 142

Sallinen, Aulis: *The King Goes
        Forth to France* 16
Sampson, Nick 155–6
Sams, Jeremy 19, 26–7, 40, 52–3,
        58, 64

Scarborough, Adrian
    Poins (*Henry IV Parts 1 and 2*)
        126
    Silence (*Henry IV Part 2*) 126
Schiller, Friedrich 23
    Don Carlos 21–2, 35, 40, 60, 62
Schmidt, Michael 21, 29, 32, 35
Scofield, Paul
    Judge Thomas Daforth (*The
        Crucible*) 96
    Volpone 63
Scott, Richard and Phillips,
        Anthony: *Alice* 19
Scottish Opera 15
Sedgwick, Kyra: Olivia (*Twelfth
        Night*) 86, 93–4
Segal, Victoria 120
Seymour, Di 19, 25–27, 29–32, 34
Shaffer, Anthony: *Murderer* 18
Shaftesbury Theatre, London 85
Shakespeare, William 3
    cutting Shakespeare 12, 23–4,
        26, 50, 63, 70–1, 92–3,
        115, 117, 126–7, 129,
        139, 153–5, 165, 180
    eclectic productions 23, 62, 89,
        99, 120, 122, 129, 180
    modern-dress productions 23,
        66, 88, 100–1, 108,
        120, 129, 140, 149,
        157, 163–4
    plays
        All's Well That Ends Well
            171–3, 176
        As You Like It 3, 21–36, 40,
            92, 129, 155
            characters
                Adam 30
                Amiens 26
                Celia 22, 24, 30, 34
                Charles the Wrestler 30
                Duke Frederick 25, 30, 35
                Duke Senior 29–31
                Orlando 27–8, 30, 32
                Rosalind 22, 24–5,
                    28–30, 34
                Touchstone 22
        Comedy of Errors, The 5, 171,
            173

Coriolanus 154–5, 173
Hamlet 7, 25, 88, 107, 129,
        139–47
    characters
        Claudius 140–5
        Fortinbras 140–1, 143
        Gertrude 142–3, 146
        Guildenstern 145
        Hamlet 48, 140–3, 145–7
        Horatio 142–3, 145
        Laertes 141–2, 144
        Ophelia 140–2, 144–6
        Osric 143–4
        Polonius 140, 144
        Rosencrantz 145
        The Ghost 142–4, 146–7
    First Quarto 145
    Folio 145
    Second Quarto 145
Henry IV Parts 1 and 2 8, 56,
        107, 114, 119–29, 131,
        138, 148
    characters
        Blunt 123
        Douglas 127
        Falstaff 114, 123–8
        Hal 114, 123–8
        Hotspur 123, 125–7
        King Henry IV 124–5
        Justice Shallow 56, 126
        Mistress Quickly 8
        Poins 124, 126–7
        Prince John (Lancaster)
            127
        Silence 125
        Vernon 127
        Worcester 127
Henry V 7, 25, 85, 88,
        107–21, 123, 129, 131,
        138, 141, 148, 155,
        157, 160, 169, 172
    characters
        Alice 113, 117
        Archbishop of Canterbury
            110, 112, 117
        Bardolph 112, 114, 116
        Chorus 109, 111–13
        Exeter 116
        Falstaff 114

Fluellen 115–17
Grandpré 117
Henry 7, 84–5, 108–19,
    165
Mountjoy 116
Nym 112
Pistol 111–12, 117
Princess Katherine
    112–13, 117
Rambures 117
The Dauphin 110
The Hostess 111, 114
The Queen of France 111
Westmoreland 111
Williams 114–15
Folio 117
King Lear 9, 39, 56, 58, 65,
    66–82
characters
    Albany 67, 69, 72, 75
    Burgundy 78
    Cordelia 69, 72–3, 75,
        78–80
    Cornwall 71–2, 75, 78
    Edgar 69, 77, 79
    Edmund 67, 77, 79, 138
    Fool 67, 77, 79–81
    France 78
    Gloucester 69, 71–2, 76–9
    Goneril 70, 74–8, 80
    Kent 69, 72–3, 77, 79
    Lear 39, 56, 67–82
    Regan 71, 74–8
Folio 69–71
Quarto 69–71
Love's Labour's Lost 11–12,
    63
Measure for Measure 7, 9, 17,
    38–47, 57–9, 61–2, 66,
    84–5, 87, 92, 94, 102,
    113, 120, 129–30, 158,
    171
characters
    Angelo 7, 39–40, 43,
        45–6
    Claudio 45–6, 84
    Elbow 45
    Escalus 39, 45
    Froth 45

Isabella 42–3, 45–7, 84–5,
    102
Lucio 44
Pompey 45
The Duke 39–44, 46–7,
    102
Merry Wives of Windsor, The
    5–6, 131
characters
    Falstaff 6
    Master Ford 5–6
Midsummer Night's Dream, A
    22, 88, 155, 175
Much Ado About Nothing
    107, 128–9, 131–9,
    180
characters
    Beatrice 131, 133–6, 180
    Benedick 131–6, 138, 180
    Claudio 132–8
    Dogberry 137
    Don John 137–8
    Don Pedro 132, 135
    Friar Francis 133
    Hero 133–7
    Leonato 135, 137
    Margaret 135
    Ursula 135
    Verges 137
    The Watch 137
Othello 3, 25, 88, 107, 129,
    138–9, 147, 157–67
characters
    Brabantio 158
    Cassio 158, 160–3, 165–6
    Desdemona 158–62,
        164–6
    Emilia 160–2, 166
    Iago 157–61, 163–6
    Othello 18, 157–66
    Roderigo 158
Pericles 175
Romeo and Juliet 7, 8, 171,
    175
characters
    Juliet 8
    Nurse 8
    Samson 8
Tempest, The 7, 10, 38–9, 45,

47–59, 61, 66–7, 75,
87–8, 94, 102, 113,
120, 129, 158
characters
Alonso 53
Antonio 57, 102
Ariel 10, 50, 52–4
Caliban 48–49, 51–4, 57
Ceres 54
Gonzalo 53
Iris 54
Juno 54
Miranda 48–9, 56
Prospero 7, 10, 21, 39,
47–51, 53–5, 57, 74,
102, 126
Stephano 10, 49
Trinculo 10, 49
Timon of Athens 25, 63, 88,
107, 129, 139, 147–57
characters
Alcibiades 149, 153–5
Flaminius (Flaminia)
155–6
Flavius (Flavia) 155
Jeweller 150, 156
Lucilius 155
Lucullus 151
Painter 150, 156
Poet 150
Sempronius (Sempronia)
151
The Senator (Lepidus) 151
Timon 147–53, 155–6
Ventidius 151
❧ *Twelfth Night* 45, 52, 57,
85–95, 98, 113, 129,
132, 135, 171, 175, 177
characters
Antonio 90–1
Feste 91
Malvolio 86, 89, 91,
93–4
Maria 91, 93
Olivia 86–8, 90–1, 93–4
Orsino 86–91, 93–4
Sebastian 87–91
Sir Andrew Aguecheek
87, 89, 91, 94, 135

Toby Belch 89, 91, 94
Viola 86, 89–91, 93
Winter's Tale, The 7, 57,
98–105
characters
Archidamus 102
Autolycus 99, 100–1,
104
Camillo 102
Florizel 99–101
Hermione 7, 102–4
Leontes 99, 101–4
Mamillius 102–3
Old Shepherd 103
Paulina 102, 104, 156
Perdita 7, 99–104
Polixenes 102–4
Time 102–3
Sonnet 12 102–3
Shakespeare Memorial Theatre,
The 134
Shakespeare Schools Festival
177
Shakespeare Survey 120
Shaughnessy, Charles 14
Shaw, G. B.
Major Barbara 17, 176
Mrs Warren's Profession 12
Shaw, Jonathan 159, 161–3
Sheffield Crucible Theatre 140
Shenton, Mark 163–4, 166
Sheppard, E. H. 65
Shewey, Don 90
Shorter, Eric 42, 52, 54
Shrapnel, John: Angelo (*Measure
for Measure*) 46
Shrimpton, Nicholas 25, 57, 73–4,
79
Shulman, Milton 43, 49
Shuttleworth, Ian 143, 149, 153,
166
Sierz, Aleks 119
Simon, Josette: Isabella (*Measure
for Measure*) 43, 45–7,
84–5
Simon, Neil: *Barefoot in the Park*
18
Singhateh, Faz: Westmoreland
(*Henry V*) 111

Skinner, Claire: Hermione (*The Winter's Tale*) 102, 104
Smallwood, Robert 41, 45
Smedley, Richard 114
Smith, Maggie
  Lady Bracknell (*The Importance of Being Earnest*) 97
  Miss Shepherd (*The Lady in the Van*) 97
Sobol, Joshua: *Ghetto* 17, 37, 58–61, 64–5, 79, 83
Spencer, Charles 55, 60, 63, 67, 74, 77–8, 81, 99, 100–1, 105, 110–11, 119, 121, 125, 128, 130, 135, 145, 164, 166
Stageworks 118
Starr, Nick 172, 178–9, 181
Stear, Rick: Sebastian (*Twelfth Night*) 90
Stoppard, Tom
  Hard Problem, The 107
  Jumpers 19–22, 27, 40
Storey, Graham 9
Suchet, David: Timon of Athens 148
Szalwinska, Maxie 152, 156

Taylor, Gary 109
Taylor, Paul 60, 62–4, 101, 113, 121, 130–1, 133, 135, 149, 156–8
Tchaikovsky: *The Queen of Spades* 15
Tesori, Jeanine 92
Thames Television 14
Thomas, Richard and Lee, Stewart: *Jerry Springer the Opera* 1, 2
Thompson, Emma 80
Thompson, Mark 19, 22, 39–40, 44, 62, 65–6, 121, 129
Thornber, Robin 22, 29, 35
Thorpe, Vanessa 174
Till, Nicholas 14
Tinker, Jack 42, 46, 52–3
Tippett, Michael
  *King Priam*15
  Knot Garden, The 16

Tommasini, Anthony 92
Tony Awards 61
Travelex scheme (NT) 105, 108, 121, 170, 172
Troughton, David: Kent (*King Lear*) 79
Truss, Lynne 65
Turner, Lyndsey (dir. *Hamlet*) 173

Varsity 10, 12–13
Vaughan, Alden T. 49
Vaughan, Virginia Mason 49
Verdi: *The Force of Destiny* 97
verse speaking 28–9, 122–3, 165
Vieusseux, Annette 136
Vinall, Olivia: Desdemona (*Othello*) 166

Wadham, Julian 19, 103
Wagner: *Rienzi* 15–16
Walker, Tim 139, 158, 164–6
Walter, Harriet: Beatrice (*Much Ado*) 134
Walters, Julie 20
Wanamaker, Zoë: Beatrice (*Much Ado*) 133–7, 139
Warchus, Matthew (dir. *Winter's Tale*) 100
Wardle, Irving 44
Warner, David: Hamlet 7
Warren, Marc, Bonario (*Volpone*) 62
Watson, Edward 150
Weill, Kurt and Brecht, Bertold
  Rise and Fall of the City of Mahagonny, The 10, 13
  Threepenny Opera, The 13
Weinstein, Philip M. 100
Wells, Stanley 51, 70
Wesker, Arnold: *Chips with Everything* 19
West End (London) 19, 60, 95
Wexford Festival Opera 15
White, Lee 113, 118, 119
Wilde, Oscar: *The Importance of Being Earnest* 97–8
Williams, Clifford 5
  dir. *As You Like It* 30
  dir. *The Comedy of Errors* 5

Williams, Hugo 63
Williams Tennesee: *Orpheus Descending* 98
Woddis, Carol 124, 128
Wolf, Matt 44, 63, 101, 157, 164
Wood, John 39, 66, 126
    Justice Shallow *(Henry IV Part 2)* 56, 126
    King Lear *(King Lear)* 39, 56, 66, 68, 70, 72–6, 79, 81, 126
    Prospero *(The Tempest)* 39, 47–9, 55–7, 74, 126
Woodall, Andrew, Don John *(Much Ado)* 138
Woodvine, John: Gens *(Ghetto)* 59

Wrede, Caspar 7
Wright, Max: Sir Andrew Aguecheek *(Twelfth Night)* 94
Wright, Nicholas
    Cressida 98
    His Dark Materials 107
    Travelling Light 107
Wycherley, William: *The Country Wife* 21–3, 40, 59, 62, 130

Young, Toby 119
Young Vic Theatre 14, 148

Zuber, Catherine 89